D1597617
978 1014300621

AUTHORS DEAD

&

LIVING

"AUTHORS DEAD & LIVING"

BY

F. L. LUCAS

(Frank Laurence)

FELLOW OF KING'S COLLEGE

CAMBRIDGE

LONDON

CHATTO & WINDUS

1926

TO
MY FATHER

Preface

My thanks are due to The New Statesman for permission to reprint these articles; and to its literary editor, Mr. Desmond MacCarthy, without whom they would never have been written. Indeed I owe more than can be put in prefaces to that quick, kindly, unpedantic mind. In some cases these pieces have been enlarged with matter for which there was not room at their first appearance; in a few others criticisms of the same authors written at different times have been combined: a fuller revision than this might have made them completer treatments of their subjects than, as they are, they have any claim to be; but there would have been danger of destroying their original character, such as it is. They were launched at first, like paper boats, to swim their day and disappear; as they proved seaworthier than their maker had expected, and friendly messages showed they had even floated across the Atlantic, I have been encouraged to launch them here a second time; but there would have been little sense in trying to recast paper boats in bronze. If they reach so far as to send some readers back to creative literature with renewed interest, they will have served their end.

Contents

x   *Contents*

PLATO denounced art as twice removed from reality; words would surely have failed even that eloquent philosopher at the idea of criticism of criticism of criticism of art—a diversion distant from reality three removes further still. And yet this sentence too will be read, though those who read it know quite well that they will never have time to read a tithe of the world's masterpieces before they die; that they are seated at a banquet of incredible richness and variety which they must at any moment leave half-tasted, never to return. Why have we this impulse to spend our span thus sipping at sauces and toying with side-dishes? Is it that they are so nourishing? Is it our love of truth, our hope to discover what really is best of all that has been said and written? That would be a dignified reason. Yet if it is truth we seek, what has criticism established since Aristotle? The fallibility of critics. It has not even been able to agree about its own terminology. Does poetry connote metre? 'No,' cry in chorus Aristotle, Dryden, Coleridge, Wordsworth, and Shelley. 'Yes,' retort Scaliger, Hegel, and the ordinary man. And after three thousand years we are still debating whether art should instruct or not instruct, whether it should imitate everything or nothing, whether it should be built on emotion or above emotion. 'Tragedy,' says Aristotle, whom trusting Lessing was proud to believe no less infallible than Euclid, 'produces its effect through pity and fear'; 'Pity,' replies Hegel, 'is an insult to the

* Contemporary Criticism of Literature. By Orlo Williams. Parsons. Latitudes. By Edwin Muir. Melrose.

truly tragic character.' For with Hegel the function
of tragedy is to show that all things are as they ought to
be ; whereas with Schopenhauer its function is to show
that all things are as they ought not to be, and with
Nietzsche, to pretend that all things are not as they are.
When we pass from general judgments to particular,
there is more apparent harmony, because literary critics
are discreeter about attacking proved reputations than
philosophic critics about tilting at theories which are
incapable of proof. For it is realised that if in practice
a writer pleases powerfully, he must have power. And
yet Dr. Johnson pronounced that *Lycidas* was ' disgusting '
and Gray popular merely because he was ' dull in a new
way ' ; Coleridge, that the Porter-scene in *Macbeth*
could not possibly be Shakespeare's, that Gibbon could
not write prose nor Tennyson verse ; Goethe, that
England had never produced a genius to be compared
with Byron ; Carlyle, that England was undone when
such a ' despicable abortion ' as Lamb could be called a
genius at all ; Ruskin, that *Aurora Leigh* was the greatest
poem, in any language, of its century ; Arnold, that
Villette was ' disagreeable ' and *Enoch Arden* the best
thing Tennyson had written. Is it hard, after this, to
understand Blake's impatient protest that every man was
a judge of pictures who had not been ' connoisseured out
of his senses ' ; or the growl of Morris that a damned
good piece of work was a damned good piece of work,
with no more to be said, and that a man should go and
do likewise if he could, and hold his tongue if he could
not ?

Yet we continue to read criticism. Partly because
in this hasty age we read everything at a run and, if

some one will tear the heart out of the book for us, are only too glad to leave the rest ; partly because we wish to have read every new thing, or at least to give our friends that impression ; partly (a more serious reason) because in the accumulated welter of literature we genuinely want to know what to read and, with older or more difficult books, what to look for in reading them ; but really and above all we read criticism—because we like reading criticism. It amuses us ; that is the best of reasons ; and there is an end of it. This indeed is not the critics' usual view of their business ; yet were they only a little more self-critical, they would realise how often, when they think they are reforming the world, they are merely (and is that so inferior ?) adding to its pleasures ; how often, when they speak to instruct, they are heard because they entertain. For the critic is, after all, no better nor so much worse than his victim, the artist ; he is an artist himself ; he, too, must please or be ignored. He may be useful ; please he must. ' What is the function of criticism ? ' ask both Mr. Williams and Mr. Muir ; and Mr. Muir answers with admirable truth, though some exaggeration—

Its justification is that it fulfils no use ; that it is, like art, expression. But if a thing is not useful, it cannot be important ? This is the great orthodox heresy about the universe which makes it such a dull place to live in.

That is all true of part of criticism, and partly true of all ; only, what exactly is criticism ? It means so many things, and such muddle ensues. Mr. Williams divides criticism in general into three categories ; there are creative or self-expressive critics, scientific critics, and practical critics. But, though a step in the right direction, this does not go quite far enough.   First, we may say, there are those who write imaginatively about litera-ture, who treat their subject as a mere peg on which to hang purple patches of their own, like Pater rhapsodis-ing on Leonardo's *La Gioconda*.   Such writing may be magnificent, but it is hardly criticism, unless we are pre-pared to call Swinburne's dirge for Baudelaire or Keats' ' Ode on a Grecian Urn ' criticism too.   And the danger of it is that there is always a tendency to confusion be-tween the mental process a work of art thus inspires in a particular writer and the general effect it may be expected, and was meant by the artist, to produce on the ordinary intelligent person.   It leads the muddle-headed to read into a poem or a picture things that were never intended to be there ;   and criticism has suffered too often from the fanatic who fathers his pet doctrines on his pet authors, or the aesthete who imports beauties of his own wherever he goes, and will have it that he can hear the grass growing with an exquisite sound denied to grosser ears.

Secondly, there are those who write philosophically about art, and these too, like the first class, deceive them-selves and become a nuisance, if they imagine (as they often do) that they are being *useful* or their meditations more than an end in themselves.   Aesthetics may provide delightful inquiries for inquiry's sake ;   but let us not persuade ourselves that ever writer wrote, or reader re-sponded, the more perfectly for having studied all the lucubrations of a Hegel or a Croce.

Then there are those who write biologically about literature, as Taine when he established a connection between the abundance of poetry and of water-meadows in England. This is a fascinating pursuit, but not to be confused with criticism proper.

Fourthly, there are those who write anatomically of literature, like Mr. Percy Lubbock ; who display before our astonished eyes the anatomies of novels or quintessences of styles. They, too, are ends in themselves ; they are entertaining, but that they contribute much to our appreciation of literature itself, I doubt. The form of a work is vitally important as the human digestion is vitally important ; it is when it goes wrong that you become aware of it ; and it is not normally desirable to be more than sub-conscious of its existence. So that the trouble with these anatomists is that they fall in love with their own art and insist on flaying and dissecting everything for your delectation, on the ground that beauty really is more than skin-deep.

Lastly, apart from the writers of literary history and biography, who are, on the contrary, generally useful and sometimes pleasing, there remain the critics in the narrowest sense, whose business, as their name denotes, is ' to judge.' They, too, may be useful, as well as pleasing. True, their disagreements prove them fallible ; but it is not only because they are fallible that they disagree. There is no one truth about literary estimates. For different temperaments different authors not only seem good, but are good ; and such hierarchy as exists of the writers who are recognised as great, is like one of Galton's composite photographs, a thing fabricated out of the varying opinions of the great body of intelligent men. Thus, for Arnold and those of his temperament Shelley was and is ' ineffectual ' ; the loss is theirs perhaps —but not certainly. Had Arnold loved Shelley more, he might have loved Goethe less. One cannot have everything. And accordingly the critic is not the Daniel come to judgment, the legislating Lycurgus, he seemed to the admiring eyes of past generations, and to some, perhaps, even now. How can he legislate when literature breaks triumphantly through any laws that can be laid down for it—except for such broad generalities as that a writer who is mentally defective, emotionally dishonest, or slovenly in execution, is unlikely to endure ? (And one could name modern writers who flourish, for the time being at least, even with these endowments.) Criticism, then, is a form of art which deals not primarily with life, but with other art—a charming parasite ; it is a form of expression which allows us to overhear the introspection of an intelligent person into his own reactions in response to a work of art. This may be extraordinarily valuable ; it is possible to return from ' Q ' to Shakespeare, from Mr. Strachey to Racine, with eyes opened and a new desire. But though valuable, it remains a luxury. Greece and Rome and the Middle Ages produced their literature and enjoyed it with hardly a critic at their ears to tell them how ; what its predecessors had done without critics, the Renaissance achieved in the teeth of them. And since then it has often been the same ; criticism has tried to encourage the good, yet Keats was no exceptional victim ; to stamp out the bad, as Macaulay is supposed to have finished Montgomery— yet chronology proves that Macaulay had little effect and Montgomery's reputation died only of Montgomery in the end.

Criticism, in fine, has often proved but a barren fig-tree. Yet civilised people do not bless trees only as a source of nutriment ; even a barren fig-tree can please the eye and make a landscape. This minor art, with all the dissensions and pretensions of those who practise it, is neither to be taken too seriously nor yet despised. It was a sound instinct which made Sainte-Beuve call his writings '*Causeries*' ; for the best criticism has the spontaneity, the sincerity, the acuteness, and the urbanity of good talk, not riding high horses, not striving to improve nor to impress, but simply to express what the speaker feels and his hearers will wish to hear. And there is little exaggeration, really, in the dictum of Anatole France : 'When I say I am going to criticise Shakespeare or Racine, I mean that I am going to talk about myself in relation to Shakespeare or Racine.'

Mr. Williams' book is a sensible rather than brilliant work, which gives a fair-minded survey of the most important living critics. Mr. Muir's, on the other hand, is a work not always sensible, but—undeniably—brilliant. It is unwise of him to spoil the reader's appetite at the outset with a preface saying that this essay is wrong in its facts and that one in its conclusions ; it only invites the comment—'Why not rewrite them, then?' ; and one wishes one might at least have been spared this disillusionment until *after* reading them. It is unwise, again, to talk about Burns as 'the sanest of all poets, saner than Shakespeare or Goethe,' on the ground that *Macbeth* shows disgust with life. For it is impossible to tabulate poets in order of sanity, and there is nothing insane in being sometimes disgusted ; the abnormality would be in never being disgusted at all. Such a statement, too, as 'Only what is gloomy should be refuted' is itself not even worth refuting. Nor is it true that in literature a strong sense of fate and of form always go together. The fact is that classical literature generally shows both, romantic neither ; but what about Scandinavian literature like the *Volsunga Saga*, so shadowed with destiny, so rambling in its construction ? These are the slips of a brain with the French gift for wide and lucid generalisations ; for the French mind sees the world as through the wrong end of a telescope, with a clearness and compactness that are perfectly fascinating ; only, it is liable to leave things out of its field of view. None the less, theirs remains one of the most delightful of all kinds of intellect, and the central essays of this book, on philosophy and criticism, are most excellent reading. Of their slightly Butlerish quality of mingled wit and shrewdness a few aphorisms gathered from these pages will give the best idea.

Tradition.—For the truths of the fathers, alas ! are visited upon the children to the third and fourth generations, even of those that hate them.

Religions.—' How unutterable is your longing for us ! ' they have said ; and men have one day discovered within them an unutterable longing.

Philosophy.—A philosopher who has laboured so badly as to land himself in a *cul-de-sac*, will never be convinced that the truth is not in it along with him.

Dostoyevsky's Russians.—How many incredible impulses will come out of one man, like rabbits out of a conjurer's hat, given a certain situation, or given none at all : that question entranced him. . . . Nothing in them is typical, for every decision they make is an exception to a rule which they do not know.

Croce's *Æsthetic*.—He submitted art once more to the slavery from which he had freed it. . . . The particular meanness of philosophy, the meanness of fitting everything into its place, where it has to sit still with folded arms eternally, lies like a damp shadow on that sunny, rarefied, and emancipating book.

Old Age.—As a dog or cat grows older, it does not become wise ; it becomes careful. Man also.

Our Age.—Our general character can be described in a few words ; everywhere and always we feel mystery rather than curiosity before things. To say this is to say we are superstitious. . . . Greece and the Europe of the Renaissance believed, and it was the chief source of their glory, that mysteries could be solved.

Add occasional pinches of salt to taste—and what a pleasant feast of reason this is !

> The gale it plies the saplings double,
>   It blows so hard 'twill soon be gone,
> To-day the Roman and his trouble
>   Are ashes under Uricon.

In this age of literary resurrections, when so many of the most mortal of authors are laboriously exhumed to grace our feasts of culture with their insignificant death's-heads, there still remains unknown to the general world a certain obscure collection of poems written not only by, but for, men long dead and forgotten, and preserved, not in yellow old pages of monkish writing, but by the mason's chisel on stones as old as the Rome of the Cæsars itself. The epitaphs written by the poets of Greece, from Simonides to the Byzantines, are still familiar enough ; of reading them and of trying to render their perfectness into tongues less perfect the modern world has never yet grown weary. But these Latin fragments from the gravestones of the Republic and the Empire still lie obscurely tumbled together in the darkness of two uninviting volumes of Teubner.*

They are, let it be said at once, often illiterate, often crude, often ridiculous ; yet from the obscure stones of this vast democracy of death there breaks ever and again some strangely moving cry. There may be little here of the silvery grace of the Greek, but there is also little of the leaden atmosphere of an English churchyard with its time-dishonoured tags and stony pieties. No doubt these Roman dead have likewise their threadbare

* *Anthologia Latina, II. (carmina epigraphica), 2 vols., ed. by F. Buecheler. (Leipzig, 1895-97.)*

formulas, their undertakers' catchwords ; yet even in death they somehow keep something of the diversity, the individuality, the naturalness of life. Even in the tomb life's hundred colours are not bleached for them into moral black and white ; even in the tomb they show a criticism of life, now grim, now gay, not our sheepish acceptance—a sense of the poetry of its poignancy, in place of our pained virtue in affliction.

The interest of these epitaphs is indeed wholly personal ; they offer amazingly little to the historian. Of the wars that reverberate with one long thunder-roll for a thousand years through Livy, Tacitus, and Gibbon, hardly an echo penetrates the stillness of these vaults. They retain far more memories of the poetry of Virgil than of all the Cæsars. So that here is justified indeed that proud claim for the immortality of Art alone, made in one of Flaubert's letters : ' Ah oui, l'amour de Glycère ou de Lycoris passera encore par-dessus les civilisations futures.' The rise of Rome, the long agony of the Empire, the clash of rival creeds, the ' drums and tramplings ' of Goth and Hun, scarcely make a whisper in the records of these dim lives. There are a few exceptions, like the tombs of the Scipios ; and even they testify less to the rise of Roman greatness than, in their proud brevity, to the spirit which made Rome great. Greece has the charm of perpetual youth ; but here are the epitaphs of a race that was never young. Thus, for instance, runs the characteristic epitaph of an unknown daughter of the Claudian house :

Hospes, quod deico, paullum est, asta ac pellege.
heic est sepulcrum hau pulcrum pulcrai feminae.
nomen parentes nominarunt Claudiam.
suom mareitum corde deilixit souo.

gnatos duos creavit.   horunc alterum
in terra linquit, alium sub terra locat.
sermone lepido, tum autem incessu commodo.
domum servavit. lanam fecit. dixi. abei.

Short is my say, O stranger.   Stay and read.
Not fair this tomb, but fair was she it holds.
By name her parents called her Claudia.
Her wedded lord she loved with all her heart.
She bare two sons, and one of them she left
On earth, the other in the earth she laid.
Her speech was pleasing and her bearing gracious.
She kept house : span her wool.   I have said.   Farewell.

(ROME, 2ND CENT. B.C.)

With time indeed the spirit of the race grows less austere,
though never younger ; and in this close of a poor in-
scription, misspelt and mis-scanned, over a slave-girl of
twelve under Augustus, the change of tone is clear
enough—

Sed tu adulescens, quem Phrygia edidit tellus,
    Desiste lamenteis me exciere.
Namque tua officia grata mihi in luce fuerunt
    Et nunc demum ad cinerem.

Dear Phrygian lad, call back my ghost no more
    With tears of vain regret ;
That love which sweetened all my life before,
    Sweetens my ashes yet.

(ROME, B.C. 12-11.)

Here shows itself not only a new pathos, but also the new
cosmopolitanism.   The city has become a world ; and
under the Empire, to which most of these epitaphs belong,
the old sternness is replaced by the gentleness of a deeper

pity, or the bitterness of a deeper pessimism, or by the
unconscious comedies of upstart ostentation.   The
humour, indeed, is often conscious too : as in the line—

Derisori qui vixit bene et consummavit bene.

Here lies a scoffer, who had a good life and made a good end.

And of an old gentleman of seventy-seven we read :

Hic fuit ad superos felix, quo non felicior alter
aut fuit aut vixit, simplex bonus atque beatus.
numquam tristis erat, laetus gaudebat ubique.
nec senibus similis mortem cupiebat obire,
set timuit mortem nec se mori posse putabat.

Happy on earth he was—the happiest
That ever lived—good, simple, truly blest.
He never grieved, his heart was always high,
He never cried for death as old men cry,
He was afraid of death and thought he 'd never die.

(OSTIA, 3RD CENT. A.D.)

Less intentionally amusing are an ancient Wife of Bath,
who bids the world not weep for one so lovingly interred
by her seventh husband ; and the matron who, charmed
by the pathetic custom of praying earth to lie lightly on
children dead in tender age, has inscribed on her monument with more truth than taste—

Earth, lightly lie upon my *middle* age.

Others, here as in other times and lands, cannot take
leave of life without a parting homily to posterity ; the
curiosity lies in the extraordinary advice they bequeath.
Thus a gladiator of Milan makes his final exit with the

ferocious maxim, that in the arena ' the vanquished ought *always* to be put to the sword by the victor '; and the successful business man warns posterity of the importance of forming the habit of early rising. But the strangest trait of all, to the modern mind, is the obsession of these generations with the need of being well buried; not the Bishop of St. Praxed's himself cherished a more vivid expectation of continuing consciously to enjoy his sepulchral splendour—

> Aedis aedificat dives, sapiens monumentum.
>   hospitium est illud corporis, hic domus est.
> Illic paulisper remoramur, ad hic habitamus.

> The rich man builds a house, but the wise a tomb.
> For that is but our lodging; this our home.
> There for a while we sojourn; here abide.
>   (ROME : NOW AT CASTLE-HOWARD.)

Experience however taught them the imprudence of trusting too much to one's heirs. And so a wiseacre from Carthage boasts, just like Trimalchio in Petronius—

> Dum sum vitalis et vivo, ego feci sepulcrhum (*sic*)
> Adque meos versus, dum transeo, perlego et ipse.
> Quisque sapis iuvenis, vivo tibi pone sepulcrhum.

> While I was still alive, I built my tomb,
> And passing by would read my epitaph.
> If wise, young man, you 'll build yours while you live.

Similarly a son who had erected over his father in Tunisia a vast mausoleum, complete with even a sky-scraping weathercock, breaks out into a perfectly Juvenalian storm of righteous indignation at the vicious extrava-

gance of those wantons who waste on good living the
money that might have made them magnificent through
an eternity of death.

And yet this clinging to the shadowy immortality of
being remembered which, if it satisfied Samuel Butler,
seems to most of us a lame and sorry comfort enough,
acquires here by its very intensity a tragic side.   For
these men so hungry ' to subsist in bones and be pyramidally
extant ' cannot forget that monuments too are mortal.
The irony of time has filled the chilly galleries of our
museums with a multitude of dumb voices that still vainly
implore the wayfarer to read who lies beneath, or the
scribbler to turn elsewhere his defacing hand ; or that
curse, almost in our Shakespeare's words, whoever dares
to desecrate their dust.   Some of these dead even parade
a ghoulish malice towards the living posterity they so
futilely envy.   Leering through the centuries beside the
Appian or Flaminian Way their spectres called after
the unheeding traveller—

Heus tu, viator lasse, qui me praeteris,
Cum diu ambulaveris, tamen hoc veniundum est tibi.

Ho you, weary wayfarer, ho you that hurry by !
Hither, when your travel 's ended, you shall come at last to lie.
                                        (CREMONA.)

Eus tu viator, veni hoc et quiesce pusilu.
Innuis et negitas ? tamen hoc redeundum tibi.

Ho, traveller, come and rest you a little space !
Do you shake your head and refuse ?   Yet here shall be your
      resting-place.

                                        (CAPENA.)

Elsewhere indeed a kindlier spirit prays—

> Bene sit tibi qui legis et tibi qui praeteris.

> Blessings alike on you that read, and you that hurry by.
> (VELLETRI.)

and a wearier one—

> Lege pauca verba, paululum et dolens vade,
> Aut nil doleto ; nil mali est ubi nil est.
> Laboris est ut occubas tibi finis.

> Read these few words and, grieving a little, go—
> Or grieving not.   Nought ails where all is nought.
> 'Tis thy toil's end to lay thee down at last.
> (N. ITALY.)

This is a gloomy sort of immortality. Yet they doubted of any other. Among the more ignorant, no doubt, the old religion glimmered on, and the coin for Charon was still laid between the pale lips of their dead. But the phrases, ' if the dead know,' ' if the dead can feel,' recur with a pitiful insistence :

Quod potui, miserandus homo, me iunxi sepulchro,
Kara, tuo, donec mihi mea vita manebat.
Credo tibi gratum, si haec quoque Tartara norunt.

All that I could—unhappy heart—I made my grave by thine,
By thine, dear love, in days while yet the breath of life was mine,
Trusting my care was sweet to thee, if aught the dead divine.
(ALGERIA.)

From the ashes of others, again, there flames out a sudden anger of protest against the cruelty of the Universe :

> Manus levo contra deum qui me innocentem sustulit.

> I lift my hands against the God
> Who gave to death my innocence.

Dii irati aeterno somno dederunt.

The gods in anger gave me to eternal sleep.

Others take refuge in the resignation of a tragic fatalism—

Quit mea damna doles ? fati non vincitur ordo.
Res hominum sic sunt : ut in arbore citrea poma
Aut matura cadunt aut immatura leguntur.

Mourn not my loss ; tears change not destiny.
Thus is man's life ; as from the lemon-tree
The ripe fruit falls or green is gatherèd.
                    (AIX IN PROVENCE : 2ND CENT. A.D.)

Nunc quoniam omnes mortui idem sapimus, satis est.

Since all we dead are wise alike, 'tis well.
                                        (ROME.)

Finer still is the terse—

Non fui, fui ; non sum, non desidero.

I was not, I was ; I am not, I would not be.

Yet others in that darkening world turn to death as an
evil not greater, less perhaps, than life—

Effugi crimen, longa senecta, tuum.

I have escaped, O lingering age, thy shame.
                                        (PADUA.)

Such is the consolation of a girl dead in early youth.
So, too, speaks Q. Octavius Primus—

Quaerere consuevi semper nec perdere desi :
    nunc ab utroque vaco.
hic mea composito requiescunt ossa, quiescit
    et labor a puero qui mihi semper erat.
nunc labor omnis abest semper curaeque molestae,
    nec scio quit nunc sim, nec scio quit fuerim.

B

I toiled for wealth, I lost it without cease,
    My cares I now resign.
For here at peace my bones are laid, at peace
    All the long toil that was since boyhood mine.
My work is ended—all that troubled me.
I know not what I am, nor what I used to be.

                                        (VERONA.)

Surely these are the accents of the man himself ; for who
would allow another to write so of his life's long futility ?
More sardonically runs another, also from Catullus'
Verona—

Quod superest homini, requiescunt dulciter ossa,
    nec sum sollicitus ne subito esuriam,
et podagram careo nec sum pensionibus arra
    et gratis aeterno perfruor hospitio.

Last state of man, my bones are softly laid,
    I have no cares about my daily bread,
No pangs of gout, distraint for rent unpaid,
    But gratis now for ever board and bed.

On some of the wearier spirits even the feverish passion
to be remembered has lost its hold.   Just as our Marston
inscribed his tomb 'Oblivioni sacrum,' so here a philosopher dedicates his ashes to 'Eternal Sleep,' and a
poet of the sonorous name of Claudius Diadumenus
boasts that he never heeded fame ; adding of himself
with an anticipation, almost, of the words of Gray's
Elegy—

sed semper modicus rexsit ubique tenor.

                        Through life
He kept the modest tenor of his way.

But the complete passivity of extremest pessimism sits
uneasily on most human shoulders and, as was to be ex-

pected, amidst all this lamentation rings out also the
defiant ' Let us eat and drink ' of the Epicurean—

> Quod comedi et ebibi tantum meum est.

> Now only what I ate and drank is mine.

> Balnea vina Venus corrumpunt corpora nostra,
>   Set vitam faciunt balnea vina Venus.

> Women and wine and baths bring life's decline.
> Yet what *is* life but women, baths, and wine?   (ROME.)

In hardly soberer prose two brothers similarly sum up
their life and its lesson—

> Voluptates secuti sumus omnes, vitae nostrae a nobis num-
> quam quitquam negatum est. Ita tu qui legis, bona vita
> vive sodalis, quare post obitum nec risus nec lusus nec ulla
> voluptas erit.

> We pursued every pleasure, through life we denied our-
> selves nothing ever. So, you who read, live like a jolly
> fellow : seeing that after death there shall be neither smile
> nor merriment nor pleasure any more.   (C. ITALY.)

And beside this echo of *Ecclesiastes* may be set another of
Omar Khayyam—the last prayer of a *bon viveur* of
Southern Spain—

> heredibus mando etiam cinere ut m[era vina ferant], volitet
> meus ebrius papilio, ipsa ossa tegant he[rbae et flores, hic ut]
> si quis titulum ad mei nominis astiterit, dicat [quod non rapuit]
> avidus ignis, quod corpore resoluto se vertit in fa[villam, bene
> quiescere].

> I bid my heirs pour wine even on my dust ; let my soul's
> butterfly be drunken in her flight, my bones be so thickly
> overgrown with grass and flower, that whoso reads this stone
> which bears my name, may say : ' Whatever the devouring
> flame has spared, whatever turns to ashes when the body
> burns, here slumbers well.'   (NEAR CORDOVA.)

All this may not furnish a very edifying philosophy of life; but such utterances have at least a personality and a variety that will be sought in vain in the sanctimonious rigmaroles, the catalogued virtues so hard to forgive, of our parochial *Hic jacets*. And doggerel as much of this sepulchral verse naturally is, there are moments when the monumental roll of the Latin tongue reasserts its grandeur and the commonplaces of the lapidary are lifted into poetry. The young wife of Megethus mourns that the end came for her with the young flowers of the year, ' And ah! Death's hand polluted April's spring.' ' Death has reft all,' wails another, ' the dreadful sleep of men '—*dira quies hominum.* Flavius Dalmatius prays the unknown possessors of his home in years to come that they will lay rose and lily still upon his dust. Arphocrates of Carthage promises to return in dreams to the wife he has left desolate; the dead boy-slave that he will follow his master always, be it eastward to far Assyria or westward to Spain; and the charioteer buried by the wayside entreats a flower from the passer's hand in momentary remembrance—

> Favisti vivo forsitan ipse mihi.

> Maybe you cheered me when I was alive.
>
> (TARRAGONA.)

Rich parents mourn that of all their wide lands they could give but a grave's length to the child that should have been their heir; and the slave pours on his young lord's bones the long-stored wine his living lips were destined never to drink. It is indeed on those cut off in their first flower, here as in the *Greek Anthology*, that some of the most loving care has been lavished—without

any of that mawkishness peculiar to modern sentiment
about children.   Once more the supreme secret is simply
simplicity.   Such are three lines on a child-slave of five,
from Arles—

> Inspexi lucem, subito quae erepta est mihi,
>   ita neque domino liquit e me gaudia
> percipere nec me scire quid natus forem.

> I looked on the light, and straight 'twas snatched from me ;
> So fell it that my lord could have no joy
> Of me, nor I know wherefore I was born.

With the same thought mourn the parents of an infant
girl at Mentz—

> Ne tu fuisses si, futura tam grata,
>   brevi reverti unde nobis edita
>   nativom esset.

> Would you had never been, if, grown so dear,
> Back to return so swiftly whence you came
> Was your nativity !

And again—

> rosa simul florivit et statim perit.

> The rosebud flowered and faded straight away.

> Ut rosa amoena homini est, quom primo tempore floret,
>   Quei me viderunt, sic ego amoena fui.

> Lovely as is the rose to men, when first it flowers in spring,
> So to their eyes that saw me, I too was a lovely thing.
>   (VIA AURELIA : AGE OF AUGUSTUS.)

> Namque dolor talis non nunc tibi contigit uni,
> haec eadem et magnis regibus acciderunt.

> Mother, thy loss hath not been thine alone.
> This selfsame sorrow mighty kings have known.
>   (ROME.)

Or with crowning brevity—

> Noli dolere, mamma, faciendum fuit.
>
> Grieve not, mamma, it was to be.

But of all these children of two thousand years perhaps
the most winning is a certain Agathe, aged five, from
Rome—

> Dum vixi, lusi, sum cunctis semper amata :
> nam pueri voltum, non femine, crede, gerebam,
> quam soli norant Agathen qui me genuerunt,
> rufa coma, tonso capite posttrema (*sic*) remisso.
> convivae cuncti nunc mi bona pocula ferte
> diciteque ut semper meo corpori terra levis sit.

> All my life I played, and all were fond of me,
>   For, know, I had a boy's look, not a girl's—
> Only my parents knew their Agathe—
>   Close-cut before, behind streamed my red curls.
> O feasters all, drink to my name to-night
> And say, ' Upon her may the earth be light ! '

Even the beasts that perish are not forgotten—the horse,
once swifter than the wind, now stalled for ever in the
grave, the carriage-dog who keeps a last vigil over his
own charred bones.

The charm of these vague relics of the Empire is a
double one—their nearness to us and their distance.
There is, on the one hand, the surprise of finding those
feelings of every day, which each generation assumes
peculiarly its own, to be after all but echoes of two thousand years ; these people are so human, so understandable and close to us—like that ancient princess a sixteenth-
century Italian chronicler describes as discovered in his
time, still fresh with a bloom as of yesterday.   Here is
none of that sinister, defeating remoteness of the Egyptian

dead who rise again on our unfamiliar world from the
Valley of the Kings—

> Then, 'twas before my time, the Roman
> At yonder heaving hill would stare :
> The blood that warms an English yeoman,
> The thoughts that hurt him, they were there.

On the other hand, the last words of these obscure
dead, which make the inscriptions of Westminster Abbey
seem so vulgar, bring home to the reader in a new and
unstaled sense how tremendous a thing was this vanished
civilisation which moulded to its own tongue for centuries the utterance of the life of Europe from the Lothians
to the Sahara, from the Land's End to the Euphrates, and
filled Hades itself with the roll of the Latin tongue.   But
most striking of all is the quick feeling these inscriptions
show for the essential tragic point in each individual
destiny, the poetry of ideas which breaks through all their
poverty of expression, their illiteracy of style.   The
thought, for instance, of the dead charioteer, that the
wayfarer who passes by his resting place at the final goal
may perhaps be one of those who once shouted him on in
the race, shows a dramatic sensitiveness which some may
call forced, but which after all is one of the great consolations of life.   For if life be a tragi-comedy, it is something
to be able to appreciate those tense instants when chance
does seem to work with the poignancy or the irony of a
great playwright's calculated skill.   If act we must, it
is something to bring understanding to our parts.   That
sense for situations these pagan epitaphs possess ;   and
the value of the best of them is that they seem to perceive,
in all their decadence, the force or the beauty of life as a
Drama, where the darker ages that followed found only
a medley of Mystery and Morality.

In the days when the Venerable Bede was writing church history in Northumbria, and Charles Martel hammering Saracens at Tours, and Leo the Isaurian smashing images in Byzantium, the intelligent Chinese were writing poetry. And when, just a thousand years later, a selection was made from the still surviving verse of this Tang dynasty (seventh-ninth centuries A.D.), even the anthology included nearly fifty thousand poems in nine hundred books (which may teach our sorely tried generation that others have suffered even worse) ; and of the twenty-three hundred poets there enrolled, the greatest was Li-Po (*c.* 700-762 A.D.).

All this sounds like a matter-of-fact fairy-tale ; and the poet's own life is of a piece with it. On the night of his birth his mother dreamed of the planet Venus—whence his name. In his teens he retired with a hermit to the mountains, where, like St. Francis, he drew the wild birds to feed from his hand. In China, however, such accomplishments bring not the halo of sainthood, but the offer of a post in the Civil Service. Li-Po declined and contented himself with wedding the daughter of an ex-minister, who later left him in a well-justified despair of his ever attaining official eminence. The poet, undismayed, became one of the Six Idlers of the Bamboo Valley, leading a troubadour life of wandering, wine, and song. At length his triumph came : he was presented to the Emperor in the Hall of Golden Bells, feasted at the Table

* *The Works of Li-Po. Translated by Shigeyoshi Obata. Dent.*

of Seven Jewels, and became one of the Eight Immortals of the Wine-Cup. However, the course of true fairy-tales never runs smooth. One day when Li-Po was drunk, a chief eunuch was ordered to pull off his shoes ; the chief eunuch, in revenge, became a critic and pretended to discover in a panegyric of the Emperor's chief mistress a hidden satire. So the poet went back to his happy vagabondage for ten years more. Then came civil war ; Li-Po had the misfortune to be patronised by the wrong side, and was banished to the extremity of the Empire. A pardon, indeed, overtook him on his long and leisurely journey to the place of his exile ; but he died not much later in the City of Taiping, whether through trying to embrace the moon's reflection in the water, or being carried off to the celestial realm on the back of a dolphin, or, says a drier chronicler, from too much wine. Of his habits we are told that he ' ate like a hungry tiger,' as well as drinking like a fish ; that his big voice could be heard in heaven ; that he was a warrior, by his own account at least, in youth, and politically minded in his middle age—

> In the middle of the night I sigh four or five times,
> Worrying over the great empire's affairs.

The same medley of faery and realism runs through his poetry ; perhaps such a combination is characteristic of the race which both invented gunpowder and yet found no use for it except to make fireworks. The nineteenth century thought such unprogressive innocence a great joke ; the twentieth, surfeited of high explosives, smiles less complacently, and has come, indeed, somewhat like the eighteenth, to find much to admire and something to envy in this Eastern mixture of simplicity and wisdom, urbanity and love of nature, childlikeness and immemorial experience. It is like sinking into the cool stillness of a country evening after a morning in London, and an afternoon in a third-class smoking carriage, to turn to poetry like this from the stuffy *salon* atmosphere of much modern verse, with its second-rate intellectuals torturing second-hand psychology into fourth-rate literature. Here once more—

> Aus alten Märchen winkt es
> Hervor mit weiszer Hand.
> Da singt es und da klingt es
> Von einem Zauberland.

But this very magic lies in the perfect mixture of familiarity here with the strangeness. Were the strangeness greater, perfect sympathy would cease : were it less, we should be disappointed of new experience. As it is, the Western mind immediately finds itself happily at home in this pleasant ' far away and long ago ' of eighth-century Cathay—

> Why do I live among the green mountains ?
> I laugh and answer not, my soul is serene :
> It dwells in another heaven and earth belonging to no man.
> The peach-trees are in flower and the water flows on. . . .

Surely this is rather remarkable a thousand years before Wordsworth. These people find in nature, so wonderfully coloured in their land, a never-ending delight. They even ascend mountains for the view, which is more than I can remember of any Greek or Latin, except a certain general in Livy ; while Christian theology left that

pursuit to the Devil.   True, Li-Po was no rock-climber
and would have shared Gray's horror of the precipices of
Borrowdale—

You cannot clamber over these jutting rocks. . . .
You shall hear no voice but the cuckoo's calling in the moonlight
    by night, calling mournfully in the desolate mountains. . . .
The lofty peaks shoot up cloudward in rows.   If one foot higher,
    they would touch the heaven.
The dead pine-trees cling to the cliff, hanging head foremost
    over the abyss.

Here again, in some lines ' On a Picture Screen,' is
the very spirit of the ' Ode on a Grecian Urn '—

How many years since these valley flowers bloomed
To smile in the sun ?
And that man travelling on the river,
Hears he not for ages the monkeys screaming ?
Whoever looks on this
Loses himself in eternity.

This shadow of Keats is pale and frail indeed ; but then
one must in justice remember that it is only a translation—excellent translation as it seems to be.   For, though
there are one or two slips in the English of Mr. Obata's
introduction, considering that he is a Japanese translating
from one foreign language into another, the style of his
actual version is amazingly good.

Of other echoes of the West—of Sappho, of Horace,
of Browning even—here is no space to speak.   The
kinship between Chinese ideas and ours has been noted
long since by Mr. Lowes Dickinson ; and, similarly, in
one of Mr. Waley's renderings of Tao-chien there is a
striking counterpart of Lucretius at his best.   So far an

East is, indeed, half West. The same impassive stars rise on their heaven, though the Great Bear has become the Golden Dipper ; on the same waxing and waning beauty of the earth these men looked once with sadness as deep, as clear-eyed as our own. Here are none of the brain-sick miasmas of Indian mysticism. There is wine in plenty in these pages, and intoxication, but a sober sense of life.

> The rabbit in the moon pounds his medicine in vain . . .
> Man dies, his white bones are dumb without a word,
> When the green pines feel the coming of the spring.
>
> .   .   .   .   .   .
>
> Hush, hush, all things pass with the waters of the east-
>   flowing river.

The rabbit is to us a little stranger ; he, it seems, poor thing, is according to the legend for ever trying to compound the elixir of life. But how familiar is the rest ! Wine, wine, wine—but it is forgetfulness they seek as much as ecstasy, forgetfulness of the perpetual partings from friend and lover ; being not saints nor visionaries nor ascetics, but merely human, and knowing it is theirs to live but for a little and to suffer much.

> If you can only make me drunk, mine host, it is enough ;
> No longer shall I know the sorrow of a strange land.
>
> .   .   .   .   .   .
>
> It is three years since you went. The perfume you left
>   behind haunts me still.
> The perfume stays about me for ever, but where are you,
>   beloved ?
> I sigh—the yellow leaves fall from the branch.
> I weep—the dew twinkles white on the green mosses.

Or again—

> Do you know your footmarks by our gate are old,
> And each and every one is filled up with green moss ?
> The mosses are too deep for me to sweep away
> And already in the autumn wind the leaves are falling.
> The yellow butterflies of October
> Flutter in pairs over the grass of the west garden.
> My heart aches at seeing them.

Even the clouds bring back memories of friendship and separation—

> The white clouds gather and scatter again like friends.

Even the flight of the swallows recalls human loneliness, as the cry of the cranes at ploughing-time reminded Theognis of Megara that the fields of his fathers were his to till no more—

> Swallows two by two—always two by two,
> A pair of swallows are an envy for man.

Even the flowers that star the silence of peaceful waters are a symbol of unkindly distance and decay—

> In the deep, sequestered stream the lotus grows,
> Blooming fresh and fair in the morning sun.
> Its growing petals touch the clear autumn water
> And its thick leaves spread like blue smoke.
> Alas ! in vain its beauty excels the world.
> Who knows, who will speak of its rare perfume ?
> Lo ! the frost will come, chilling the air,
> And its crimson must wither, its fragrance fade.
> Ill it has chosen the place to plant its root.
> Would it could move to the margin of a flower pond !

Among these partings are some of a kind that we, likewise, have learnt to know too well. There is here no romance about war ; but from the far frontiers of the fairy empire we hear the howlings of the barbarians of Tartary, and the fading tramp of men who march away. Thirty thousand died in these years in the Gobi Desert ; two hundred thousand are said to have fallen in the marches of Yunnan—

> And upon his sword the desert frost blossoms.

How much there is in that one line—the desolation where nothing flowers but the frost : and it flowers upon a sword !

> In the tiger-striped gold case he left for her keeping
> There remains a pair of white-feathered arrows
> Amid the cobwebs and dust gathered of long years—
> O empty tokens of love, too sad to look upon !
> She takes them out and burns them to ashes.

Twelve centuries have passed since then. We kill a little better ; we write a little worse ; we suffer the same.

ONCE, before they recognised themselves as kindred forms of fiction, there lay a feud between Poetry and Philosophy ; but that was healed long since, and a hundred years ago, when Keats drank confusion to Newton, destroyer of the mystery of the rainbow, a new quarrel had begun —between Poetry and Science. Wordsworth looked forward to a reconciliation, Tennyson attempted it ; but no second Lucretius has come and indeed this new opposition strikes far deeper than the old. For though, Heaven knows, Science too sometimes strays still on to the fairy ground of fiction, she moves there in extreme discomfort, with her endless chain of facts dragging at wrist and ankle, and escapes the moment she can see her way back to the service of that severely virgin Truth who never suffers herself to swoon in the arms of Imagination.

Yet it has not always been so. Turn to the Middle Ages and you will find Science a charming infant, innocent of the apple of Knowledge, and wandering poetically in a childish Paradise, where truth is not stranger than fiction, being indeed the same. Nor did it matter very greatly ; seeing that no one ever experimented whether, in fact, ' if any man bind the right eye of a wolf on his right sleeve, neither men nor dogs can hurt him,' no one was much the worse for believing it. The bag was religiously handed down from age to age and, as no one ever pried into it, the cat never got out. Men were so greedy for knowledge that they could not wait a single instant to test if any of it were true. It almost passes belief how the learned copied for fifteen centuries, what Pliny had copied from every book he could lay hands on with an energy that it took an eruption of Vesuvius to extinguish, without ever apparently making trial of anything, until at last it occurred to Bacon and others that everything found in books is not inevitably true. It is largely to this brilliant notion that, for better and worse, modern civilisation is due. But to the mediæval scientist, the more antiquated the evidence, the more certain it was. Thus Topsell, after relating how unicorns are caught by means of virgins in whose laps they at once proceed to lay their heads, forget their fierceness, and go to sleep, adds in a grumbling tone : 'Concerning this opinion we have no *elder* authority than Tzetzes, who did not live above five hundred years ago, and therefore I leave the reader to the freedom of his own judgment to believe or refuse this relation.' How judicious it sounds ! Really, between the Greeks and the seventeenth century the scientific mind hardly existed ; and that the Greeks were by no means all they might have been, witness their greatest, Aristotle, who might, one would think, have found out for himself whether men and women really differed in the number of their teeth. Still, this is nothing to the feats of the mediæval intelligence. Says Topsell : 'In the heart of horses there is found a bone most like unto a dog's tooth ; it is said that this doth drive away all grief or sorrow from a man's heart ' ; and again, Albertus Magnus states that a woman will confess all her secrets if only you lay a frog's tongue in the region of her heart when she is asleep ; and Pliny (Pliny indeed would swallow most things, but then it took the Middle Ages to appreciate him properly), that if you have a great journey to go and take a staff of myrtle in your hand, you shall never be weary. Was this world of theirs so happy,

that men had no sorrow, and women no lovers jealous of
their secrets, and wayfarers no weariness ?   It is not as
if horses' hearts or frogs or myrtle were recondite things
to come by ; had it been the yolk of a phœnix's egg that
the recipe required, one could understand ; as it is, the
wonder is not ' Why did they never try ? ' but ' How
could they possibly refrain from trying ? '   And yet even
things false on the face of them are painfully transmitted
to posterity by writers who can never have laid down
their pens for one moment to think.   Topsell says of
lizards : ' The old one devoureth the young ones as
soon as they be hatched, except one she suffereth to live,
and this one is the basest and most dullard ; yet, notwith-
standing, afterwards it devoureth both his parents.' Never,
clearly, was such a perverted creature ; yet how did
Topsell suppose that there were any left in the world, if
their numbers were halved at each generation ?   The
original pair that came out of the Ark would have had
no grandchildren—unless he thought they were also spontaneously generated.   But it is far more likely that he
never thought at all.   As one person in *The Cloister and
the Hearth* says to another who asks what is the meaning
of the uproar in the street—' Just a miracle.'

And yet, incredibly childish as all this may seem, it is
not so self-evident that our scientific precisians have really
been more blessing to us than curse, that we can afford
merely to sneer at these curious mediæval minds.   They
are often charming ; and this is not just quaintness—they
are so human, so fanciful as well.   Not having sacrificed
their imaginations to the matter-of-fact accurateness of
our age of apothecaries, they have live ideas, as delightful
as they are delightfully expressed.   Towards them poetry

C

could feel no enmity, nothing indeed but indebtedness ; for how much would the Elizabethans, and Shakespeare himself, have lost, if the science of their time had been already Baconian, and banished unicorn and basilisk and baleful comet from the vividness of real things to the fusty lumber-room they have since come to occupy as mere poetic 'properties' ! It was indeed by way of Elizabethan poetry that I came on the fascinating collection of mediæval lore which suggested this essay.* Such science was itself really half an art, aiming largely at the amusement of mankind, as it imagined the Creator Himself to have aimed. 'Some beasts be ordained,' says the thirteenth-century Bartholomew, familiar to the Elizabethans in two Tudor translations from his Latin, 'for man's mirth, as apes and marmosets and popinjays ; and some be made for exercitation of man, for man should know his own infirmities and the might of God. And therefore be made flies and lice.' In the art of amusement these zoologists certainly succeed, often beyond their intention, as in the description of the goat doctoring himself with 'Dragon Tea,' or this opening sentence of Topsell on the mouse : 'Of the vulgar little mouse : Concerning their manners they are evil, apt to steal, insidious and deceitful.' After which terrific moral indictment, he continues with obvious satisfaction : 'A Mouse watcheth an oyster when he gapeth, and, seeing it open, thrusts in his head to eat the fish ; as soon as ever the oyster feeleth his teeth, presently he closeth his shell again, and crusheth the Mouse's head in pieces. A Man took a Mouse, which Mouse he fed only with the flesh of Mice, and after he had fed it so a long time, he let it go, who

* *Natural History in Shakespeare's Time. H. W. Seager. (London, 1896.*

killed all the Mice he did meet, and was not satisfied with them, but went into every hole he could find, and ate them up also.'   Or there is Pliny's description, in Holland's translation, of the religion of hens and the memory of magpies.   ' The Hens of country houses have a certain ceremonious religion.   When they have laid an egg, they fall a-trembling and quaking, and all to-shake themselves.   They turn about also, as in procession, to be purified.'   ' Pies take a love to the words they speak. . . . It is for certain known that they have died for very anger and grief that they could not learn to pronounce certain hard words ; as also, unless they hear the same words repeated often unto them, their memory is so shittle, they will soon forget the same again.'

Yet it would be unfair to ascribe the delightfulness of such passages simply to ' quaintness,' that is, to being old-fashioned. The real charm lies in a very simple, but very vivid, imagination ; their naïve form of it happens to be almost dead among us now ; but it is not valuable because it is dead, but because it was so extremely alive. For absolutely fantastic imaginativeness it would be hard to beat the statement of the *Hortus Sanitatis* that ' the mussel (not our shellfish, but another fish) is the male of the whale.' ' The mussel and the whale,' it continues, ' are examples of friendship, for as the whale's eyes through the great weight of its brows are closed, the mussel swims before it and points out those things which might be harmful to its bulk.' Then there is Topsell's story of the deliverance of Britain from cockatrices by a man who went about dressed in looking-glasses, so that the cocka-trices died of the sight of their own faces ; or Bar-tholomew's wolf, who ' may not bend his neck backwards

in no month of the year, but in May alone, when it
thundereth. And when he goeth by night for to take
his prey, if it happeth in any wise, that his foot maketh
noise, treading upon anything, then he chastiseth that
foot with hard biting. His eyes shine by night as lant-
horns. And he beareth in his tail a lock that exciteth
love.' There is poetry, too, as well as absurdity, in the
same writer's picture of the ostriches, who refuse to
lay, till 'they heave up their eyes and behold the stars
that hight Pleiades'; or his mole, to whose blindness
death alone brings light—'and some men trow that
that skin breaketh for anguish and for sorrow when
he beginneth to die, and beginneth then to open the
eyes in dying that were closed living'; or his peacock,
that 'hath foulest feet and rivelled (wrinkled). And
he wondereth of the fairness of his feathers, and
reareth them up, as it were a circle about his head, and
then he looketh to his feet, and seeth the foulness of his
feet, and, like as he were ashamed, he letteth his feathers
fall suddenly, and all the tail downward, as though he
took no heed of the fairness of his feathers. And hath a
voice of a fiend, head of a serpent, pace of a thief.' There
is something more than childish in such vivid prose as
this; and one may greet a flash of the sublime rhythm of
Job in Bartholomew's lion—'he hideth himself in high
mountains, and thence espieth his prey'—or in his bees,
that 'have an host and a king, and move war and battle,
and fly and void smoke and wind, and make them hardy
and sharp to battle with great noise.' It would be easy
for a poet, not to say a psycho-analyst, to find a sad parable
in Greene's ape, who 'ever killeth that young one which
he loveth most with embracing it too fervently'; and

poets have drawn on Bartholomew's picture of the adder resisting the snake-charmer, when she ' layeth her one ear to the ground, and stoppeth the other with her tail, and so she heareth not the voice of the charming, nor cometh out to him that charmeth, nor is obedient to his saying.'

There is perhaps, strictly speaking, more fancy than real imagination in these brightly coloured embroideries of truth ; like Chaucer, the background of whose world was just such a tapestry, they have not, it may be complained, ' high seriousness.' Be it so ; we shall not close our Chaucer. When the Middle Ages were serious, they tended either to the tedious or the ghastly ; there is no midway halting-place for them between the grotesque devils of their cathedrals and their drama, and the too real ones of their Infernos, between eating black-puddings on the altar at the Feast of Fools and burning heretics in the square outside. As cruel as children, as unreasoning as children, they have childhood's charm and its vitality ; and so it comes that they can write at times more tiresomely than the modern mind can easily conceive, at times with a freshness it cannot hope to recapture. This is Bartholomew on the flea : ' The flea . . . is a little worm of wonder lightness, and scapeth and voideth peril with leaping, and not with running, and waxeth slow, and faileth in cold time, and in summer time it waxeth quiver and swift. And the flea is bred white, and changeth as it were suddenly into black colour, and desireth blood, and doth let them that would sleep with sharp biting, and spareth not kings, but a little flea grieveth them, if he touch their flesh. And to fleas wormwood is venom, and so be leaves of the wild fig-tree.' If one were asked to analyse why exactly this is so pleasant, I suppose the answer would be : ' Partly it is the pleasure of good words and phrases like " quiver and swift " ; partly because the author, unlike us with our terror of the obvious, describes it with such delighted zest that we realise how extraordinary the obvious really is—the incredible, grotesque oddity of the flea. And lastly, there is that sudden glory when the writer leaps from the dust of commonplace to the canopies of kings.' The same qualities go to the making of an even better description of that overworked creature, the lamb ; Wordsworth talked enough about simplicity, but in practice what a hash he made of his lambs compared with this ! ' The lamb hoppeth and leapeth before the flock, and playeth, and dreadeth full sore when he seeth the wolf, and fleeth suddenly away ; but anon he is astonied for dread, and stinteth (stoppeth) suddenly, and dare flee no further ; and prayeth to be spared, not with bleating, but with a simple cheer, when he is taken of his enemy. Also whether he be led to pasture or to death, he grudgeth not, nor pranceth not, but is obedient and meek. It is peril to leave lambs alone, for they die soon, if there falleth any strong thunder ; for the lamb hath kindly (by nature) a feeble head.'

Here is something, nothing very great, but something, that English can never do again. English literature has become literary ; the highest literature must be that— conscious in its art ; Homer already was. But the gain is not quite pure gain and there is some payment to be made—

Nothing can be as it has been before.
Better, so call it, only not the same.

Part of the price of Milton and Gibbon is the Ballads and Bartholomew.

'HONEST OVID AMONG THE GOTHS'*

In the spring of 1480 Caxton, who had set up his press
at Westminster three years before, finished his translation of Ovid's *Metamorphoses*. Whether he ever printed
it remains very doubtful ; if there ever was such an
edition, it has vanished without trace ; and of his rendering the last six books alone survive in a manuscript of
unknown origin, possibly Caxton's autograph, now in
the Pepysian Library at Magdalene College, Cambridge.
It is this which is here printed, with a bibliographical
introduction by Stephen Gaselee and a literary one by
H. F. B. Brett-Smith.

With such a book it is a case of love at first sight. The
Shakespeare Head Press has produced a work as pleasant
to look at as it is to read—sometimes even pleasanter.
For though Caxton is charming, Ovid's butterfly lightness of touch was not for him. Read running, his version
is a delight ; but the run must not be too long. After
all, this is natural enough ; of an overworked man of
business, with the raciest gift of self-expression but the
most modest claims to style, one cannot expect too much
—least of all when one remembers his amazing output
of over eighteen thousand books and four and a half thousand pages of translation. And so between Caxton and
Caxton's French original, Ovid finds himself at times
very much among the Goths. Of the innumerable mis-
translations a single instance will suffice. Describing

* *Ovyde hys Booke of Methamorphose. Books X-XV. Translated by*
W. Caxton. Blackwell (Shakespeare Head Press).
  Fanshawe's Loves of Dido and Æneas. Edited by A. L. Irvine. Black-
well.

39

how Mount Tmolus came to judge between the fluting
of Marsyas and Apollo playing the lyre, Ovid had
written—

> From his ears he brushed the trees ; only an oak
> Wreathed his dark locks and let its acorns hang
> About his hollow temples.

But Caxton sees a very different picture—

> Tymolus the montayne . . . for to here the dysputacion
> unstopped hys eerys whyche were shadowed with trees and
> put from hym all maner trees sauf onely an Ooke laden and
> charged with akehorns whych he retened and satte upon.

Here are the *Metamorphoses* metamorphosed indeed ;
never again shall I hear the familiar crackling of basket-
chairs under old gentlemen of generous proportions
without a vision of Caxton's mountain sitting down
heavily upon its single oak.   Still less could he be bothered
about proper names ; Anaxarete disguises herself as
‘ Anapareces,’ Erebus and Chaos become ‘ Crevy and
Cao ’ ; Tarpeia alters her sex to ‘ Tarpee the foole,’ and
‘ Yrys ’ changes hers from sentence to sentence with
more than feminine caprice.   For Caxton followed his
French manuscript through thick and thin, and where
it was illegible or ambiguous, just hoped for the best.
Our modern accuracy was one of the few superstitions
which did not trouble the Middle Ages : and after all
these things have a charm of their own, like the crazy
overhangings of the houses of Caxton's century, and
there is something refreshing in that entire indifference
to literary property or propriety which can interpolate
without a word of warning, now a mediæval account of

the seduction of Helen, now an allegorical explanation of the myths of Orpheus or Atalanta—

> By the fayre Athalanta, with whome many men ranne and deyde for her love, may be understande the delytes of the worlde, chaungeable, which alway flee withoute beynge ferme and faste. And they destroye them self, that must put hem self to payne and travayll to gete and have it.

Here we breathe another air than Ovid knew, and the stern Hill of Calvary rises between us and that fairy pagan world. In such an atmosphere we cease to wonder when our author couples Polymestor with Iscariot, and makes Pan spring ' vauntynge hyme of the horne-pype of Cornewaylle ' ; or when he hides Achilles ' in an Abbaye ' and pokes into that hero's shield a whole enchanting Mandevillian catalogue of countries—Barbarye and Cathaye, Bretayn and Lorayn, Northweye and Southweye, ' and Jherusalem beynge sette in the ryght Centre of all the erthe '—and, with these, the figures of ' the seven Scyences liberal,' headed by ' Gramare betynge the children ' !

Strange fate that brought, of all poets, Ovid the neat, the debonair, that brilliant, light-hearted, ill-fated butterfly, into the hands of this solid Englishman of the Kentish Weald ! One feels at times as if *The Rape of the Lock* or *The Importance of being Earnest* were being paraphrased by Mrs. Beeton. Now and then Caxton's sledge-hammer smashes the egg-shell out of recognition, and Ovid's silk purse seems really turning into a sow's ear. And yet the result is often surprisingly successful ; it is never Ovid, but it can be magnificent in quite a new way of its own, as Mr. Brett-Smith points out in an introduction, of which the only fault is that he has picked out the best of Caxton with so sure an eye that the reader is a little disappointed when he comes to Caxton as a whole. For Caxton at his best can write like this—

> The nyght was fayre and stylle. And the Mone and the Sterris shone when Mirra emprysed her wodeness (madness) for to goo an evylle voyage . . . thryes she stombled and thryes brayd on her the Owle in sygne of shrewde tydynges. Yet for all this that she sawe or herd she wolde not leve her waye.

And again—

> The hows of this gode (Sleep) was in a most still place of the worlde in the bottom of the kreves of a mountayne, where as the sonne never shyneth, where as it seemeth aleway is betwyn day and nyght. There slepeth this god. Ther is neyther noyse ne lyghte may dystrowble hys reste. There resowneth nothynge but a swete wynd amonge rosyers. And a lytil broke of water soundeth, whych renneth and murmureth upon the gravell that it resowneth forto gyve appetyte to sleep.

And even if Caxton himself often nods and sometimes snores, still a volume like this is to be read rather than read through and, on a shelf or off it, is a pleasant thing to possess.

Mr. Irvine's little book contains the Latin text of *Æneid IV*, with Sir Richard Fanshawe's seventeenth-century English on the opposite page, followed by an interesting set of notes for the not too learned reader. These notes indeed are made even a little more amusing than they are meant to be by the editor's admirable determination to bring in somewhere, by hook or by crook, his favourite little bits of information ; the following appears, for instance, on line 412—

> This line may recall to readers of Lady Fanshawe her husband's exclamation when, awaiting the attack of a Turkish

galley during a voyage to Spain, he suddenly finds his wife at
his elbow, wearing a blue thrum-cap and tarred coat which
she had bribed a cabin-boy to lend : ' Good God, that love
can make this change !' She adds : ' And though he
seemingly chid me, he would laugh at it often as he
remembered that voyage.'

Readers of Lady Fanshawe are few, and the connection
somewhat tenuous ; but this foible, if it be a fault at all,
is too pleasant in its results to be wished away.   Equally
amiable is Mr. Irvine's resolve to exalt the good Sir
Richard's verse.   It is so easy (*peccavi*) for an editor to
love his author not wisely but too well.   Fanshawe was
no goose ; but I cannot find so tuneful a swan as Mr.
Irvine suggests, in one who could write—

> And yet, perchance, you lying in his breast
> With a wife's rhetoric may his counsels sway ;
> Then break the ice ; I 'll second the request.

And if Caxton was not clever enough for Ovid, Fanshawe
is far too clever for Virgil, whom he finds it necessary to
improve now and then with detestable fancies of his own,
such as—

> They comb'd with oars great Neptune's curled head,

or
>   The sad ambassadress
> Carries her tears, and brings them back again
> (As brackish tides post to and from the main).

There are two fine lines—

> When every one was parted to his rest
> And the dim moon trod on the heels of day—

but, though Fanshawe's general level is far from bad, I
do not think there are many more.   The Spenserian
stanza is dangerously difficult, with its quadruple rhymes,

and dangerously rigid for reproducing Virgil's Miltonic play of pause and paragraph. These may not be fatal obstacles ; indeed it is perilous in literature to call anything impossible ; but Sir Richard was not the man to overcome them.

There remains one other controversial point—the usual anxiety to whitewash Æneas' treatment of Dido. Mr. Irvine hunts hotly on this trail, and argues once again how much more Rome mattered than a mere woman, and how it follows that if Virgil is a great poet, then his hero must be a great hero, and so forth This has long been one of the great cruces of literature ; yet I doubt if the character of the good Æneas is worth all the pother that has been made about it. One might as well hang oneself as read the *Æneid* for the sake of its hero ; after all there is no literary law that heroes *must* be heroic. We read Virgil far more for the character of Virgil himself than of the son of Anchises—for the sake of his splendour of sound and language, that intensity of beauty Flaubert could hardly bear ; for the sake of his wistful pity ; for the sake of the story and its episodes and its memories. As for the Dido business, the apologists for Æneas always forget that it is not only what one does that matters, but how one does it. It is the manners of Æneas that are the intolerable thing ; to say to a forsaken woman, ' After all, you know, I never said anything about marrying you,' is a little too cheap. Let those who hold that the Romans never knew how to behave, suppose that the poet, whom men called ' The Maiden ' for his gentle sensitiveness, was callously blind to this. What lowers Aeneas is not that his love yields to duty, but that it yields so easily. Did he really care ? Did it cost him

much ? Virgil could have torn his hero from the arms
of Dido with as little dishonour as Racine his Titus from
the arms of Bérénice ; but the Roman poet had in his
memory a very different pair—the Medea and Jason of
Euripides. And as the Greek Medea has inspired some
of Dido's angry eloquence, so, I believe, some of the base-
ness of Jason's casuistry has cast its shadow on Aeneas ;
and I believe also that Virgil himself, like his hero, was
seduced into momentary forgetfulness of Rome itself by
the tragic splendour of his Carthaginian queen. How
many of the most living characters of fiction have re-
fused to behave exactly as their creators intended ! Was
not Milton tempted of his own Devil ? The plan of the
Æneid may suffer ; but it suffers less than its greatest
episode has gained ; and if Æneas is damaged, after all,
like Dido who perishes, he too is but a means to that one
great end which is Rome. Things are like that. ' With
Æneas goes the *Æneid*,' pleads Mr. Irvine ; that is precisely what it does not do, any more than *Paradise Lost*
depends on Adam. Mr. Chesterton has well said of
the Old Testament view of life, that if God chooses to
use a man or a mammoth for His purpose, it does not
necessarily entail any peculiar consideration for man or
mammoth in themselves. And indeed Delilah's Samson
and the ignoble jawbone of an ass were enough for the
salvation of Israel and the glory of its God. ' Que mon
nom soit flétri, que la France soit libre '—it was a nobler
than Æneas who uttered that ; but Virgil would have
understood. Æneas remains a worthy character ; no
amount of ink will whiten him to a splendid one. An
Achilles can ruin an empire ; it needs an Æneas to
rebuild one.

For why the soule being divine alone,
Exempt from vile and gross corruption,
Of heavenly secrets comprehensible,
Of which the dull flesh is not sensible,
And by one onely powerfull faculty,
Yet governeth a multiplicity,
Being essentiall, uniforme in all ;
Not to be sever'd nor dividuall,
But in her function holdeth her estate,
By powers divine in her ingenerate. . . .

I pray thee, love, love me no more,
　　Call home the heart you gave me ;
I but in vain that saint adore
　　That can, but will not, save me.

Between these two fragments there might lie two hundred years. It is as though some creaking fifteenth-century waggon, loaded with overgilt mediæval furniture and imitations of imitations of Chaucer's day, were suddenly overtaken on the road and passed in a whirl of dust by the racing canter and jingling bit of some cavalier flushed and gallant from Whitehall. And yet, incredible as it may seem, the two passages come from one and the same hand.

Drayton never rose to be a great poet, except for fourteen lines so consummate that some have been found to deny that any but Shakespeare himself could have written them ; but if he kept close to the ground, he covered a vast amount of it ; and no man was ever more

* *Endimion and Phœbe.* By Michael Drayton. Edited by Prof. *J. W. Hebel.* Blackwell (*Shakespeare Head Press*).

of a self-made poet, so far as unending effort and experiment can make poets at all. To write poetry was the first ambition that fired his childhood ; and the whole of his long life was one patient apprenticeship in ever new ways of writing it. With more than Elizabethan spaciousness, through a career of forty years, he set his hand to poems religious, historical, geographical, and pastoral, to sonnets, to satires, to odes, to epistles, to burlesques, to panegyrics, to stage-plays. In his own charming words—

> My wanton verse ne'er keeps one certain stay,
> But now at hand, then seeks invention far,
> And with each little motion runs astray,
> Wild, madding, jocund and irregular.
>> Like me that list !—my honest merry rhymes
>> Nor care for critic, nor regard the times.

And if these forty years were largely spent wandering in wildernesses whither few follow him now, still he pointed the way to more than one land of promise that lay ahead—to the smoothness of Waller, to the weight of Dryden's couplet, to the Miltonic ode, to the lyrics of the cavaliers, to Tennyson's ' Light Brigade ' with its feebler imitation of his ' Agincourt,' and even, as Professor Elton has pointed out, to the wild tripping dance of some of Swinburne's ecstasies—

> Give her th' Eoan brightness,
> Wing'd with that subtle lightness
>> That doth transpierce the air :
> The roses of the morning,
> The rising heaven adorning,
>> To mesh with flames of hair.

And yet, for all his labours, Drayton is seldom quite

good enough ; he was in too great a hurry. Patient with a more than Roman persistency in performance, he showed himself, too often, inconsiderate in what he undertook. He was in a tearing haste to become a poet, even before he was one ; indeed, nothing ever quite became his literary life so charmingly as the beginning of it, as told in that pleasant description of his Warwickshire childhood in the household of Sir Henry Goodere, which his old age penned to Rainolds—

> In my small self I greatly marvell'd then,
> Amongst all others, what strange kind of men
> These poets were ; and, pleased with the name,
> To my mild tutor merrily I came
> (For I was then a proper goodly page,
> Much like a pigmy, scarce ten years of age)—
> Clasping my slender arms about his thigh,
> ' O my dear master, cannot you (quoth I)
> Make me a poet ?   Do it if you can,
> And you shall see I 'll quickly be a man.'

And yet, his childish ambition duly accomplished, he ruined himself from a worldly point of view by this same eagerness, which drove him to congratulate James on his accession with a haste that the Court considered indecent ; so that when the due measure of official tears had flowed for Elizabeth, the King's returning smile was reserved for rivals, and Drayton was left to vent his anger in a satire on the palaces of princes, and to find what comfort he could in his own abiding sturdiness of heart—

> Yet had not my clear spirit in fortune's scorn
> Me above earth and my afflictions borne,
> He, next my God on whom I built my trust,
> Had left me trodden lower than the dust.

But even this was not the end of his disappointments ; other patrons he could find, but not readers for his life's work on the legendary glories of the English countryside. For the second part of *Polyolbion*, indeed, he could hardly discover a publisher, and his wounded pride and patriotism find vent at last in the half-superb, half-laughable cursing and swearing of its preface—

Some of our outlandish, unnatural English (I know not how otherwise to express them) stick not to say that there is nothing in this Island worth studying for, and take great pride to be ignorant in anything thereof ; for these, since they delight in their folly, I wish it may be hereditary from them to their posterity, that their children may be begg'd for fools to the fifth generation until it may be beyond the memory of man to know that there was ever other of their families.

But there was no help. Even the longer-suffering public of that day was not to be bludgeoned into reading a guide-book to England versified in thirty books of Alexandrine couplets. Drayton, however, now in his sixties, instead of bowing his grey hairs in disappointment to the grave performed the last of his amazing transforma-tions. The mountain suddenly begins to skip like a young ram ; and, vital and versatile as ever, the aged poet bursts into the mocking, midget laughter of *Nymphidia*. Here, at all events, stretching one fairy hand back to Shake-speare, one on to Herrick, danced a fantasy that could and still can bewitch the most frivolous ; it does not seem, however, to have made much material difference to the old man himself. ' Honest Mr. Michael Drayton had about some five pounds lying by him at his death, which was *satis viatici ad coelum* ! ' And so to his rest at West-

minster ; where a better epitome of the man to set above
his bones in the Abbey than the stock undertaker's
couplets attributed to Jonson, would have been his own
proud lines of years before—

> No fatal dreads, nor fruitless vain desires,
> Low caps and court'sies to a painted wall,
> Nor heaping rotten sticks on needless fires,
> Ambitious ways to climb, nor fears to fall,
> Nor things so base do I affect at all.

England has had many greater poets than Drayton ;
and yet in Drayton can be seen with unusual clearness
that strangely ordinary, quiet temperament which has
given to England poets greater, not only than Drayton,
but than those of any other land but Greece. You
would never guess from the faces you see in an English
market-place, or in a carriage on the Underground, that
ours was the race which could claim, beyond question,
this proud pre-eminence. You will notice far more
superficial poeticalness abroad ; only read, for instance,
the rhapsodies with which Fascism plasters the streets
and railway stations of Italy ; and yet the paradox remains, that this temperament, so easily dismissed by
quicker races as stolid and almost stupid, holds hidden in
its finer types the unsuspected power of attaining in its
moments of fanciful humour such delicacy and brilliance,
in its moments of passion such undreamed-of heights and
depths. The Drayton in the National Portrait Gallery
wears almost the mien of a respectable bricklayer on a
Sunday, highly serious but unconvincing in his laurel
wreath ; the later engraving in the 1619 edition of his
poems shows much more character, indeed, in the grim

pursing of the disgruntled mouth, but hardly more intellect.

'Since there's no help, come let us kiss and part'—was it from such prosaic-looking lips that this supreme cry first broke? True, the portraits are very likely unlike; but one could not possibly assume it. Was it not Hazlitt, who, asked about the countenance of Wordsworth, replied, 'Have you ever seen a horse?'?

Few of us in our comfortable obscurity will envy Drayton his career, with its hopes deferred only to be disappointed, its long labours for so slight reward; but we shall not grudge him, either, a title to a greatness of his own. Ben Jonson said to Drummond, who doucely popped it into his notebook, that 'Drayton feared him; and he esteemed not of him'; but we may well doubt the first of these statements, and esteem Jonson himself none the better for the second. For of Drayton also is true that fine sentence of Mrs. Browning on herself— 'I have loved poetry more than my successes in it.' Whatever his own achievement, this blunt Warwickshire Englishman kept to the end unswerving devotion to his art—

> When heaven would strive to do the best it can
> And put an angel's spirit into man,
> The utmost power it hath, it then doth spend
> When to the world a Poet it doth intend.

Like one of his own personified Midland rivers, he goes winding on, quiet, strong, unruffled, through a country-side ever changing, but always typically English, with clear waters that mirror in turn on their calm surface the sunset and dawn and sunset of Middle Ages and Renaissance

Endimion and Phœbe is an early work and a poor one.
Marlowe had produced his *Hero and Leander*, Shakespeare his *Venus and Adonis*; so Drayton must needs
follow suit with a similar love-idyll; only, the love should
be platonic, like the poet's own passion for Mistress Ann
Goodere. The result is a sticky, sickly stream of sweet-
nesses which makes the reader feel like one of the unfortunate inhabitants of the treacle-well in the Dormouse's
story in *Alice* or, indeed, like the Dormouse himself.
Marlowe's magnificent impetuousness hurls itself onward
through the bad taste and *niaiseries* of his poem, like the
white body of Leander threshing through the weltering
Hellespont. If the characters in Shakespeare's tale leave
us cold and cloyed, yet there remain for ever the splendour
of his horse and the pity of his hunted hare, the pure poetry
of his lark and snail. But Drayton's piece has neither
passion nor pity; it has no story, only a thin thread on
which to string his coloured beads of word-painting.
The narrative is more like a series of magic-lantern slides
jerked on and off the screen, than any sort of moving
picture; and the individual episodes vary from the blank
mediæval tedium of the extract which heads this essay,
to the Elizabethan prettiness of the following—

> And *Cynthia* sitting in her Christall chayre,
> In all her pompe now rid along her Spheare;
> The honnied dewe descended in soft showres,
> Drizled in Pearle upon the tender flowers;
> And *Zephyre* husht, and with a whispering gale,
> Seemed to hearken to the Nightingale,
> Which in the thorny brakes with her sweet song,
> Unto the silent Night bewrayd her wrong.

But as a whole *Endimion and Phœbe* is typical of those

youthful periods of development when the appetite for sugar seems perfectly inexhaustible. The best that can be said of it may most fitly find expression in the lines of its author's *Polyolbion*—

Even in the aged face where beauty once did dwell
And nature in the least but seemed to excel,
Time cannot make such waste, but something will appear,
To show some little tract of delicacy there.

As man and as poet Donne has been exhaustively treated by Sir Edmund Gosse and Professor Grierson. Mr. Fausset, who is not primarily interested in poetry or men, has approached his subject from a different angle—as a 'Study in Discord.' Harmony with ultimate reality, with the creative Life-force, and, on the other hand, the contrasting discords through which Donne laboured all his days in search (little as he himself realised it) of that harmony—these are the real subjects of this biography. In fact the book is a logical continuation of Mr. Fausset's earlier works on Keats and Tennyson. Keats, in Mr. Fausset's view, after throwing off his charming juvenilia, the Sonnets, Odes, and the rest, was just reaching harmony with the Life-force in 'The Induction to Hyperion,' when death took him. Tennyson, we gather, proved an even sadder failure, for not death, but his own weakness, prevented him fulfilling the true poet's only function, in attaining this same harmony. But Donne, it seems, after flinging off like the other two his youthful effusions, did not die young like Keats, nor sink into the degenerate serenity of Tennyson, but lived out his life lacerated indeed by the wild discords of his soul, yet discords which at a few happy moments—for instance, during the agonies of the fever which almost proved fatal to him in 1623— would appear to have been temporarily resolved into the ultimate harmony. This is, we are told, less strange than might perhaps seem : ' In the delirium of the fever patient, as in the visions of many ecstatics, glimpses of pure reality are found co-existing with every kind of

* *John Donne : A Study in Discord.* By H. I'Anson Fausset. Cape.

confused hallucination. . . . So akin is such a state to
mystical illumination, that we are tempted to suppose the
existence of some element of fever as necessary for the
release of the imagination from the clutch of the flesh.'
Unhappily such 'states of grace' (a term which, Mr.
Fausset complains, 'has been often clouded by association with formal creeds or conventional sanctity') were
short-lived in the Dean of St. Paul's. Once more his
health rallied. He became petulantly anxious about his
recovery. His black horrors of death returned upon
him. And had he really got well again, it is likely that
Mr. Fausset would once more have been compelled to
regret, as two years previously, that improvement in
health had brought with it deterioration of character—
that is to say, renewed interest in social intercourse and
political small talk, and fresh flatteries of patrons in the
hope of preferment. However, during the last gloomy
eight years of his life, Donne never properly recovered ;
and yet, even so, Mr. Fausset tells us, harmony was never
safely his. Discord still gnawed the roots of his character.
' And so his style, whether as poet or preacher, never
achieved either the fresh, effusive gaiety or the assured
serenity of Absolute Beauty. He could not create beauty
out of life ; he could not even see the beauty in which
the limbs of life were veiled . . . because he lacked
harmony in himself.'

But though Donne, it appears, 'could not create
beauty,' he has special interest for our age. 'We, in a
different way, are in danger . . . of becoming dwarfed
and mechanical for want of that apprehension of creative
purpose in the universe, which invites to self-forgetfulness.'
And yet the battle is not quite so fierce for us ; we are

milder; and, besides, 'we approach life with less assurance and less arrogance.' This last is a statement which Mr. Fausset himself does not make it very easy for us to believe.

In writing such stuff he is merely abusing his talents. It is very well to know what one thinks; it is important also to think what one knows. This sort of glib dogmatism, like facile generalisations about women's instinct, 'eager for enslavement,' leads nowhere. Mr. Fausset should decide whether he wants to write philosophy or biography, to follow M. Bergson or Mr. Lytton Strachey. He cannot do both. It will always be a poor sort of biography that is interested less in human beings for their own sakes than to prove some thesis or other; and it is a poor sort of criticism that decries the 'Ode to a Nightingale,' or 'Tithonus,' because they are wrong about the Life-force, or that hurries past Donne's early poems as if they were milestones on the road from perdition, with so little appreciation of their astonishing qualities as to suggest that their author 'could not create beauty,' or that his prose is more poetical. Parnassus is not Sinai.

It is curious to watch Mr. Fausset's theories, as one might expect, twisting his facts. If the young Donne shows eagerness for aristocratic society, it is not really necessary to suppose that he was seeking in convention and etiquette curbs for the wild beast within him. It is simpler to conclude that he liked aristocratic society. Or take that blistering poem 'The Apparition '—

> When by thy scorn, O murd'ress, I am dead,
> And that thou think'st thee free
> From all solicitation from me,
> Then shall my ghost come to thy bed,
> And thee, feign'd vestal, in worse arms shall see . . .

Mr. Fausset for some reason identifies the object of this invective with that married woman whom Donne in his youth seduced, and sees in the poem the pitiless farewell of the ' moralist newly risen from the ashes of the brute ' ; whereas it seems clear enough from the poem itself that no such identification is possible, and it is merely a savage parting fling at some ' feign'd vestal ' who had rejected Donne's advances. Again, it is extremely misleading to drag in evolution in connection with that curious poem, ' The Progresse of the Soule ' (from Eve's apple through mandrakes and fishes and apes, into the body of Queen Elizabeth), and to talk about ' the mysterious force of life gradually driving it upward to the higher plane of humanity,' when it is a simple application of Pythagoras to satirise the heretic sovereign with the attribution of so degraded a soul, and the poet cynically doubts, as the soul passes from an ape to a woman, whether the move were upwards or downwards in the scale of things. Lastly, a better taste would have spared such a comment as this on Donne's famous invocation—

> I have a sin of fear, that when I 've spun
> My last thread, I shall perish on the shore ;
> But swear by Thyself, that at my death Thy Son
> Shall shine as He shines now, and heretofore ;
> And having done that, Thou hast done,
> I fear no more—

' Unfortunately, the Deity is not given to swearing oaths, even for the reassurance of agitated Deans.'

The effect of this irritating, interesting book is to make one feel how little value remains in the record of Donne's life, as compared with the living portion of his work ; and feel, also, the irony that this should be so. The verses of his reprobate youth, the verses he would never publish, which only a saving relic of vanity saved from the flames, are the most precious things that tortured life has left. To Donne in his old age they were abominations; but to us they are the real Donne still—'The stone that the builders rejected.' And similarly with his other great bequest to posterity, the sermons. Written and delivered in agonies of hope and fear, so vivid that the spell-bound congregations in St. Paul's seemed to see the heavens open above them, and felt beneath their feet the roaring of the furnaces of Hell or the cold writhing of the undying worm in the coffins of the crypts below—they are read now for their style. The thorns that anguished spirit wove together to scourge itself, lie quiet to-day in the flower-garland of the anthologist.

Donne was not a great man nor a particularly good one; he had not the nobility of prouder, the pity of kindlier, souls; but he was an amazing poet, one who stands, still, in the whole world's literature, unique and alone. Others have had his astonishing agility of mind; others his passionate intensity; but none has combined quite in Donne's way realism and unreality, directness and abstruseness, spontaneity and affectation, the lightning and the will-o'-the-wisp, the audacity, the cruelty, and the charming irritability of youth.

> Busy old fool, unruly Sun,
>   Why dost thou thus
> Through windows and through curtains call on us?
> Must to thy motions lovers' seasons run?
>   Saucy, pedantic wretch. . . .

For God's sake hold your tongue and let me love !

. . . .

Love, any devil else but you
Would for a given soul give something too.

. . . .

For the first twenty years, since yesterday,
I scarce believed thou couldst be gone away.

. . . .

If yet I have not all thy love,
Dear, I shall never have it all.

. . . . . .

Hope not for mind in women ; at their best
Sweetness and wit, they are but Mummy, possest.

Had the soul of Catullus danced for ages on the point of
the mediæval Schoolmen's needle, or spent the centuries
talking with their subtle spirits in some anguished circle
of Dante's Hell, it might have breathed again in the young
Donne.   Physical of the physical, he can be ethereally
ideal ; now, at his touch, abstract becomes concrete and
the soul like a ' great prince in prison lies,' now concrete becomes abstract—

That one might almost say *his* body thought.

It is interesting that, as Sir Edmund Gosse points out,
he makes allusions, rare in his age, to Dante, Rabelais, and
Albrecht Dürer ; the dark intensity, the blunt grossness,
the macabre realism of these three unite themselves in
him. ' Twisting iron pokers into true-love knots,' he
remains not one of the greatest poets but, as Ben Jonson
said, ' the first poet in the world *in some things*.'   Strong

though he was, rather than sweet, to deny him beauty is absurd, and to be prim about him, impertinent—

> Surely you were something better
> Than innocent.

Better, indeed, in many ways, had he died young, had he indeed been laid to sleep with that ' bracelet of bright hair about the bone,' not perpetuated through a harsh eternity in his grotesque, unhappy winding-sheet of stone. Some prefer the sermons to the poems ; for to some minds the poems are shocking. To others the sermons are considerably more so. No sensuality on earth is so disgusting as cruelty ; and under the splendour of Donne's prose lie ideas that would outrage an intelligent savage. Again, Donne in his writings was always given to hyperbole ; and that fault is easier to forgive in the lover and the youth. And, lastly, with all their majesty, the sermons have an unreality, an antiqueness, that many of the poems with their amazing modernity do not show ; they ' date ' ; their theological cummin-splitting, their efforts to stampede humanity into virtue by brandishing painted devils, their insane morbidity belong to a dead order of things. We grow so weary of the worms, worms, worms. It was part of the spirit of that age, no doubt. In Webster and his like exists also this same ' wormy circumstance ' ; but with a difference. For in Webster's tragedies human courage confronts undaunted the horrors of the tomb ; in Donne's sermons it is bidden cringe and grovel before them.

> Those are my best days when I shake with fear.

Still, there they are : let us be thankful for the organ-thunders of their Dead March also. They remain the last great English literature over which Terror reigns ; and that spectral figure of the great Dean, risen from his death-bed to preach his own death-sermon, with all its theatricality, seems to speak the epilogue of the age of English Tragedy. To the congregation that watched it, this emaciated shape waving its gaunt arms in the Gothic shadows of old St. Paul's, it must already have seemed a relic of an outworn time. For us, with the impressiveness mingles a repulsion ; as when we look on Donne's effigy, which by some strange chance escaped the Great Fire and holds still its incongruous place, a last fragment of the Middle Ages, within the classic precinct of Wren. Too truly he cried—

> Nothing but man of all envenom'd things
> Doth work upon itself with inborn stings.

Strange vanity of human self-torment—that troubled dust sleeping so sound at last, the fires of Hell forgotten, while the old London it had known, the old cathedral it had once made to echo with warnings of eternal torment, staggered and crashed above it into a sea of real flame. Even yet the stony immortality of that barbaric genius, that demoniac among the tombs, awes us with its stare ; until, with an impulse of revolt, the mind turns from its savagery to remember instead the balance and the self-command of Greece and Rome, the nobler sadness of races that never dealt in death's-head and skeleton, the quiet beauty of the tombstones of the Cerameicus, the indomitable dignity of those great bastions of the Imperial dead along the Appian Way.

MICHELET, as he brings to a close his story of the long martyrdom of Joan of Arc, losing all at once his cold, judicial bitterness, flares out into a passionate denunciation of our race, that startles not so much by its suddenness even, as by its definition of the supreme English sin —unbending, unchristian, unalterable pride. ' C'est le seul peuple qui n'ait pu revendiquer *l'Imitation de Jésus* ; un Français pouvait écrire ce livre, un Allemand, un Italien, jamais un Anglais. De Shakespeare à Milton, de Milton à Byron, leur belle et sombre littérature est sceptique, judaïque, satanique, pour résumer, anti-chrétienne.' He calls to witness the very aborigines of America, ' qui ont souvent tant de pénétration et d'originalité ' ; have not they, too, a legend that Christ was a Frenchman crucified at London, and Pontius Pilate an English magistrate ?

We may admit this charge of pride ; we may prove it the truer by being rather proud to admit it ; but there remains one period when our ' fine and gloomy literature ' did produce great Christian poetry. Granted that Milton's, in the eyes of Michelet, forms no part of it ; yet Milton had contemporaries whom that historian has forgotten. Our seventeenth century is indeed a strange medley. So mediæval still, yet at times so modern, that Donne can express us better than most poets of to-day— the unearthliest of our centuries, yet, from the charnels of Webster to the burial-urns of Browne, the earthiest— it produced a succession of writers who wrote difficultly

* *Henry Vaughan : Poems and Prose. Nonesuch Press.*

and yet plunged with an un-English ease through ' the
deep, but dazzling darkness ' of the mystic's way. The
Middle Ages and the Renaissance were dying, victor and
vanquished, side by side ; and in that twilight of the elder
gods, from Donne to Vaughan, our poetry seems for
once to find naturally the Christian mystic's ecstasy.
When in 1695 Vaughan died he had long outlived
himself in a new world which was not ecstatic nor mystic,
not very poetical nor particularly Christian ; in the very
next year there appeared, typically enough, the *Psalms*
of Tate and Brady, and Toland's *Christianity not Mysterious* ; only a century later did the forgotten Silurist
wake echoes in the mind and verse of Wordsworth.

From birth there was perhaps a Welsh gift for mystic
fervour in Vaughan's blood ; he had, we are told, an
elder kinsman who conversed familiarly with spirits which
revealed themselves in the strange form of scarabees.
And the frivolous may recognise another supposed racial
character, of a less admirable kind, in Aubrey's comment
on Vaughan's father : ' A coxcomb and no honester than
he should be ; he cozened me of fifty shillings once.'
The poet's own life was blankly uneventful. From
Jesus, Oxford, he passed to London to study law and
medicine, diversified with those juvenile poems which he
liked to imagine, after his conversion, as so much naughtier
than they had ever been. For in later years Vaughan
came to speak with harshness, though a musical harshness,
of the singing follies of his youth :

> Let it suffice my warmer days
> Simpered and shined on you,
> Twist not my Cypresse with your Bays
> Or Roses with my Yewgh ;

Go, go, seek some greener thing,
    It snows and freezeth here ;
Let Nightingales attend the spring,
    Winter is all my year.

It is indeed a standing miracle through what chrysalis all
medical students pass from the noisiest to the quietest of
God's creatures : Sir Thomas Browne might well have
discussed it among his *Vulgar Errors*—though it be none.
At all events, by this time-honoured process the sonneteer
of Amoret became for fifty years a devout country doctor ;
and from the peace of Brecknock and Norwich at the
quiet extremities of a troubled England there stole into
the world *Olor Iscanus* and *Religio Medici, Silex Scintillans* and *Urn-Burial.*

Vaughan's prose essay from the *Mount of Olives* included in this edition, gives a measure of the likeness and
the difference between the two physicians.   Its cadences
seem a fainter echo of Browne, when the Welshman
describes the dissection of hibernating animals in their
' dark state of dormition ' ;   when with a sudden touch
of poetry he pities the brief life of man, outlived ' sometimes by a flower of his own setting ' ;   or when he
writes, ' The contemplation of *death* is an obscure,
melancholy *walk*, an Expatiation in *shadows* and *solitude*,
but it leads unto *life*, and he that sets forth at *midnight*,
will sooner meet the *Sunne*, than he that sleeps it out
betwixt his curtains.'   Yet there is a gulf between the
kindly East Anglian, who could never bring his mind
to dwell on the idea of eternal torment, and this fanatic
revivalist warming his hands with complacent ingenuity
over the ancient fires of Hell

' Suppose,' he writes, paraphrasing an admired author

of his, ' that this whole Globe of earth were nothing else but a huge masse, or mountain of sand, and that a little Wren came but once in every thousand yeers to fetch away but one grain of that huge heap ; what an innumerable number of years would be spent, before that world of sand could be so fetcht away ! And yet (alas !) when the damned have laine in that fiery lake so many yeers as all those would amount to, they are no nearer coming out, than the first hours they entered in.'

So might have meditated the horrible genius of Donne, or Burton diverting his melancholy with speculations on the cubic content of Hell ; but never Sir Thomas Browne. Vaughan is an inspired poet, but a smaller man. At the moments when he becomes supreme, the reader feels a sudden astonishment—' Was there so much in him ? ' But when Browne reaches *his* heights there is no wonder in our admiration ; we knew he could do it all. Vaughan, at such instants, seems transfigured by a glory not earthly nor his own. The spark leaps, but the flint is still a flint. And when the drone of devotional verse is broken by such things as his vision of Eternity, or

> I see them walking in an Air of glory
>   Whose light doth trample on my days ;
> My days, which are at best but dull and hoary,
>   Meer glimering and decays,

or

> Thou art a toylsom Mole, or less,
>   A moving mist ;
> But life is, what none can express,
> *A quickness, which my God hath kist,*

then it seems as if the poet, schoolboy-like, had been given somehow unfair help by a master far above himself. And

E

the feeling is just, to this extent—that Vaughan's poems do generally, as they go on, lose their opening ' clouds of glory ' and fade before they end.   Too often his own words come true—

> But (ah !) my soul with too much stay
> Is drunk and staggers by the way.

It is simply that he has little to say—he attains vision sometimes, conceits often, but his range is small and his reason not his stronger part.

> Alas, my God, take home Thy sheep.
> This world but laughs at those that weep—

so he longed ; and as he grew nearer his long home, his songs grew dimmer, so that in his last volume little that is memorable remains.   The Christian has plucked out eye and ear, and put from him the pied world of the senses ; but the true poet must be of this world, even when he sings the next.   Gold is earthliest, most mundane of transitory things ; yet with it, not with good intentions, imagination has paved the streets of Sion.   It has indeed been well said of Vaughan : ' No English poet of his rank is so constantly in search of a subject.'   Still, when he does turn from groping in the clouds to concrete, material things, he can be charming ; thus there is a strange and, for him, unusual tenderness in his description of the dead, dry log that has long lost the green of life—all but life's old, premonitory dread—

> Sure thou did'st flourish once ! and many Springs,
> Many bright mornings, much dew, many showers
> Past ore thy head ; many light *Hearts and Wings*
> Which now are dead, lodg'd in thy living bowers. . . .

But thou beneath the sad and heavy *Line*
Of death, dost waste, all senseless, cold and dark ;
Where not so much as dreams of light may shine,
Nor any thought of greenness, leaf or bark.

And yet (as if some deep hate and dissent,
Bred in thy growth betwixt high winds and thee,
Were still alive) thou dost great storms resent
Before they come, and know'st how near they be.

It is beautifully done, but after it inevitably follows the usual dull moral, a tail without a sting. ' Silex Scintillans '—he chose well his emblem ; beautiful in the darkness is the out-springing of the flint's hidden seeds of flame ; but though they can kindle, they cannot warm.

A TAME OAT FROM EPICURUS' GARDEN*

SEEDLINGS of the Garden of Epicurus have never greatly flourished in England. There is something in the climate too austere. We have bred a Milton but never a Horace, a Bacon but no Montaigne, a Hardy but no Heine, a Shaw but no Anatole France. Between *Rasselas* and *Candide*, children of the same age and the same pessimism, is fixed the same eternal gulf; and though Weeping Philosophers and Stoics, Sceptics and Platonists throng the pages of English literature, how rare is that true Gallic blend of the life according to Epicurus with the philosophic laughter of his master, Democritus! We once had indeed a 'Democritus Junior,' but he wrote an *Anatomy of Melancholy*. We are like the youth in Mr. Yeats—

She bade me take life easy, as the leaves grow on the tree,
But I being young and foolish with her would not agree.

And though we think ourselves the most humorous nation in the world, we keep our laughter mostly out of our philosophy, if we have one, taking seriously our pleasures, our poetry, and especially ourselves. So that Matthew Arnold was only being very English, pupil of Sainte-Beuve as he was, when he made his famous demand for 'high seriousness' and 'criticism of life' as the essentials of great literature—a dogma in part truism, in part untrue.

Yet, things were not always thus. The mediæval Englishman was not more reproached by the world for

* *Poems of Charles Cotton. Edited by John Beresford. Cobden-Sanderson.*

68

his notorious possession of a tail than for his equally
notorious lack of gravity—just as Chaucer himself was
to be given a bad mark by Arnold for his want of the
required ' high seriousness.' But these happy days soon
passed. There is little laughter in the sordid annals of
the fifteenth century. The Elizabethans were too
young, too breathless with the excitement of all the new
worlds that were unfolding before them, to be frivolous.
Under the Commonwealth our grey skies turned to
black ; the eighteenth century was too aristocratic, pre-
serving its dignity even through dullness, its etiquette
despite its ennui ; and the nineteenth was too middle-
class, sobered with all the life-is-real-life-is-earnestness
of a respectability which believed progress proved and
itself the main demonstration.

But there remains in our history one light-hearted
interlude, when for a little while it became common for
English writers, instead of believing that the heavens
would fall if they shrugged their shoulders, to forget that
life was highly serious, and to devote their main criticism
of it to the need of gathering its rosebuds. Herrick,
Cowley, Butler, Hobbes, Pepys, Cotton and the dramatists
of their day are, no doubt, of a lower stature than ' the
giants before the flood,' or after it ; but with all their
individual differences they have this in common, that they
represent a unique, untypical, but not unattractive mood
in English literature. They were what they were, in
part because, like the one first-rate English writer who
shares at all their rotund Epicureanism, Chaucer, they
had tasted what Lord Tennyson so pompously called
' poisonous honey brought from France ' ; in part because
the Puritans had surfeited even English solemnity. They

are never sublime nor passionate nor tragic ; nor yet are
they urbane and conventional and 'connoisseured out of
their senses,' as the generations that followed came to be.
Cotton and his fellows view life with no high enthusiasms,
but yet with a considerable zest. They do not dream
that earth is Heaven nor cry that it is Hell. Worldly-
wise but not world-weary, frivolous but not foolish,
middle-aged but vigorous, they have that humour which
is middle age's chief compensation, wiser in their generation than many of our poetic children of light. They
dwelt in the Garden of Epicurus ; but it cannot be
denied that they cultivated it. To the blind Samson in
Bunhill Fields Cotton was doubtless but one more 'son
of Belial ' ; and our modern Puritans, like Mr. Shaw,
who has trounced Dr. Johnson himself for ' trifling with
literary fools in taverns, when he should have been
shaking England with the thunders of his spirit,' would
doubtless agree. But we are not all Ram Dasses with
fire in our belly to burn up the sins of the world. Self-
indulgent, spendthrift, sensual, Mr. Charles Cotton of
Beresford Hall was neither a saint, a hero, nor an economic
man, but a kindly, pleasant soul ; a Captain of Foot who
would not have touched a fly—save for the sake of a
trout ; on occasion a charming poet ; and, always, the
dear friend of Izaak Walton—one, as he describes
himself—

> Who with his angle and his books
> Can think the longest day well-spent
> And praises God when back he looks
> And finds that all is innocent.

Things were not invariably quite so idyllic ; but the

Recording Angel, when all was written, can have had
no great cause to complain of Charles Cotton.

Mr. Beresford's edition (complete except for the
Travesty of Virgil, the long *Battle of Ivry*, and some of the
translations) contains three hundred and sixty pages of
text—a pretty heavy banquet of verse, which may move
the guest to groan, in anticipation, as loud as any loaded
table. But the entertainment proves on the whole surprisingly easy to get through, if not very nourishing.
Wisdom, in Scripture, is justified of her children ; but
in Cotton, frivolity. Where he does set out to be philosophic or religious, when he embarks on epics or dramatic
choruses or Pindaric odes, he becomes merely ridiculous,
and his metrical mountains give birth to blind mice that
cannot even run.

> Who the world's wrongs does either feel or see,
> That possibly from passion can be free,
>   But must put on
>   A noble indignation
> Warranted both by virtue and religion ?

is indeed ' criticism of life,' but in the vein of that Lord
William Lennox who so originally observed that
' feathered bipeds of advanced age are not to be en-
trapped with the outer husks of corn.' And though no
sentiment could be more ' highly serious ' than—

> Methinks I 'm now all sacred fire,
>   And wholly grown
>   Devotion.
> Sensual love 's in chains,
> And all my boiling veins
> Are blown with sanctified desire,

it seems less appropriate to a lover than to the frog of
fable who burst herself in the effort to look like an ox.
The moment Cotton becomes really serious, it is impossible to treat him seriously. Clouds that ' clap their
liquid hands,' ships that are almost sunk by the weight of
the crew's despair, flocks that

> bite
> The smiling salads in our sight,

are a little staggering even for that age of conceits. It
is only when Cotton is content to be his naïve, quaint,
flibbertigibbety self that he becomes readable—often
entertaining, sometimes charming, occasionally really
graceful. When he describes his Nymph with her
lute—

> And every snowy finger, as she played,
> Danced to the music that themselves had made

(not the ' little silver feet ' of the fawn of Marvell's other
Nymph are prettier), or when he builds in his Phyllis'
bower

> Casements of crystal to transmit
> Night's sweets to thee and thine to it,

then one forgives and forgets even his Pindarics. The
' Morning,' ' Noon,' ' Evening,' and ' Night Quatrains,'
with their solemnly absurd exaggerations, every one
knows ; but there is another description of night in the
' Entertainment to Phyllis,' in which Cotton produces
more real poetic effect, with less help from the smiles of
his readers and the quaintness time has lent him—

> Now Phœbus is gone down to sleep
> In cold embraces of the deep,

> And Night's pavilion in the sky
> (Crowned with a starry canopy)
> Erected stands, whence the pale Moon
> Steals out to her Endymion ;
> Over the meads and o'er the floods
> Thorough the ridings of the woods,
> Th' enamoured Huntress scours her ways,
> And through Night's veil her horns displays.

But between his highest levels and the dismal flats of his most pompous attempts, lies a stretch of honest, open country, in which the attractive thing is the amusing, kindly figure of the author. What a difference between his attempts to be Pindar and Marcus Aurelius in one, and this spontaneous outburst at the New Year—

> Pox on 't ! the last was ill enough,
> This cannot but make better proof ;
> Or at the worst, as we brush'd through
> The last, why so we may this too ;

or between his ethics on a high horse, and the half-naïve, half-sly confession—

> He fain would be just, but sometimes he cannot,
> Which gives him the trouble that other men ha' not !

He has, indeed, no false shame and not much true ; and thanks to the absence of either, we come to know him with moments of an almost Pepysian intimacy, now innocently pursuing his trout 'beside the springs of Dove,' now pursued in his turn and, less innocently, evading in his private grotto the attentions of creditors and duns ; now posting from London to the Peak (and on a Sabbath), or from the Peak to Holyhead, with a quite Borrovian thirst and eye for inns; now turning Montaigne into English or Virgil into scurrility—

> And now I'm here set down again in peace
> After my troubles, business, voyages,
> The same dull Northern clod I was before,
> Gravely enquiring how ewes are a score,
> How the hay harvest, and the corn was got,
> And if or no there's like to be a rot;
> Just the same sot I was ere I remov'd,
> Nor by my travel nor the Court improv'd,
> The same old-fashioned squire, no whit refined,
> And shall be wiser when the Devil's blind.

He died in London in 1687, not inopportunely for an old Cavalier, on the eve of a less loyal and politer age.

His shade has not lacked recognition. We may discount the cousinly partiality of Sir Aston Cokayne—

> The world will find your lines are great and strong,
> The *nihil ultra* of the English tongue.

But even his *Travesty of Virgil* was found by Pepys 'extraordinary good'; Wordsworth approved of 'Winter,' and Lamb loved his 'New Year.' With this complete collected edition he comes finally into his own, and his work has its fair hearing. Most of it no one will want to hear twice, indeed it would be likelier to last with the general public were there less of it. Cotton must hope for occasional reincarnation in the selections and anthologies that every generation or two will find it needs to make afresh. What their editors include will vary with the veering taste of ages: but it will be a sorry time that can no longer enjoy at least such a piece as this—

Caelia, my fairest Caelia, fell,
 Caelia, than the fairest, fairer,
 Caelia (with none I must compare her)
That all alone is all in all
Of what we fair or modest call,
Caelia, white as alabaster,
Caelia, than Diana chaster,
This fair, fair Caelia, grief to tell,
This fair, this modest, chaste one fell. . . .

But if you 'll say my Caelia fell,
 Of this I 'm sure that, like the dart
 Of Love it was, and on my heart;
Poor heart, alas! wounded before
She needed not have hurt it more;
So absolute a conquest she
Had gain'd before of it and me,
That neither of us have been well
Before, or since my Caelia fell.

ANDREW MARVELL*

I⟨T⟩ is but a few years since the city of Hull was celebrating the tercentenary of her poet's birth with every conceivable form of acclamation, from the silver tongue of Mr. Birrell to the metallic thunder of two new tramcars adorned with the Marvell arms, with symbolic personages, and with ' flights of seagulls in gold on a black ground.' There is a certain piquancy in such a combination ; and yet the very incongruity of this united *Magnificat* by everything from a critic to a tramcar is really rather happily appropriate to commemorate a poet whose own life and genius were most strangely compounded of contraries, and whose poems doubly deserve their title of ' miscellaneous.' For Andrew Marvell stands on the frontier of two sharply severed periods, between the lyric dream that was dying and the common sense that was coming to birth, between John Donne and John Dryden, between the kingdom of poetry and the kingdom of prose. In him died the last of the Metaphysicals ; the English lyric was not to reach such heights again till, over a century later, there appeared at Kilmarnock the first volume of Robert Burns ; but on the other hand, unlike his friend Milton, he crosses the dividing line into the new age, and there are passages in his political verse which might have come from the hand of his junior colleague in the Civil Service, John Dryden. Much of it (like Dryden's indeed) is sad stuff. But when, for instance, the inspiration of Cromwell's personality breaks the long rumble of their decasyllables with a sudden

* *Miscellaneous Poems of Andrew Marvell. Nonesuch Press.*

lightning-flash, the likeness of manner is unmistakable between Marvell's

> He without noise still travell'd to his End,
> As silent Suns to meet the Night descend,

and Dryden's

> His grandeur he derived from Heaven alone,
> For he was great ere Fortune made him so;
> And wars, like mists that rise against the Sun,
> Made him but greater seem, not greater grow.

Marvell is an intermediate figure in other ways as well. For this poet of the Puritans was the son of an Anglican clergyman ('the hunger-starved whelp of a country-vicar,' as Bishop Parker less politely put it), and ran away from Cambridge to join the Jesuits in London. Tutor of Fairfax's daughter, then of Cromwell's ward, he was none the less a friend of Lovelace the Royalist and thought the Parliamentary cause 'too good to have been fought for'; and the assistant of Milton in the Foreign Office of the Commonwealth, the stinging satirist of the Restoration, yet devoted some of his noblest lines to the memory of Charles the First. The Protector he honoured, praised, knew personally; but he reports to his constituents in Hull the resolution of the Commons that Oliver should be exhumed and hanged at Tyburn, with a calm absence of comment that goads Dr. Grosart, his editor, to sorrow and anger.

So with his writing. Bishop Burnet calls him 'the liveliest droll of the age,' and Tennyson is said to have made Carlyle laugh for half an hour with the satire on the natives of the Netherlands—

> Glad then, as Miners that have found the Oar (ore),
> They with mad labour fish'd the Land to Shoar.

Yet Mr. Eliot could praise him the other day as more serious than William Morris—which is saying a good deal. In his poetry the sublime is jostled by the ridiculous, imagination trips momentarily into puerility. In his soul the last ghosts of the Middle Ages still struggle with the ordered urbanity of Rome. With a survival of that mediæval childishness which could caricature an enemy as a stone monkey amid the glories of a cathedral front, he follows the matchless 'To his Coy Mistress' with this description of the birth of an unfortunate infant who 'ere brought forth, was cast away '—

> Till at the last the master-Wave
> Upon the Rock his Mother drave ;
> And there she split against the Stone
> In a *Cesarian* Section.

And he can mix, in one and the same poem, that lovely lament for the Civil War—

> O Thou, that dear and happy Isle
> The Garden of the World erewhile,
> Thou *Paradise* of the four Seas,
> Which Heaven planted us to please . . .
> Unhappy ! shall we nevermore
> That sweet *Militia* restore,
> When Gardens only had their Towrs,
> And all the Garrisons were Flowrs ?

with a comparison of distant kine at pasture to pimples on a face or fleas under a magnifying glass. Such enormities the next generation could no more have committed than it could have written 'The Garden.' And yet surely some of the urbanity and refinement of the

Augustans might have been expected from the author of the best imitation of Horace in the English language.

Once more, lover of unspoilt nature as he is and herald in his degree of the Romantics (so that his soul with a quite modern sympathy of imagination 'into the boughs does glide,' and sits there birdlike, just as Keats felt himself becoming one with the sparrow before his window), there remains a curious artificiality even in his passion. Artifice was of course second nature to his age ; but it is enough to contrast with his work *L'Allegro* or *Lycidas*. Marvell, like Milton, the sea had left mourning ; his own father perished in the Humber, while he was at Cambridge, in a strangely tragic way. For with him were drowned a pair of lovers going to be wed ; and, as the boat put off, old Marvell (so runs the story) with a sudden premonition cried, ' Ho, for heaven,' and flung his staff back to the shore. Yet Marvell's nearest approach to *Lycidas* is a slightly rococo nymph's lament for her fawn.

In fact there is almost as much diversity in Marvell's life and writings as in the wildly discrepant portraits of the man himself. He remains something of a riddle. Even his lyric verse is far from self-revealing ; and all of it that counts was written within the years 1650-52 and left by his indifference unpublished when he died. At all events during the last eighteen years of his life the poet was swallowed up in the Member of Parliament ; and the folio here reprinted dates from three years after his death under the hands of a bungling physician. The reprint makes a charming book to possess, and it will be very odd if there is any difficulty in finding eight hundred and twenty-five would-be possessors. Of the one flaw

—the retention of all the original misprints which the poet himself was not alive to correct—the less need be said, as it has already been the subject of a tart correspondence. This 'faith unfaithful' certainly seems particularly pointless in a text with no pretensions to be an *exact* facsimile (since the letter 's' is throughout substituted for 'f'), and is, indeed, too like the proverbial blacking oneself all over in order to play Othello.

But though this edition makes Marvell attractive as never before, it will hardly add to his real fame. The anthologists have between them left little to glean. As Mr. Chesterton says of Swinburne, 'You never know who is an inspired poet till the inspiration goes'; and there can be no doubt that, in this equivocal sense, Marvell was one. It is illogical, but inevitable, that he should seem to lose some of his greatness, when one finds that he can be as trivial as Cotton, as far-fetched as Cowley, as disgusting even as the youthful Dryden's description of Lord Hastings' smallpox. There is a slight compensation in finding that he could write prose not unworthy to be contemporary with *Religio Medici*—

> But the dissoluteness of grief, the prodigality of sorrow is neither to be indulged in a man's self, nor comply'd with in others. If that were allowable in these cases, Eli's was the readiest way and complement of mourning, who fell back from his seat and broke his neck. . . . Upon a private loss and sweetened with so many circumstances as yours, to be impatient, to be uncomfortable, would be to dispute with God and beg the question.

Perhaps the greatest poetic gain of this complete edition lies in having 'Upon Nun Appleton House' in full. It is uneven, and the forcible marriage of ideas that mortal mind can never have associated before begets some incredible intellectual abortions ; but on the whole, as Johnson observed of the Metaphysicals, ' If their conceits were far-fetched, they were often worth the carriage.' And yet after all it is the half-dozen old, familiar pieces that matter—the ' Coy Mistress,' especially, stands out more transcendently beautiful than ever amid much that is grotesque, a princess among metaphysical goblins. That masterpiece Palgrave and prudery omitted from the *Golden Treasury* (some people cannot understand why this generation is sometimes irritated by the Victorians), but it alone is golden enough to make the fortune of any poet short of the greatest, for ever and ever, or at any rate

Till the Conversion of the Jews.

> C'est le bon sens, la raison qui fait tout,
> Vertu, génie, esprit, talent et goût.
> Qu'est-ce vertu ?   Raison mise en pratique.
> Talent ?   Raison produit avec éclat.
> Esprit ?   Raison qui finement s'exprime.
> Le goût n'est qu'un bon sens délicat
> Et le génie est la raison sublime.

THERE could be no clearer manifesto than these lines by M.-J. Chénier of the eighteenth-century attitude towards Art and Life ; and the interest for us wiseacres after the event lies in watching the essential nature of great poetry—imagination, wonder, mystery, what you will !—being pitchforked out by Reason through these seven lines, only to slip lightly back again at the end under the cloak of that one final word—'sublime.' The same process, prolonged through a century, is the theme of Mr. Doughty's book. In lyric the eighteenth century is certainly poorer than the two centuries that preceded it or the two that have followed—

> Ask not the cause that I new numbers choose,
> The lute neglected and the lyric muse.

We do ask ; but the answer is not as obvious as it may seem.   For Mr. Doughty the root of all the evil is Reason.   'Reason *versus* Emotion ; that was the dominant question in Eighteenth-Century Literature in

---

* *The English Lyric in the Age of Reason.* By *Oswald Doughty, M.A.* O'Connor.

  Forgotten Lyrics of the Eighteenth Century. By *Oswald Doughty, M.A.* Witherby.

England '—so cries his wrapper for him that runs to read. Head and heart, he thinks, are born enemies; this misguided century wanted to be all head (Dryden and Pope) and, failing, grew disillusioned (Collins and Gray), then rallied (Johnson and Goldsmith), and lastly died and was eaten of worms (Miss Seward and the Della Cruscans). Of course there is truth in this; but it is unfair to a great age to talk about ' the classical midnight of Dryden and Pope ' and its ' failure '; and it is unfair to Reason to saddle it with the imbecilities of a Young or a Blackmore. For whatever did induce Addison to write ' O the pleasing, pleasing, pleasing, pleasing, pleasing anguish ! ' it was certainly not Reason; and among the many faults of ' Rule Britannia ' and ' God Save the King,' we never heard it mentioned that they were ' highbrow.'

It is, of course, easy to quote from the verse of Akenside and others glorifications of passionless reason; but it is dangerous arguing from ideals to realities, from what an age wants to be to what it is; and Mr. Doughty himself, when he comes to particular cases, with that fine fairness to individuals which is the saving of his book, admits as much, especially of Johnson. As Mr. Lytton Strachey in his *Landmarks in French Literature* has said of Voltaire's supposed coldness, one might as well ' infer that a white-hot bar of steel lacked heat because it was not red.' No, the eighteenth century is not to be dismissed as a battleground of sense and sensibility, in which the wrong side (in Mr. Doughty's, not Jane Austen's, view) carried the day.

Suppose some curious change of taste gradually confined musicians almost entirely to playing the flute. It would not be hard, nor yet very helpful, to observe that the ensuing degeneracy of music was doubtless due to this change—because there are many things that cannot be expressed on the flute, many that cannot be played on it without thinness or monotony past endurance. The real difficulty would be to understand why, then, people continued to tolerate the tyranny of the flute at all. Similarly with eighteenth-century poetry. Here too it is easy enough to point out how mediocre most poets were bound to be in a century which confined them almost entirely to three or four conventional metres, a rigidly syllabic scansion, and an equally artificial diction. But why — the difficulty remains — was the age content, and more than content, with such a state of things? And, further, what makes the minor poetry of the period so unsatisfactory, even of its kind? For if Pope proved what heights the couplet, with all its limitations, could attain, yet those heights are strangely seldom approached by other poets of his time and after him.

This general inferiority it is indeed the fashion of the moment to deny, and there has recently been a series of attempts to magnify the minor poetry of the eighteenth century ; for it has seemed to provide a last unexhausted field for those who labour to discover lost treasures of our literature—or, if not to discover, to invent. Yet even after a couple of pleasant hours over Mr. Doughty's *Forgotten Lyrics* the ordinary reader is likely to remain of the opinion that if the sections of eighteenth-century verse in our anthologies are thin, and half filled out, at that, with poems which are in revolt against the verse standards of the eighteenth century, this is after all merely just and as it should be.   But why should it be ?   What was wrong with them ?

To us poetry means the successful expression in rhyth-mical language of emotions we can value, whether they are excited by the fall of Cæsar or of a sparrow.   The emotion may be perfectly familiar, for instance praise of a mistress's eyebrow, so that we learn nothing but simply enjoy the way it is expressed ; or it may be strange to us so that we cry inwardly in response not only, ' How true ! ' but ' How new ! '   That is to say, it may either *be* new, because it is something we have never felt, like the longing of the Prisoner of Chillon to get back to his dungeon, or the ecstasies of Crashaw, or the charnel-broodings of Beddoes (though we are, of course, able to imagine them, with the help of fragments of our own re-membered experiences, otherwise the poem remains mere sound and fury) ; or the emotion may *seem* new, though half familiar too, because we have never so deeply or subtly analysed it in ourselves, like the tangle of passions in *Modern Love* or the agonised sensitiveness of the poetry of Hardy.   Similarly novelist and playwright have their choice of recreating familiar types, like the lover or the miser, or creating new ones like Hamlet or Hedda Gabler. (In practice the wise do both.)   Now, if the emotions expressed are perfectly familiar, the value and interest of the poem must lie entirely in its treatment of them ; here style becomes everything, whereas it seems to matter less where there is the fascination of the unknown as well.   And yet even the unheard-of soon grows commonplace and people find, like Grant Allen, that they themselves take the impossible Hedda ' down to dinner twice a week ' ; so that here too style counts vitally in the end. It is no longer as startling as when Keats was young, to wish ' to cease upon the midnight with no pain ' ; it occurs to undergraduates ; but the style remains.

The feelings, however, which find expression in typical eighteenth-century verse neither are nor seem new in the least. This is not just because they are more than a hundred years old ; Donne and the *Sonnets* of Shakespeare are a century older still. Not only the practice but the theory of the Neo-Classic age insisted on the familiar and eschewed the new. It was not for the poet to reveal unnoticed streaks in a tulip or a soul, but to renew the thoughts of elder poets and the universal feelings of mankind. For him the unknown was No Man's Land ; and a character like Iago was an artistic as well as a moral monster ; for it is notorious that soldiers as a class are really ' honest ' men. All this was very hampering ; yet it need not in itself have been fatal. The deepest things in life are familiar. There is nothing novel in the feelings which brought Horace's poetry to birth ; but he remains one of the great poets of the world, because, if his ideas are common as flies, the happiness of his style and his personality has made them as rare and as immortal as flies in amber. But it was impossible that the common poetic style of any age as a whole should possess the happiness or the individuality of that little, plump, lovable character. The style of eighteenth-century poets is, in general, ' a pity ' ; and as for personality, Nature bestowed on few of them anything very striking (Dryden does give an impression of greatness, but then Dryden half belongs to an earlier and greater age) and poetic fashion discouraged the display of what they had.   In short, the minor verse of the period consists largely of hackneyed feelings in hackneyed verse, things often thought but never worse expressed.   And an extra curse of their conventionality of heart and tongue is that it makes them seem less sincere than sometimes they really are.   We suspect those who have all the right sentiments of having no feelings at all, and those who talk in *clichés* of not even meaning what they say.   This is often unjust ; but it is quite inevitable.   The eighteenth century was as fanatical as it was capable of being about anything on the subject of the proper style for gentlemen to use in poetry ; but it is impossible that such a thing should even exist.   ' Le style c'est de l'homme ' ;   and any style common to a whole epoch is doomed to be commonly bad.   This may be granted without going to the opposite extreme of Verlaine—

> Car nous voulons la Nuance encor,
> Pas la Couleur, rien que la Nuance ;
> Oh ! la Nuance seule fiance
> Le rêve au rêve et la flûte au cor.

It results that the minor verse of the Neo-Classics is seldom more than wittily pretty or prettily witty ;   and, since wit is rare in any age, is more often tedious and disgusting. Even the great poets are different from those of other periods.   Even Pope, like lightning — the flickering play of summer lightning in the distance or the dazzling flash overhead—amuses or amazes, blasts perhaps, but never warms ;   even Gray, outside his ' Country Church- yard,' that magnificent Dead March of commonplaces, seems to me more interesting in his letters.   And what an eighteenth-century minor tended to make of the

'Country Churchyard,' witness this passage quoted by
Mr. Doughty from the Rev. James Fordyce's 'Soliloquy
Written in a Country Churchyard '—

> Time was, these ashes lived—a time must be
> When others thus may stand—and look at me,
> Alarming thought ! no wonder 'tis we dread
> O'er these uncomfortable vaults to tread.

That thrill down the spine, that quickening of the pulse,
that wonder, that momentary sense of intenser life, as at
a vision of some Beauty never born before starting from
the changeless sea of things—these even the lesser poets
of the English centuries since Chaucer can give, but our
Classic Age, whatever other pleasures it provides, but
seldom and to few.

This is what seems lacking in eighteenth-century
poetry which is really typical (it is mostly its rebels that
we read) ; but why was it ? ' Because they had a
horrible style.'   But why did they have a horrible style ?
' Because their England, like the prosaic fifteenth-
century England of the Pastons, was materialistically
absorbed in material progress—with " commerce settled
on every tree." '   But so was the England of the Victorians.   ' Because they lived on a theory that reason was
good and emotion bad.'   Read their lives !   Really, of
course, there were more reasons than it is possible to dis-
entangle—the reaction from seventeenth-century law-
lessness, in mind, as well as in metre and language ; the
overgrowth of the critical spirit ; the depressing influence
of the glory of Dryden and Pope, as well as the Ancients,
which crushed succeeding poets into a mixture of imi-
tativeness and inferiority-complex, as the Augustans

crushed Silver Latin literature and Chaucer the writers of the fifteenth century. All this we have heard a hundred times. But there are two other reasons of which more can be said. Their theory of the essence of the poet's aim was different ; and, partly in consequence of this, some of the most poetical things in eighteenth-century literature are not in verse at all, but in its prose.

Poetry, said they, should imitate Nature ; Nature is the way sensible people behave and believe the world to behave ; and the most sensible people of all were the Ancients. After the frenzies of Fifth Monarchy men and the orgies of the Restoration, the importance of good sense had been rediscovered ; and, further, the value of Science and the scientific intellect was being discovered for the first time. Accordingly new-found faith in reason plunged these people into the supreme unreason of forgetting how illogical an animal man is, and how important that side of him always remains ; they even persuaded themselves that the Universe itself was quite obviously rational. Hence Dryden's remark, amazing when one stops to think what it implies, that ' the composition of poetry is and ought to be of Wit.' It was not nearly so much that they repressed their emotions, as that they thought them neither very important nor very decent to dwell upon and discuss, except in their most traditional and general aspects. Hence that terrible impersonality and unintimacy of most of their poetry. We complain of them, as Queen Victoria of Mr. Gladstone, that they address us as if we were a public meeting, their human individuality and ours lost in one undivine average. In real life even those whose conversation on

every other subject is utterly tedious, become fascinating
when they pour out to us their hidden hopes and sorrows.
But under this theory of poetry just those intimate sad-
nesses and agonies, which have given life to the utterance of so many minor poets in other eras, were sternly
ruled out.   It was like their social canons.   'One might
have gout, but one must walk about all the same without
making grimaces.   It was part of good breeding to hide
one's sufferings.'   No pageants of bleeding hearts, no
sonnet-keys to unlock them—indeed there were no
sonnets.   Dr. Johnson was particularly severe with
Boswell on this subject of seeking sympathy by con-
fidences ; pity, said that stern reason, could do him no
good.   And it was equally typical that Boswell's betrayal
of an emotional imagination in the remark, that hearing
music made him wish to rush into the thickest of the
battle, only called down the snub—' I should never hear
it, if it made me feel such a fool.'   Indeed Johnson would
probably have felt much the same irritation, had he lived
to read the emotion roused in a certain Mr. Wordsworth
by the song of a Scotch Reaper (such as he had heard
himself with mild interest on his trip to the Hebrides)
with its memories of battles long ago.   Arnold's summary
of Gray, that he ' never spoke out,' applies in a different
way to the poets of his century in general.   They were
forbidden to give themselves away ; whereas the careers
of Byron and Wordsworth and Shelley consisted of little
else.   Indeed it is one of the essential things about poetry
that it enables people to do that.   But there seemed a
sort of emotional immodesty about such behaviour in the
eyes of that most civilised of societies whose passing
away was to be marked, and hastened, by the abashless

exhibitionism of Rousseau.   Goethe knew that atmosphere—

> Gute Gesellschaft hab' ich gesehn, man nennt sie die gute
> Wenn sie zum kleinsten Gedicht keine Gelegenheit giebt.

It was because of this mental attitude of the eighteenth
century, that such a colourless diction of *clichés* gained its
hold ;   and naturally, the vicious circle once formed, this
artificiality of diction helped to make spontaneous self-
expression harder than ever.   Poetry became a sort of
poetry-game for gentlemen (as Dryden remarked, the
civilest men are commonly the dullest) ;   and poetry
remained in bondage longest of all literary forms because
it was more traditional than the rest, and more bullied by
the Ancients.   Hence, a certain amount of poetic power
must have died unheard for want of outlet (what could
a Webster have done in such an age ?), a certain amount
must have expressed itself in prose.

Here lies in part the answer to Mr. Iolo Williams'
argument that the English, being the most poetical race
in the world, simply cannot have produced for a century
poetry mostly bad.   The syllogism is questionable in
other ways, and the best poetry does not need logic to
prove it good ;   but there is also this consideration—that
the most poetical part of the literature of the century was
not always its verse.   ' Cousin Swift, you will never be
a poet,' said Dryden, with a truth that was not forgiven
him ;   yet what tragic poet ever conceived more fearful
moments than Swift fashioned for himself in that long
tragedy of his life—Vanessa, Stella ;   the envelope found
after his death, marked with bitter simplicity, ' Only a
woman's hair ' ;   the birthdays spent as days of mourning

with the Bible open at Job's curse on the night in which a man-child was conceived ? So too in pages of their great novels, in moments of Goldsmith and Sterne, there are far more poetic visions of human character and human life than in all the dreary verse-drama of the day. ' " I thought love had been a joyous thing," said my uncle Toby.' How many professional poets of his generation could challenge the majesty of Johnson's sadness or the imaginative splendour of the periods of Burke ? And, lastly, if we look for the Epic of the age, we must turn, not to Pope's *Homer* but to the *Decline and Fall.* Just as the history of Tacitus has far more poetical quality than all the scrubbed and polished hexameters of the first century of the Roman Empire, so Gibbon's narrative of that Empire's age-long destruction is, with all its utter difference, the only counterpart for epic grandeur and magnificence that our Neo-Classic literature can offer to Milton's story of the Fall of Man.

While Julian struggled with the almost insuperable difficulties of his situation, the silent hours of the night were still devoted to study and contemplation. Whenever he closed his eyes in short and interrupted slumbers, his mind was agitated with painful anxiety ; nor can it be thought surprising that the Genius of the Empire should once more appear before him, covering with a funereal veil his head and his horn of abundance, and slowly retiring from the Imperial tent. The monarch started from his couch, and stepping forth to refresh his spirits with the coolness of the midnight air, he beheld a fiery meteor, which shot athwart the sky and suddenly vanished. Julian was convinced that he had seen the menacing countenance of the god of war ; the council which he summoned, of Tuscan Haruspices, unanimously pronounced that

he should abstain from action; but on this occasion necessity and reason were more prevalent than superstition; and
the trumpets sounded at the break of day.

The historical value of that last clause, for instance, is
nothing; yet how it rounds the whole! It was not
the English of the eighteenth century that were un-
imaginative or passionless or unpoetical; it was only
their poetry. In short, if there is any clear contest it is
not between reason and emotion so much as between
common sense and imagination. The Elizabethans had
discovered the strange effectiveness of mad scenes where
fantasy runs absolutely riot; the same device recurs in
Herrick's ' Mad Maid's Song,' and in the ' Tom o'
Bedlam ' of *Percy's Reliques*; and the romantic revival
is not only a resurgence of democracy, of the Middle
Ages, of a new poetic diction, but also of poetic madness.
Collins, Cowper, Smart, Blake all hovered on the con-
fines of insanity, to say nothing of the opium of Coleridge
and De Quincey. These new men were not more
emotional than the Augustans; it was not that their
hearts had run away with their heads; they do not super-
sede reason, they merely supplement it with a judicious
mixture of unreason. Hear Coleridge himself, for
instance. ' Poetry is certainly something more than
good sense, but it must be good sense at all events.' Nor
does the Augustan Age stand condemned because it
decayed; death is the wages not of sin but of existence.
Neo-Classicism perished because it had been alive and
grown old—it needs no elaborate *post-mortem* with a
verdict of degeneration of the heart. Indeed, it has its
vitality still. There is a time for all things, and a mood

among others when from the flutter of Shelley's wings in the void one may turn with relief back to these generations of our fathers who passed urbane, human, self-possessed lives without thinking or needing to think that life consists in running to a fire. The peace of the Augustans is not a desolation. Belief in reason is not a curse, nor all frenzies fine, nor all intuitions true.

THE POEMS OF HAMLET*

> True, I am a forest and a night of dark trees, but he who is not afraid of my darkness will find banks full of roses under my cypresses. NIETZSCHE.

THE year which presented the world with that curious pair of twins, Mr. Wordsworth's *Lyrical Ballads* and the Rev. Malthus's *Essay on Population*, saw also the birth in a remote, hill-perched hamlet of the march of Ancona between Adriatic and Apennine, of an obscure little count. Seventeen years later, while Europe gazed on Waterloo, behind its back the heir of the Palazzo Leopardi, humped and undersized, was squandering his remains of health and sight and youth in following up the *History of Astronomy* he had written at fifteen, with those treatises on Plotinus, on the rhetoricians of the Empire, and on the errors of the Ancients, which were to extort from the astonished Niebuhr the recognition of the boy as Italy's one great philologist. Did he not pause, one wonders, as he pored over his rhetoricians, at the fate of their 'Phœnix,' Hermogenes, who was, like himself, a master at fifteen, only to become an idiot at five-and-twenty, and whose heart, Professor Saintsbury assures us, 'was covered with hair'? At all events the warning was lost until too late; the prodigy who had taught himself Greek, French, English, German, and Spanish, who disputed in Hebrew with the rabbis of Ancona, was not indeed to go mad, but to become a poet, and the most miserable of poets.

* *The Poems of Leopardi. By G. L. Bickersteth, M.A. Cambridge University Press.*

He had cause. His father was bigot and fool, his mother bigot and saint—one of those saints in stone who hold themselves fit foundations of the Church that was to be builded upon a rock. This salvation by petrifaction was all she had to give her children. If they had childish sorrows, let them ' offer them to Jesus.' Did they long for friends ? Friends would but ' distract them from loving God.' Her own devotion to Him only Mammon shared ; to restore the lost finances of the Leopardi was her dream ; and the Count, who in his youth had squandered them, was left a nonentity in his own household with a stingy dole of pocket-money. He might indulge his reactionary crotchets by being the last of all his peers to wear a sword ; by having, like a dotard out of Ibsen, a lay figure in rusty armour to stand sentinel at his door ; but he was impotent to do even what he would for the children he loved in his bewildered, owlish way. In the words of his only daughter : ' Somehow when I was still a baby, and perhaps before I was born, my father's legs got entangled in my mother's skirts, and he has never since been able to free himself.' As for the young Leopardi, liberty to ruin his life by seven years of frenzied study was the only liberty he knew. Even at the age of twenty, he and his brother were not allowed to go out by themselves ; the next year he made an attempt to run away ; and only at twenty-four was he at last allowed to go to Rome. Dante went living down to Hell ; Leopardi was born there.

Meanwhile at eighteen his imagination had suddenly awakened. Was this life ? Sickly, ugly, alone, ' il gobbo de' Leopardi,' he saw the world revealed as by a lightning flash—his own death-bed. Then came the first of his unhappy loves, threatened loss of eyesight, utter loss of faith. Like Paul he had a vision, but the vision was not Paul's. The veil was rent before his intuition, and behind it appeared the horror of one vast Nothingness. He was ' converted '; and his unfaith endured unshaken through the eighteen years of life that remained.

That period was one long, frantic, and at last successful struggle to escape, by hackwork, by charity, by the generosity of friends, from being dragged back into the living grave of his home at Recanati. We see him at Rome, finding his ' first and only pleasure ' there in the tears he shed on Tasso's tomb; at Bologna, fortified against its winter by encasing himself to the shoulders in a sack of feathers; or, with his tortured eyesight, stealing out only after dark into the streets of Florence, ' like a bat.' When in 1837 he died, the last four years of his life had been spent under the care of his devoted friend Ranieri at Naples, harassed only by his physical misery and extravagant eccentricities, such as dining at midnight and going to bed at dawn.

The same year crowned the lifework of the Countess Adelaide; at last the finances of the house of Leopardi stood on an economic basis once more. Her son's last letter had been addressed to her, a begging appeal for ten dollars. ' God forgive him !' was henceforth her sole comment on the dead genius and atheist she had given to the world.

Unpardonable it may be, but it is tempting to suspect that Leopardi's personality is really of more interest than his poetry. It was not the pure poet or philosopher in him that so stamped his image on the memories of men, but the fanatic of despair, who made no compromise with hope, no reservations in his evangel of darkness, who not only shared our common boredom, but was bored to frenzy. His name stands wrapped in a sinister sanctity, such as the old Romans gave to ground that the thunderbolt had blasted. And apart from mere superstitious awe, what a self-communing Hamlet was this who has left 4526 pages of close-written reflections, over two-thirds of which date from two years of his life alone ! The analogy goes further. The plain person will never understand by what strange logic one who thought of life as Leopardi did, refrained from suicide. His reasons to the contrary seem mere excuses ; the truth being that Leopardi, like Hamlet, both introspected because he failed to act, and failed to act because he introspected. As about taking life, so about love ; Leopardi is said to have been so ugly that he was foredoomed to sigh in vain. This explanation, accepted by Mr. Bickersteth, is very rightly questioned in another quite recent book on Leopardi, by Karl Vossler ; and it surely betrays some ignorance of human psychology. Wilkes only asked half an hour's start with any woman to make up for his ill-favoured face ; charm and devoted friends Leopardi had in abundance ; and the sculptured head, which forms Vossler's frontispiece, idealised or no, is rather attractive —certainly far from any Socratic standard of ugliness. And even Socrates was loved. No, the youth of nineteen, whose first step on falling in love was scientifically to catalogue his minutest sensations in a *Diario d'Amore,* may well have had other than physical reasons for the failure of the three great passions of his life. Here was no Catullus nor Burns, but one whose feelings used themselves up in being felt. The tragedy does not, perhaps, become less, but it becomes a different one—the tragedy of the thinker whose thoughts by their very force and fertility become not a means to action, but its substitute. He found love and put it on paper. He clamoured for death from the age of nineteen ; and died in his bed twenty years later, on the point of fleeing from a cholera epidemic.

This is not very consistent, even for a human being ; as Leopardi himself partly felt. But where Heine with his sense of humour would have burst into charming laughter at his own expense, Leopardi talked of suicide as beneath the dignity of the ' magnanimo '—as if, in a world of utter vanity, ' l'infinita vanità del tutto,' magnanimity were any less an illusion than everything else. His main view of life as a fiendish farce in the eyes of reason, to be relieved only by those noble dreams of poetry and the heart, which make us forget the truth for a moment, but do not palter with it like the comfortable lies of the religions, may be true enough. But he spoils his case by overstatement. All mankind does not in fact languish perpetually in the abysmal misery or ennui that he supposes ; and when people told him as much, it was inadequate to retort that they were poltroons and hypocrites. He spoils his case also by excessive re-statement. It is necessary to be interested in order to interest. Leopardi, in his poetic moments, was indeed desperately interested in his own boredom ; but not even the boredom of a Leopardi is inexhaustibly thrilling. Homer took nearly as dark a view of life in its essentials as the Italian ; but he had other strings to his lyre. He saw existence as a tragedy ; but he saw also that a tragedy requires action and a hero, not mere choruses of lamenta-

tion ; and instead of pointing out testily to mankind
that they were more miserable than they knew, he pointed
out with equal truth that they were also nobler.   Heine
took as dark a view ; and a mattress-grave does not lend
itself to high romance like the plains of windy Troy ;
but he had the humour to see the comic relief of the
tragedy—

And the feather-pate of folly
Bore the falling sky.

'Laugh, my young friends,' said Nietzsche, 'if you
are at all determined to remain pessimists '—how wisely,
let the example of Horace and Omar, Hardy and Housman,
James Thomson and Shakespeare witness.   'As for that
threatening,' said Sir Gringamor, 'be that as it may,
let us go to our dinner.'   There are worse answers to
life.

Exaggeration and a certain bleating monotony are,
then, the two defects of Leopardi's poetry.   Passion he
has and dignity, sincerity and artistic restraint, with some
of the steely, inevitable directness of Dante : and the
beauty of the language of Italy gives an almost unfair
advantage to her poets.   His descriptions, sparingly used
and kept in their proper place, are all the better when
they come—the hares a-dance in the forest under the
moon, the long booming of the bell in the campanile
of Recanati, as it tells its slow hours to the winds, the
thought that dominates his soul like a gigantic tower
alone in a weary land, his Horatian vision of the future
desolation of Italy, with the fox lurking in the cities of
Latium and the plough furrowing once more the Seven
Hills—

Tempo forse verrà ch'alle ruine
Delle italiche moli
Insultino gli armenti, e che l'aratro
Sentano i sette colli ; e pochi soli
Forse fien volti, e le città latine
Abiterà la cauta volpe, e l'atro
Bosco mormorerà fra le alte mura.

The time perhaps will come when sheep shall feed
Among the ruined piers
Of proud Italian palaces, and the plough
Shall furrow the seven hills ; ere many years
Have rolled, perhaps the timid fox shall breed
Where stood the towns of Latium, and where now
Rise lofty walls, thick forest trees shall wave.

And though many of his odes are too abstract and too diffuse, he can rise at passionate moments to the laconic simplicity of Sappho or Catullus. Thus, on the wedding of his sister—

> O miseri o codardi
> Figliuoli avrai.   Miseri eleggi.

> Know thy sons must be
> Wretched or craven.   Choose the first.

> Morte domanda
> Chi nostro mal conobbe, e non ghirlanda.

> 'Tis not a wreath
> That one who has known our ill, desires, but death.

And to himself—

> Assai
> Palpitasti.   Non val cosa nessuna
> I moti tuoi, nè di sospiri è degna

La terra.   Amaro e noia
La vita, altro mai nulla ; e fango è il mondo.
T'acqueta omai.

Sufficient
Hath been thine agitation.   Nought is worthy
Thine agonies, earth merits not thy sighing.
Mere bitterness and tedium
Is life, nought else ; the world is dust and ashes.
Now rest thee.

Here Mr. Bickersteth's ' dust and ashes ' misses the
terse scorn of ' fango '—' filth ' ; of his edition as a whole
(which for those who can afford it must certainly super-
sede its predecessors) it is enough to say that the introduction is very competent and the notes copious, even to
excess.   In the poet's biography the anecdotard will miss
some few details he regrets, but console himself with
some others which are new ; the criticism of Leopardi's
art and thought is extremely thorough, though it gives
here and there the impression, which one associates with
some of our staider literary journals, of an elephant picking up pins.   There is also a suspicion that, under the
influence perhaps of the now fashionable terror of the
word ' pessimist,' Mr. Bickersteth would like gently to
detach that label from his hero ; which is merely preposterous.

Mr. Bickersteth's translation is almost always, as in
the specimens we have given (' undulous prairies ' and
' indulges in sweet thoughts galore ' will hardly do)
decent and dignified ; but Leopardi's subtlety, or arbi-
trariness, of rhyme-scheme does not really suit English,
and W. D. Howells was, perhaps, wiser in giving rhyme-

less versions.   Of course James Thomson ought to have done the *Canti* as well as the prose dialogues ; and yet, after all, one need not regret it too seriously.   For Thomson was better employed on that one masterpiece of his own, greater surely, in fire and splendour, strength and vividness, sublimity and sound even than Leopardi,— *The City of Dreadful Night*. The noble's and seaman's son were, indeed, alike born free of that City of unhappy slaves ; and alike they found the only anodyne of despair in the courage of despair.   Yet I always turn almost gladly from this wail of lute-strings in the languid Southern darkness to the vaster desolations of that Cimmerian city of a colder shore and a less caressing tongue.

> In fuga
> Van l'ombre e le sembianze
> Dei dilettosi inganni ; e vengon meno
> Le lontane speranze
> Ove s'appoggia la mortal natura.
> Abbandonata, oscura
> Resta la vita.   In lei porgendo il guardo
> Cerca il confuso viatore invano
> Del cammin lungo che avanzar si sente
> Meta o ragione ; e vede
> Che a sè l'umana sede,
> Esso a lei veramente è fatto estrano.

Elaborately, perfectly it goes with its swaying rhythm, like a cat treading subtly and delicately over treacherous heights.   Yet there is a certain vagueness and uninevitability about it all.   There seems no reason why those exquisite, unhappy lips should not go on modulating their melodious monotonies for ever.   They do not stamp themselves on the memory like the iron and forged finality of Thomson's stoical despair at the doom of humankind.

> They have much wisdom, yet they are not wise,
>   They have much goodness, yet they do not well. . . .
> They have much strength, but still their doom is stronger,
>   Much patience, but their time endureth longer,
> Much valour, but life mocks it with some spell.

HERMAN MELVILLE *

> We look
> But at the surfaces of things ; we hear
> Of towns in flames, fields ravaged, young and old
> Driven out in troops to want and nakedness,
> Then grasp our swords and rush upon a cure
> That flatters us because it asks not thought :
> The deeper malady is better hid,
> The world is poisoned at the heart.
>
> WORDSWORTH, *The Borderers.*

LAST night I dreamed of Moby Dick. I looked across the sea to eastward, and there he lay under a Day of Judgment sky—full length, from his head to his up-tossed tail. Closer and closer I drifted, until suddenly what had seemed his extreme tail revealed itself as but his hump. So vast was he.

I do not know what it may signify to dream of whales ; perhaps Mr. Masefield does or Dr. Freud. But to deal waking, even, with Moby Dick and Herman Melville, such strange medleys, both, of stark realism and dis-embodied dream, is in itself a matter not more of critical than of oneirocritical mastery. It is like tape-measuring the Ivory Gate or taking the altitude of that Elm within it, where in batlike inversion cling the flocks of Dreams themselves.

Melville came indeed with solidity enough behind him into this solid world. There is not much fire and air in being born of mixed Scotch and Dutch ancestry in a street of New York City in the year 1819, son to the

Herman Melville, Mariner and Mystic. By R. M. Weaver. Milford.
105

canny, prosaic Allan Melville and the florid, worldly
Maria Gansevoort. It is true that round both his
grandfathers hung the glamour of the War of Independ-
ence. The dead General Peter Gansevoort, defender
of Fort Stanwix, was a romantic memory of Melville's
boyhood ; though perhaps Herman was really more
akin to the less distinguished Major Melville, in his
youth one of the ' Indians ' at the Boston Tea Party, who
amused his latter years and got his death at eighty-one
by running to fires. For, according to the fashion of the
day, he was eminent in the local company of firemen.
' Running to a fire,' in a favourite adage of the late Pre-
sident Wilson, is just what life does not consist in ; but
if will-o'-the-wisps can be counted, Herman Melville's
was to consist in little else.

This passion for the impossible, this ' itch for things
remote,' like the yearning of Dante's Ulysses for

> l'esperienza
> Di retro al sol, del mondo senza gente,

even in the grey twilight of his day seems to have hunted
him, no longer across Atlantic and Pacific, but still onward
' through strange seas of thought alone.' The longing
is common enough in itself : it is such intensity that is
rare. Youth in general submits to have its romanticism
bludgeoned out of it betimes, and barters its expectations
in El Dorado for a treadmill in the City. A Keats indeed
builds his own magic casements in Hampstead, a Thompson his own Jacob's Ladder by Charing Cross. But
Melville, more obstinate than the crowd, more realist
than the poets, after a taste of impoverished life as bank-
clerk, store-clerk, farmer and usher, at seventeen instead

of taking to drink or respectability or the quietus of pistol and ball, took instead to the sea.

The memory of the bestial hardships of his first voyage before the mast to Liverpool and back, sustained him through three years more of schoolmastering, during which he produced some Juvenilia of quite extraordinary worthlessness. But in 1841 he 'broke out again,' as the inhabitants of Grasmere used to say of Wordsworth, and shipped on a whaler for the South Seas. When three and a half years later he landed at Boston, he had accumulated the 'copy' of a lifetime. He knew the merchant, the whaling, the naval service ; he had lived four months among the cannibals of the Marquesas ; deserter and mutineer, only the frailest chance had stayed him from dragging with him to the bottom of the sea the naval captain who had ordered him a flogging. Now Odysseus could sit down to his *Odyssey*. Here for once was a nineteenth-century writer who had also lived, and where others would be gravelled to invent, he had only to remember. As from a peak in Darien, he could annex the South Seas for literature.

From 1845 to 1852 he wrote hard and continuously. Half-way through *Mardi* (1849) begin his dreams. The book opens in the Pacific ; it ends the other side of *Erewhon*, in the despair of *Rasselas*. It was followed by *Moby Dick*, with again the same subtle transition from the hard daylight of Nantucket and New Bedford, their Quaker captains and cannibal harpooners, to the hysterical splendours of a Tom-o'-Bedlam's dreams. The series of novels closes with the nightmare disillusion, the felt darkness, of *Pierre*.

In that darkness the world lost sight of Melville. With occasional travels, twenty unregarded years in the New

York Customs and a few spasmodic literary stirrings, his life crept to its silent close in 1891. The record of those years remains tantalisingly obscure ; his biographer cannot or at least does not tell us anything in detail ; one is left to imagine a jumble of office routine, metaphysics, and attempts to write. It is as if, with his last plunge, Moby Dick had dragged into the abyss the captain of Melville's soul, the indomitable Ahab, and the dauntless jester, Stubbs ; leaving only the baffled and incoherent Starbuck to drift and drift, maimed and dumb and broken, on through hopeless years.

Of the twin volumes of later work here published,* one contains magazine articles written by Melville in the period 1850-56, the other a selection from the verse he produced between the end of the Civil War and the close of his life in 1891. It was a barren wilderness in which Melville's spirit slept or wandered for the forty years between *Moby Dick* and his death, and these prose sketches were clearly meant to keep their author, rather than to be kept, to be his quails and manna, not his monument. And yet one hoped to find something imperishable, some relic of the true Melville, even here ; with disappointment it must be owned that the manna is perished and the quails but the driest of bones. When he left the sea, Melville withered. It is not that he was one of those writers who lack the originality or invention to write any but autobiographical fiction ; the creator of Captain Ahab had an imagination like a typhoon ; but still it was an imagination seemingly confined to its element, and though it touched the heavens with its head, it was

* *The Apple-Tree Table and Other Sketches. John Marr and Other Poems. By Herman Melville. Milford.*

based and planted on his well-loved and remembered sea. Confined to the demure pages of *Putnam's* or *Harper's Magazine*, this mystic and pessimist and insurgent visionary was like a petrel with clipped wings on a domestic lawn. As he wrote to Hawthorne at the beginning of these years : 'Dollars damn me. . . . What I feel most moved to write, that is banned, it will not pay. Yet, altogether, write the *other* way I cannot. So the product is a final hash and all my books are botches ! ' Thus was the blinded Samson set to grind chaff for the Philistine ; and except at rarest moments (such as the description of his chimney as 'breaking water from the ridge-pole like an anvil-headed whale through the crest of a billow ') there lives in these tales of fiddlers and apple-tree tables no echo of the far Pacific, in this rather strained humour and forced heartiness and *cliché* sentiment no whisper of the deep-stirred despairs and ironic laughters of old, thundering on like ocean rollers over the shoreless seas of life. Doubtless these mild essays tided the readers of *Putnam's* over the month well and smoothly enough ; that was all they were meant, all they should ever have been made, to do.

With the verse it is rather different. Here there is no question of pot-boiling ; but again Melville's imagination seems to have been cramped in the chains of metre, which he so seldom succeeds in wearing lightly. There is singularly little bite, for instance, in this description of the Maldive shark with its allies, the pilot-fish—

> They are friends ; and friendly they guide him to prey,
>   Yet never partake of the treat—
> Eyes and brains to the dotard lethargic and dull,
>   Pale ravener of horrible meat.

Occasionally there are better moments, when the clay in the moulding hands quickens into transitory life—as in the opening lines on Sheridan's ride—

> Shoe the steed with silver
>   That bore him to the fray,
> When he heard the guns at dawning—
>   Miles away ;
> When he heard them calling, calling—
>   ' Mount ! nor stay ' ;

or, best of all, in ' Far Off-shore '—

> Look, the raft, a signal flying,
>   Thin—a shred ;
> None upon the lashed spars lying,
>   Quick or dead.
>
> Cries the sea-fowl, hovering over,
>   ' Crew, the crew ? '
> And the billow, reckless rover,
>   Sweeps anew.

Here is an ear, and a far from unhappy boldness ; further, whatever Melville's literary decay, the prose ' Supplement to the Battle Pieces,' in which he rams a little sense down the throats of the type of fool, common then as now, who professed moral indignation because the beaten enemy ' showed no penitence,' does prove that his sense and his humanity remained as sound as ever.

But, when all is said, there are two passages in Weaver's excellent biography which gain an added significance of irony from these reprints ; and there is not much gain beside. The first is Mrs. Melville's remark in 1859 : ' Herman has taken to writing poetry. You need not tell any one, for you know how such things get around.'

The other is Melville's own : ' No commonplace is ever effectually got rid of except by essentially emptying one's self of it into a book ; for once trapped into a book, then the book can be put into the fire and all will be well.' He had failed to reckon with the reprints of the indiscriminate adorer.

But enough of this final, St. Helena phase : Melville's memory depends on the versatile work of the eight years before it. The amazing thing is not only that the author of *Typee* should have produced *Moby Dick*, but that even the two sides of *Moby Dick* should have come from the same pen. Here, you think at first, is the admirably plain teller of a tale, extraordinary indeed, but still the accident of personal experience—life, not he, is the real author. But then one discovers that this writer, whose first manner recalls the deposition of an intelligent witness with a sense of humour, combined with disquisitions on Polynesians and whales in the vein of a clever popular lecturer, has in reserve the imagination almost of a Shakespeare. That his style recalls at times Sir Thomas Browne and Carlyle, his thought Swift and Butler, his feeling Sterne, matters little in comparison ; these are commoner, less inaccessible, not always unmixed virtues. It is the poetic imagination that a man cannot counterfeit.

> Nor when expandingly lifted by your subject, can you fail to trace out great whales in the starry heavens, and boats in pursuit of them ; as when long filled with thoughts of war the Eastern nations saw armies locked in battle among the clouds. Thus at the North have I chased Leviathan round and round the Pole with the revolutions of the bright points that first defined him to me. And beneath the effulgent Antarctic skies I have boarded the Argo-Navis, and joined the chase

against the starry Cetus far beyond the utmost stretch of Hydrus and the Flying Fish.

With a frigate's anchors for my bridle-bitts and fasces of harpoons for spurs, would I could mount that whale and leap the topmost skies, to see whether the fabled heavens with all their countless tents really lie encamped beyond my mortal sight !

And yet his finest raptures are somehow welded by Melville into a perfectly satisfying unity with the rough matter-of-factness of a whaler's deck, as his blacksmith forged Ahab's steel razors on to a shank wrought of common horse-shoe stubbs, to barb the supreme harpoon.

Still, imagination is a gift for which its possessors commonly pay in full. There was indeed but one philosophy for so clear a head and so intense a vision. The Universe is no pastoral for those who have eyes, not for courtesy, but to see with. ' Ecclesiastes is the fine hammered steel of woe. All is vanity, ALL. This wilful world hath not got hold of un-Christian Solomon's wisdom yet.' Yet he was proud, as pessimists often are, of his disillusion. ' There is a Catskill eagle in some souls that can alike dive down into the blackest gorges and soar out of them again and become invisible in the sunny spaces. And even if he for ever flies within the gorge, that gorge is in the mountains ; so that even in his lowest swoop the mountain eagle is still higher than other birds upon the plain, even though they soar.' But, unluckily, Melville had not only too much passion for Truth to palter with religious orthodoxy, whether occupied in constructing present Hells in Polynesia or future Heavens *in vacuo* ; he had also too keen an imagination to leave the Infinities alone.

He could not simply lose his faith with a *Deo gratias !*
He could neither believe nor rest in disbelief. He ex-
changed religion only for metaphysics and threw good
reasoning after bad. More ordinary men are here more
sensible ; recognition of the vanity of eating or writing
does not take away their appetite for meat or ink ; they
have less brain and more earwax, and to them the Sirens
sing supperless. But Captain Ahab is not the just man
of De Vigny, who

> Ne répondra plus que par un froid silence
> Au silence éternel de la divinité.

He is of the race of Prometheus bearding the Eternal,
of Hercules whizzing his arrows against the intolerable
sun in the zenith, of the Cimbri taking arms against the
resistless sea. Melville could find no anchorage alive.
Happiness was not for him. With all of us indeed the
closeness with which satiety treads on the heels of fruition
is the tritest of sorrows ; but with him the two things seem
to have come almost hand in hand. Not the romance of
the sea or of Typee, nor the love of Fayaway or Miss
Shaw, nor the friendship of the somewhat spineless
Hawthorne, could give him more than a momentary
respite from disillusion. Like the fabulous Bird of
Paradise he had no feet to perch on any resting bough ;
and like Dante's Ulysses he sailed into the sunset in
quest of the Happy Isles only to sight at last the Mount
of Purgatory, and there be swallowed in the gulfs. The
young Herman walking to the end of his first ship and
flinging his last penny out to sea is typically one of those
who care for all or nothing, with a heroic disdain of the
day of small things, of those minor pleasures, which yet

make life endurable. It is in the grand manner ; but the sea of life does not give up its pence to the so proudly prodigal. The same spacious Elizabethan carelessness goes into his very style, mixing up blank verse with the prose, whenever its emphatic chant suits his mood. And chant and mood are wedded, when he cries like, too like, a hero of Chapman's : ' If after all these fearful fainting trances, the verdict be, the golden haven was not gained ; —yet in bold quest thereof, better to sink in boundless deeps than float on vulgar shoals ; and give me, ye gods, an utter wreck, if wreck I do.'

And if Melville now shows unexpected signs of life, it is not because of admirable stories of whalers and cannibals ; others have written as well their experiences of ships and savages. Nor is it his philosophy, which one may recognise without finding it very new or its ' mysticism ' very deep. It is as the creator of an epic of the sea and of human life, not faultless, but, in the sense of Longinus himself, sublime. *Moby Dick* has a digressive unity that would have delighted Aristotle ; a gift of characterisation more strong than subtle, but strangely real ; a diction that at its worst is never feeble ; and enough ' hard acorn of thought ' to satisfy even Matthew Arnold. It is not an allegory spun into a story, but a story strong enough to shoulder a dozen allegories or none at all. And the handling of the Supernatural, as an example of how it should be done, can compare with *The Ancient Mariner* or *Macbeth* itself.

These things are not merely great ; they are rare ; and this book will not get lost so easily a second time. Like his mystic Fedallah, the dead Melville rises again from the abyss to the light of day, on the back of Moby Dick.

Dᴜʀɪɴɢ the American Civil War, in a Washington hospital, when one of the wounded in his agony thrust a bare leg through the bedclothes, the nurse is recorded to have fled in prudish horror from the ward. It was in an age when such things were quite possible, that Whitman had the courage to publish a poem 'To a Common Prostitute.' 'Yes,' it may be said, 'very fine, no doubt, but we have progressed since then ; half of our drama and fiction is about nothing else.' But, again, after Lincoln's murder, when the gentle Emerson was finding even in that crime the finger of a wise Providence solicitous that the defeated South should not be treated too leniently, it was left for the sanity of Whitman to write of ' Reconciliation '—

> Word over all, beautiful as the sky . . .
> For my enemy is dead, the man divine as myself is dead.

Here, perhaps, remembering our own antics of a few years ago, we may feel less superior. There was greatness in Whitman. That does not prove his poetry worth reading ; but that was one of the things which made it so. For personality cannot make great writing ; but without it the greatest writing cannot be at all. Whitman's greatness (like Tennyson's, little as the two men had in common) was streaked with pettiness ; but it was real. He found American literature a revered mummy, swaddled and reswaddled by a number of gentlemen of letters, always polite and always second-rate ; in his

* *Walt Whitman : A Study and a Selection. By Gerald Bullett. Grant Richards.*
Swinburne's Collected Poetical Works. Heinemann.

hands it became a new thing, clumsy, grotesque, but at last alive.   He did not regard his work as literature at all.   He wanted to think of himself as a poetic Melchizedek sprung suddenly on the world without ancestry or heritage from the past.   'Make no quotations, no reference to any other authors,' he adjures himself in one of his notebooks ;   for these writers of tradition were the 'pampered jades of Asia,' and he, like Tamburlaine, the Scythian Shepherd from whom a new era should begin.

> Camerado, this is no book,
> Who touches this, touches a man.

But the unforeseen happened.   It was the enemy who flocked to his banner.   Not 'These States,' but England, not his familiar dock-hands and omnibus-drivers of Brooklyn, but delicate men of letters like Symonds and Stevenson, the mild Dowden, the pre-Raphaelite William Rossetti, the pessimistic James Thomson, first gave a real welcome to his work.   This puzzled Whitman a good deal, yet it was natural enough ;   only the cultured could appreciate his reaction from culture, only the literary his defiance of literary tradition.   They were so uncertain of themselves, and here stood this genial creature, gasconading with the naïve arrogance of a giant in a fairy-tale.   They were troubled with themselves, and here was a 'natural and nonchalant person,' with no inhibitions, no self-questionings, facing life with a bravado which its sincerity and sympathy prevented from seeming cheap.   They were perplexed about God and about good, and here rose one who answered—

> I say to any man or woman, ' Let your soul stand cool and
> composed before a million universes . . .'

And I say to mankind, ' Be not curious about God,
For I, who am curious about each, am not curious about God,'
(No array of terms can say how much I am at peace about
   God and about Death).

And how assured and imperturbable his sense of his own
importance, of every human individual's importance in
the universe, as heir of all its æons !

Cycles ferried my cradle, rowing and rowing like cheerful
   boatmen,
For room to me the stars kept aside in their own rings,
They sent influences to look after what was to hold me.
Before I was born out of my mother, generations guided me,
My embryo has never been torpid, nothing could overlay it.
For it the nebula cohered to an orb,
The long, low strata piled to rest it on,
Vast vegetables gave it sustenance,
Monstrous sauroids transported it in their mouths and
   deposited it with care.

To us it seems that they were somewhat easily con-
soled ; the maladies of our time do not yield to remedies
so simple. We see to-day in Whitman no philosopher,
only a light-hearted, incoherent mystic, now lost in unity
with the universe, now defying it to absorb him, now
abandoning his individuality, now shouting it to the four
winds. The problem of evil seldom vexed that sanguine
soul ; it was necessary or an illusion, he could not remember which. ' These States,' ' the divine average,'
' the athletic American matron speaking in public to
crowds of listeners '—from such things the glamour has
departed. We doubt the divinity of averages, and as for
the athletic American matron . . . ' Camerado ' comes
the insistently repeated call, a little ghostly and pathetic

now. He points out how placid are the animals, how unvexed by our problems. But we are not animals. As pigs we should be happier, doubtless ; yet we should flee Circe, if we met her to-morrow, like the devil. ' Memo. Get from Mr. Arkhurst the names of all insects ; interweave train of thought suitable,'—so runs a note of his ; and we are left marvelling what train of thought could conceivably be suitable. What a technique ! Whitman, indeed, revelled in creation, as if he were the God of *Genesis* and had just created it ; yet he did not really understand himself. He thought he was a new phenomenon in the world, when in reality he was as primitive as the shepherds of the mountains of Arcadia, who deemed themselves elder than the moon. That is his charm. We do not believe his gospel ; but we like him. His answers to the eternal questions were childish ; but he asked the questions with a man's honesty and courage—

> I know I am restless and make others so,
> I know my words are weapons full of danger, full of death,
> For I confront peace, security, and all settled laws, to unsettle them.
> I am more resolute because all have denied me, than I could ever have been, had all accepted me,
> I heed not and have never heeded either experience, cautions, majorities, nor ridicule,
> And the threat of what is called hell is little or nothing to me,
> And the lure of what is called heaven is little or nothing to me ;
> Dear camerado, I confess I have urged you onward with me, and still urge you, without the least idea of what is our destination,
> Or whether we shall be victorious, or utterly quelled and defeated.

So modern and iconoclastic ; yet dropping, most typically, for its final cadence, into an echo of the oldest and noblest of European measures, the hexameter. He scorned the literary ; yet he had an ear and an imagination, and polished his work and toiled after the right word like any Flaubert. Because of that and for the sake of the pity, the courage, the humanity that were in him, he can still be read and, easy as his style appears, none has repeated his success. So he won his reward ; yet life did not spare him its irony at the end, the poet of the beauty of the active body paralysed in a bathchair. He fades gradually from us in that twilight, a pathetic, feeble figure, with a note of wistfulness creeping into the old buoyancy—

Soon to be lost for aye in the darkness ; loth, O so loth to
  depart !
Garrulous to the very last.

It had been supposed, to the righteous indignation of many, that he died almost penniless ; it turned out that he had spent four thousand dollars on a large and hideous mausoleum, besides leaving ten thousand and more in the bank. That lesser Whitman who had written anonymous reviews to the glory of *Leaves of Grass* and lied about its sales and touted for it by publishing a private letter from Emerson, died only, it would seem, with the death of the nobler figure that we know. But he was an extraordinary man. This beautifully-printed selection with its sensible introduction would have given him almost as much pleasure as another mausoleum ; the only criticism is that it might perhaps have been a little enlarged to contain some of the best passages from poems not worth quoting as a whole.

If Whitman had this touch of human greatness, it is perhaps the one gift Swinburne lacked. ' Isn't he the damnedest simulacrum ? ' was Whitman's characteristic comment when the poet who had hymned him as ' heart of their hearts who are free ' turned to shriek at him as a libertine (this came well from the author of *Dolores*) whose idea of love was ' a Hottentot Venus under the influence of cantharides.' By that time, indeed, a ' simulacrum ' was all that remained of Swinburne. When Mazzini and Jowett met in the house of Mr. George Howard to consult ' what was to be done with and for Algernon,' even they little guessed how successfully Algernon was going to be done for. It was reserved for Watts-Dunton to imprison what had been a great poet in ' The Pines ' at Putney as hopelessly as ever Nimue locked Merlin in the hollow oak of Broceliande. Only, the process was exactly opposite. It consisted in complete disenchantment, the destruction of all the magic which had once encircled the most dæmonic of young poets. There is consolation in the thought that perhaps his genius had almost burnt itself out in any case ; but it is hard not to blame Putney in part at least for that dreary verbiage of Swinburne's later volumes, which has made it the popular thing to regard him as the poet of wonderful sound and no sense. This view has, indeed, been restated by one of our most brilliant critics, who paradoxically regards him as both a chimæra bombinating in a vacuum of meaninglessness, and yet a remarkable poet, on the ground that bombinating in a vacuum and writing whole poems without any meaning are remarkably difficult accomplishments. They may well be ; like Dr. Johnson on a similar occasion, I wish they were

impossible.   But those who love *Atalanta* and *Chastelard*
and *Poems and Ballads*, love them because they find there
expressed with Dionysiac splendour their own most
passionate feelings.   Among the earlier poems of Swinburne there are indeed some, among the later very many,
which signify little ; and they are insignificant as poetry
in proportion.

At the present day he is not popular.   For the Philistine he will always be ' immoral ' ; the rest of the world
dislikes him for several reasons.   His rhythms are obviously and unashamedly beautiful, they do not coquette
with the ear ; and modern affectation dislikes that.   The
development of metre has followed other lines, partly
because on his it could go no further ; and thus his very
success has been against him.   Another reason is one of
Time's usual revenges.   He attacked the gods, the con-
ventions, the prejudices of his own age ; and a writer
who attacks his own age is in danger of perishing with it.
He assaulted religion : to-day religion is either accepted
or ignored by a generation tired of arguing.   He believed
passionately in liberty : to-day Mazzini has given place
to Mussolini, and men, if not weary, as *Il Duce* asserts, of
her ' decomposing corpse,' have at all events learnt not
to expect too much of her.   He believed in freedom of
thought : to-day men regard that as a matter of course—
or a superfluous luxury.   It is not because he is meaningless that Swinburne is not read ; it is because certain
things meant more to him than to us.   He was an enthusiastic decadent ; modern decadence is not enthusiastic,
only sometimes pretentious.   So it turns out that the
only strong admirer of his known to me was a middle-
aged philosopher, the late Dr. McTaggart.   The con-

ventional young scout him.   The unconventional young
think he made too much noise about liberty and too much
fuss about libertinage.

But Swinburne will outlive the young.   Some of the
things he cared about do matter ; some things he did
supremely well.   The effects that talent produces, one
can fancy oneself producing, with one's own powers
magnified ; but the effects that genius produces, you
cannot conceive yourself even beginning to create.   Such
is Swinburne at his best.   He is like the sea, but the sea
within a cave ; limited, yet sublime in its energy ; sublime
in its energy, yet monotonous at times ; majestic, but
not with the majesty of human pity ; beautiful, but not
with a human beauty.   And at last there comes the ebb.
He lacked tenderness, though in later life he sacrificed
himself, an inverted Moloch, to a maudlin worship of
infants.   He lacked force of character such as, with all his
faults, Byron had ; they were both supreme orators in
poetry, but it is a far cry from Putney to Missolonghi.
This lack of the deeper human qualities is the weakness
of his plays ; as de Reul says, ' si les hommes et les femmes
de Swinburne parlent avec ardeur, ils ne s'écoutent pas
entre eux.'   Yet at times, as a pure lyric poet, he seems
the most wonderful writer in the world ; it is mere intoxication ; but how intoxicating it is !

> Albeit I die indeed
> And hide myself and sleep and no man heed,
> Of me the high God hath not all his will.
> Blossom of branches, and on each high hill
> Clear air and wind, and under in clamorous vales
> Fierce noises of the fiery nightingales,

Buds burning in the sudden spring like fire,
The wan washed sand and the waves' vain desire,
Sails seen like blown white flowers at sea, and words
That bring tears swiftest, and long notes of birds
Violently singing till the whole world sings—
I, Sappho, shall be one with all these things,
With all high things for ever.

There 's the Irishman Arthur O'Shaughnessy—
On the chessboard of poets a pawn is he ;
   Though a bishop or king
   Would be rather the thing
To the fancy of Arthur O'Shaughnessy.

THESE lines of Rossetti's were not, of course, intended as a serious estimate of O'Shaughnessy, any more than the couplet,

   There is a young person named Georgy
   Who indulges each night in an orgy,

was a literal description of the domestic habits of Lady Burne-Jones. But it is possible to ask to-day, how far time has proved the jesting judgment true. O'Shaughnessy's place among the English poets is hardly royal, still less episcopal, even though he may have written

   I was beauteous and holy and sad.

In practice, whatever other merits his poetry possesses, of virtue it displays little except 'the lilies and languors.' But is he really only 'a pawn'? Or a captive knight, rather, —held in thrall by that dark queen of many names, Circe, La Belle Dame sans Merci, Dolores, Proserpine—that soft, morbid, melancholy mistress, whose cheeks are powdered with the dust of death—the Muse of Decadence ?

   O exquisite malady of the soul,
   How hast thou marred me !

---

* *Poems of Arthur O'Shaughnessy. Selected and edited by W. A. Percy. Yale University Press. Milford.*

Hers is the frail, pale beauty, hers also the fatal weakness, of O'Shaughnessy's work.

It was a strange union. For his business in life was the care of ichthyological specimens in the British Museum. Gods and little fishes have long been joined on the lips of men, but when before was a Muse found in such company? The records of his uneventful existence are dim, and darkened yet further by hints of a mystery. Lord Lytton, parent of one dubious poet, 'Owen Meredith,' and credited by fantastic rumour with the parentage of another very real one, James Thomson, was, if no more, the generous patron of O'Shaughnessy. Through him the boy of seventeen became an assistant in the Printed Books Department of the British Museum; two years later his appointment to a post in the Natural History Department was maintained in spite of the protest-meetings of enraged herpetologists. His first poems were published in 1870, when he was twenty-six, and won him a place in the pre-Raphaelite circle. Finally, after losing his wife and two children, he died himself, on the eve of remarriage (in a way that makes some of his poetry seem strangely prophetic), at the age of only thirty-seven.

This is a quiet life, as well as a brief one; and that it was so might well be guessed from the poems alone—

> Es bildet ein Talent sich in der Stille,
> Sich ein Charakter in dem Strom der Welt.

A cultivated talent is just what the poems show; and a strong character is just what they lack. Vitality, animal spirits, intensity of soul, it is vain to look for here; Nature did not give him these nor circumstance call them forth.   Nor again was he likely to learn them from those with whom he put himself to school.   Not that in the greater pre-Raphaelites there was wanting an innate and inextinguishable force—the sombre power of Rossetti, the frail fanaticism of his sister, the leonine strength of Morris, the chronic fever-heats of Swinburne ; but their distinctive atmosphere had always been the sweet heaviness of poppied autumn in some garden of Proserpine.   The same was true of his other master, Poe.   But it was not opiates that O'Shaughnessy needed.   His poetry suffers from a nervelessness and languor that make his very dreams grow too faint and drowsy, his murmuring monotones nod into discords.   And, after all, nothing is more tiring than eternal weariness.   When he sings

> My lips have the languid complexion
> Of the phantom loves that they kiss,

one feels it is only too true ; and as a refrain,

> Fading away, ah, fading away,
> Fading, fading away,

is so very Lydia Languish as to be more than a little ludicrous.   Another side of the same *fin-de-siècle* decadence is his blood-thirstiness.   Just as the bedridden Henley breathed swords and slaughter, so O'Shaughnessy pines for the love of young murderesses or ' the passion of a purple Nero.'   This Circe of his imagination changes him into the were-wolf of ' Bisclavaret.'   His love of colour is more savage and exotic still.   Tennyson, it is related, once tried to fire Wordsworth's imagination with an ecstatic description of a tropical island he had heard of, where the foliage was one blaze of scarlet ; Wordsworth, we gather, remained chilly. But even Tennyson's tropics and the palettes of the P.R.B. pale beside O'Shaughnessy's visions of blue islands with red love-birds and the ' flaunted glories of hundred-coloured lories.' He bursts into the lyric cry—

> O gorgeous Erumango, Isle
>   Or blossom of the sea ;

he dreams how

> The crimson bird hath fed
> With its mate of equal red,
> And the flower in soft explosion
> With the flower hath been wed ;

and there was surely something very curious about the colour-sense of the poet who could write—

> The blue effusion of a luminous kiss.

He has, too, like Coleridge in his later years, the regular dreamer's grandiosity. A writer far richer in sound than sense, he yet talks freely of ' mazes of immeasurable thought ' and the ' eternal mark ' they have set upon his face ; and this unreality is not altogether absent from one of the few poems of his which may hope to weather the year 2000, and the best known of all. When he sings—

> One man with a dream, at pleasure,
>   Shall go forth and conquer a crown ;
> And three with a new song's measure
>   Can trample a kingdom down.
>
> We, in the ages lying
>   In the buried past of the earth,
> Built Nineveh with our sighing,
>   And Babel itself with our mirth,

this expression of an idea, not in itself too romantic to be true, comes a little incongruously from a poet who, so far from being a Tyrtæus or a Rouget de l'Isle, was as incapable as any one ever born of trampling down or building anything but a city in the clouds. Even the grief is half unreal which can write—

> My sorrow was turned to a beauteous dress,
> Very fair in my weeping was I.

Well might even a minor Elizabethan have replied—

> Thy teares are dewdrops : sweet as those on roses,
> But mine the faint and yron sweatt of sorrow.

This persistent note of *fainéance* in O'Shaughnessy's writing sets narrow and definite limits to his success. His longer poems faint and flag in mid-career. Even the story of 'Chaitivel,' despite all the eerie fascination of the original legend, moves too slowly forward with the sinuous and serpentine flow of its long stanzas ; and the comparison it challenges with *The Earthly Paradise* is fatal, except for the song of Sarrazine over her lover in the grave—

> Hath any loved you well, down there,
>   Summer or winter through ?
> Down there have you found any fair,
>   Laid in the grave with you ?
> Is death's long kiss a richer kiss
>   Than mine was wont to be—
> Or have you gone to some far bliss
>   And quite forgotten me ?
>
> Hold me no longer for a word
>   I used to say or sing ;
> Ah, long ago you must have heard
>   So many a sweeter thing ;

> For rich earth must have reached your heart,
>   And turned the faith to flowers;
> And warm wind stolen, part by part,
>   Your soul through faithless hours.

Song indeed was O'Shaughnessy's one, true gift. Music he loved, and the clean, simple lucidity of French. At times he borrowed too boldly. The little bitter snakes of Swinburne he bottled in his poems, as he did the rarer reptilia at the Museum; and the artless 'quites' and 'verys' of the *Defence of Guinevere* reappear in him with a too artificial abundance.

> O woman have a care—
> What if two came to claim your hair
> Of God?—what if two shall have thrown
>   Their strong arms round your body, quite
>   Belonging with an equal right
> To each for ever?

When Sarrazine sings,

> What soft enamouring of sleep
>   Hath you in some soft way?

she rouses the mightier ghost of Rossetti's Villon:

> Tell me now in what hidden way is
>   Lady Flora the lovely Roman?
> Where's Hipparchia, and where is Thais,
>   Neither of them the fairer woman?

And clearer yet rings the voice of Rossetti's sister, with its sad, sweet austerity, in such a stanza as this:

> I made another garden, yea,
>   For my new love;
> I left the dead rose where it lay,
>   And set the new above.

J

> Why did the summer not begin ?
> Why did my heart not haste ?
> My old love came and walked therein
> And laid the garden waste.

Still it is not being inspired by others that matters, but being inspired at all. O'Shaughnessy was not just an echo. And if, as some hold, Leigh Hunt is to be adjudged the poet's name on the strength of that one line in an impromptu sonnet,

> The laughing queen that caught the world's great hands,

then O'Shaughnessy's few laurels are secure. But Mr. Percy's pruning-hook was needed ; it saves the reader most of the horrors I have quoted, though not Erumango or the explosive loves of the plants, and it preserves most of the essentials, though not Professor Saintsbury's best-beloved 'Barcarolle.' Those who care for poetry cannot afford to ignore a poet who is sometimes so good, though never great. Another singer, born in the same year as O'Shaughnessy, has described once for all the vein he chose, those 'songs of modern speech,'

> Lull'd by the song of Circe and her wine,
> In gardens near the pale of Proserpine,
> Where that Aeaean isle forgets the main,
> And only the slow lutes of love complain,

and how their honey cloys at last. Lang was right ; the Venusberg breathes too heavy an atmosphere for human beings to live in long. Yet there is a time for all things and all moods, and not least for this last rose of pre-Raphaelitism—or, perhaps rather, this arum lily, a little festered, from its grave.

THE IMPORTANCE OF BEING
EARNEST*

ATHENÆUS relates that the people of Tiryns were
incorrigibly frivolous. In time, however, finding their
own flippancy rather beyond a joke, they inquired of
Delphi how to become serious, and were bidden to throw
a bull into the sea as a sacrifice to Poseidon, keeping
straight faces the while. But at the psychological
moment of this ceremony an urchin's chance remark sent
them, unhappily, into roars of laughter ; and incurably
merry they remained thenceforth. There is little laughter
now among the grey stones of Tiryns in their sun-smitten
plain ; but while Samuel Butler lived, there was at least
one Tirynthian left on earth. When shall we see such
another combination of painstaking genius and the boun-
cing inconsequence of the dried pea in the bladder of a
fool ? Indeed, the breaking in of this flighty cheerful-
ness has done some harm to his work, and a great deal
more to his reputation ; for his flippancy has made him,
like his brilliant disciple, G. B. S., something of a laughing Cassandra. The British public is particularly slow
to realise that a shaft may strike no less straight to the
heart for being winged with goose-feathers.

There is, for instance, no more inherent absurdity in
believing—for there is no Salic Law in literature—that
the *Odyssey* was written by a woman than in supposing
the *Iliad* to have been clubbed together by a syndicate of

* *The Authoress of the Odyssey (2nd edition). By Samuel Butler. Cape.*
The Iliad, and the Odyssey (2nd edition), in English Prose. By the same.
Cape.
The Wrath of Achilleus, translated from the Iliad. By George Ernle.
Milford.

old gentlemen, unlimited. But Butler wrote his book as if it were half a joke, and one can read it as wholly one ; whereas after fifty pages of Jebb on Homer, so far from laughing at him, one feels as if one would never smile again.

The Authoress of the Odyssey sets out to prove that the poem was written by a woman, and that woman Nausicaa herself ; and that most of its scenes, including Phæacia and Ithaca itself, are to be sought round Trapani in West Sicily. The first of these theories depends on two axioms. One is, ' I doubt whether any writer in the whole range of literature (excepting, I suppose, Shakespeare) has succeeded in drawing a full-length, life-sized, serious portrait of a member of the sex opposite to the writer's own ' ; the other, ' that the mind of man, unless when he is young and lovesick, turns more instinctively to man than to woman,' and therefore the *Odyssey* with its great feminine interest cannot have been written by a man.

Did the law really stand so, Butler's circumstantial evidence would be amply sufficient to hang Homer and bring the lady into the property. Nor could one stop at that ; it would be necessary to attribute not only most of Shakespeare, in whose plays, as Mr. Shaw has pointed out, ' it is the woman who takes the initiative,' but most great drama, from the *Agamemnon* and the *Medea* to the *Doll's House*, to a ' monstrous regiment of women.' But in such a sieve of assumptions not even the wizardries of Butler can expect to keep afloat.

And then what clowning some of the detailed argument is ! It suits him to suppose that the Cyclopes were merely a Sican tribe with a perfectly good pair of eyes apiece. Then how was Polyphemus blinded? 'True, the writer only blinds one eye, but she could trust to the sympathetic inflammation which so serious an injury would excite in the other eye, and would consider that she had sufficiently blinded both by roasting one of them.' Butler had not altogether the right to take pepper in the nose at not being treated seriously himself by his opponents.

There is more solid sense and some quite solid learning in the Trapani argument. But this too is vitiated by the assumptions, first that Scheria must be west of Ithaca (north will do equally well), secondly that it or the other places in a fairy tale need be anywhere in particular at all. At precisely which port in Bohemia did Antigonus land? Because Butler invented little himself and used real places in *Erewhon* and real people in *The Way of All Flesh*, he jumped to the conclusion that other creators must do the same.

It is usual to talk about Butler's Homeric translations as if his *Iliad* and his *Odyssey* were of a piece. Actually the two are as distinct in tone as if he had set out to make his public believe not only the originals, but the translations themselves, to be by different hands. Through the *Iliad* he manages to keep serious and to produce what is probably the best English prose translation of it existing ; but in the *Odyssey* he becomes again the urchin of Litera-ture. The sneer at Wardour Street English has survived, because it meant something ; but 'before we go to Paradise by way of Kensal Green' in Butler's company, we may decide that we prefer *The Earthly Paradise*, even via Wardour Street, after all. Even Butler in a candid moment admitted that *The Old Sailor* would

not be quite the same thing as *The Ancient Mariner*.
But he chose to forget that truth while translating the
Odyssey.

To the very sound and rather priggish essay of Matthew
Arnold *On Translating Homer* sixty years have added
nothing. Of Arnold's four Homeric qualities —
rapidity, simplicity of style and of thought, and nobility—
Butler's *Odyssey* rather exaggerates the first three, and
loses the last and greatest. Emperors have died with a
line of the *Odyssey* on their lips ; but of Butler's *Odyssey* !
There is nothing here of ' surge and thunder,' no

> tales of true, long-parted lovers,
> Joined in the evening of their days again.

' The interest of the poem ostensibly turns mainly on the
revenge taken by a bald, middle-aged gentleman, whose
little remaining hair is red, on a number of young men
who have been eating him out of house and home, while
courting his supposed widow.' To this rather frowsy
humour of general attitude Butler's diction corresponds—
always bald, often comic, sometimes vulgar. ' Bless my
heart,' says Odysseus. ' Sweethearts,' says Penelope to
the suitors. Diana's nymphs are ' a whole bevy of
beauties,' and in the palace of Alcinous one ' meets all
the best people among the Phæacians.' Such things are
pure Scarron, and the *Virgil Travestied* not more blatant
travesty than this. Similarly the descriptive passages
become good *Robinson Crusoe* ; they would do excellently
for Lucian ; but to Homer they bear no relation at all.
It was typical of Butler's misogyny to produce such a
thing and pretend that a woman had done it ; and of his
dislike for greatness in general, not merely for cant about

it, to make out that the poetry of Homer was this sort of
'plain Jane and no nonsense.'

In the *Iliad*, however, Butler behaves himself. Venus
(how one wishes the editors had given the Greek names,
as Butler was prepared to do, if ever they came into current
use !) does indeed call Helen a 'hussy'; but that may
pass. The right diction for rendering Homer is, of
course, an infinitely vexed and vexing question. If the
translator aims at producing on one who knows no Greek
the same effect as the original on one who does, his style
must be, if not a little archaic, certainly not staringly
modern. Homer is definitely an ancient, in manner as
in matter, to us, as he already was to Sophocles. On the
other hand, most translators become too archaic, too full
of 'tushery'; as Ben Jonson said of archaising Spenser,
they 'write no language.' Homer is rapid; but the
Lang style is too barnacled over with antiquarianisms like
'-eth' and 'even as' to keep pace with him. Homer
never seems odd or grotesque, but always, nodding or
waking, natural. But when knights 'wallop together'
in Malory, when we come as late as the seventeenth
century on oddities like 'some darksome spelunk in the
wilderness,' here the quaintness that we enjoy is quite an
un-Homeric thing; to bring it into Homeric translation, to use expressions like Newman's 'bragly' or Butler's
own 'fruitling of my spear,' is to mix oil and water. The
reader laughs or shies; the speed and the illusion are
lost. There is much to be said for Arnold's model, the
Bible; but the main thing is surely not so much to attain
the old as to avoid the jarringly modern. In this respect
in the *Iliad* Butler does succeed. He may, perhaps, tend
to exaggerate Homer's plainness into the bleaker, terser

strength of the Icelandic Saga ; but he is splendid in his rapidity, not being muffled with any false beard of fifteenth century cut. Only, Homer's nobility here too he often fails to give. That importance of the beautiful word, which Longinus and Dante cannot stress enough, Butler, like Wordsworth, often ignores to his own undoing. ' Jove boded them ill and roared with his portentous thunder '—' there he lay in the whirling clouds of dust, *all huge and hugely* ' (instead of ' the mighty one mightily fallen ')—such things are miserably unjust to the grace of the Greek. But it is worth comparing him for a moment with what one may call the standard version ; here is Leaf's rendering of a famous passage—

> Then Hippolochos' glorious son made answer to him : ' Great-hearted Tydeides, why enquirest thou of my generation ? Even as are the generations of leaves, such are those of men ; the leaves that be, the wind scattereth on the earth, and the forest buddeth and putteth forth more again, when the season of spring is at hand ; so of the generations of men one putteth forth and another ceaseth.'

Butler's runs—

> And the son of Hippolochos answered, ' Mighty son of Tydeus, why ask me of my lineage ? Men come and go as leaves year by year upon the trees. Those of autumn the wind sheds upon the ground, but when spring returns the forest buds forth with fresh ones. Even so is it with the generations of mankind, the new spring up as the old are passing away.'

Even in these few lines the gain in swiftness and directness is immense. Again take a fragment of Achilles' great reply to the Embassy in Butler's version—

Why, pray, must the Argives needs fight the Trojans?
What made the son of Atreus gather the host and bring
them? Was it not for the sake of Helen? Are the sons of
Atreus the only men in the world who love their wives?
. . . Let him look to you, Ulysses, and to the other princes
to save his ships from burning. He has done much without
me already. He has built a wall; he has dug a trench
deep and wide all round it, and he has planted it within
with stakes; but even so he stays not the murderous might
of Hector.

Here one may contrast Mr. Ernle's version—

Danaans, why fight you the Trojans? Why has Atrides
brought you to die here, sons of Achaia? Why, on
account of Helen's bright hair! But do you believe them
singular in cherishing their wives, these children of Atreus?
. . . You, Odyseus, you princes of his, can counsel Atrides
how to protect the vessels from fierce flame, if you desire to.
Me he requires no longer—he does so bravely without me,
building a high rampart, good Gods! and delving a deep
moat under it and filling it with sharpen'd stakes to defend
him! And cannot all his efforts keep out victorious
Hector?

This last—how many will suspect it?—is a verse translation in quantitative hexameters. Prosody is in general
an uncomfortably calorific subject; but it is only fair
to summarise Mr. Ernle's idea, which is apparently one
more revival of Spedding's attempt to get over the monotony of the accentual hexameter, by calling in quantity
to redress the balance with that interplay, supposed to
exist in the ancient hexameter, between the long syllables
which have metrical stress, and the verbal accents that
now coincide, now conflict with them. This is, however,

sitting in the Siege Perilous. For one thing, the part played by accent in the Latin, still more in the Greek hexameter is by no means certain ; for another, to the ancient ear quantity was the main thing in metre, accent quite secondary, whereas with us accent has come to tyrannise over quantity, so that in a modern Greek village to hear one's host reading out one's pocket Homer to his admiring gossips is metrical torture, and in English verse the quantity of *most* syllables depends simply on their being accented or not. When Mr. Ernle proceeds to legislate to the effect that vowels followed by two consonants are, with various exceptions—(' would ' and ' should ' for instance, must be pronounced ' wŭd ' and ' shŭd ')—to be counted long, one can only echo Professor Saintsbury's bewildered ' Why ? '

At all events the proof of the pudding is in the eating ; if there are people, as there appear to be, whose ears can delight in such rhythms as

Queen Helena excepted alone, as being an Argive,

we wish them joy of it. To us the accentual hexameter, with its lack of spondees and the relentless ' jiggledy jiggle ' tied always to its tail, is too unbearably monotonous a metre ; while the quantitative hexameter does not appear to be metre at all. From the enormities of Stanyhurst—" his woords fitlye placed with his heuenly phisnomye pleasing '—and the admission of Campion that ' *Carmen Exametrum* doth rather trot and hobble than run smoothly in our English tongue,' to the verdict of Tennyson and Swinburne, this metre, with a few exceptions which are really anapæstic, has been a hothouse weed, which has borne no fruit in England   It is rather in the

iambic-anapæstic *Sigurd*-metre of Morris (without his
Anglo-Saxonisms) or the similar metre of Mr. Way that
the best native equivalent of the music of Homer is to be
sought. In prose, Butler's *Iliad*, though not ideal, has
yet to be surpassed.

UTOPICS *

HERBERT TRENCH was born at Avoncore, county Cork, in 1865, went to Haileybury and Oxford, and worked from 1891 to 1908 on the Board of Education. The next two years saw him curiously transformed into the director of the Haymarket Theatre ; then his health failed, and the last decade of his life was mainly spent in the neighbourhood of Florence, till he died at Boulogne in June 1923. The bronze bust by Antonio Maraini, reproduced in the *Collected Works*, shows a not unfamiliar, masterful type of man—flannel collar flung wide at the throat, the hair thrown back as by a violent wind all along the line of the high forehead, eyes wide apart and rather defiant, the chin a little over-resolutely set. It becomes easy, after seeing it, to understand how, though his youth produced the inevitable *Deirdre* which it appears to be compulsory for every literary Irishman to produce at some time or other in his life, Trench came to regard the Celtic twilight (says Mr. Williams) as 'sentimental mystery-mongering.' Yet he hugged all the closer a queer, mystical prepossession of his own ; the human race, he dreamed, was being safely shepherded by Destiny towards an ever-increasing realisation of the Oneness of the Many, of the absorption of all individuals in the unity of the life of the Universe. To foster this feeling of unity was the work of the family ; from that inner circle it was to spread through the race outward and outward, like the rippling rings on the surface of a pool in which a stone has sunk and lost itself. 'The family,' explains

* *The Collected Works of Herbert Trench. Edited by Harold Williams.* Cape.

Mr. Williams, 'is the glowing chalice of life expanding in " spirals of creation " in unison with other chaliced centres,

> Until with sense of all the rest inwound.'

The persistence with which Trench rides this hobby-horse of his with a perpetual clanging of ' chalices ' from its saddlebow, grows a little tiresome to the unconverted. The mystic has always longed in this way for absorption ; but the ordinary human mind is not mystical, and is left cold by this passion for getting lost in things. To feel a man's poetry it is, of course, not necessary to believe his philosophy ; but it is necessary to be able to sympathise with it for the duration of the poem, to suspend for the moment disapproval and disbelief. A good Catholic can enjoy the ' Hymn to Proserpine,' a good pagan ' The Hound of Heaven.' Were the world as the poet sees it, the same despair, the same rapture might be our own. But with Trench the difficulty goes deeper ; even sup-posing we believed that we were all going to feel less and less individual, more and more mere cellules in a greater organism, we cannot imagine ourselves in ecstasies over the prospect. Absorption ! Meredith, with his jaunty pæans to Nature, was worshipping a tiger ; but this is to adore a sponge. We are told it is a superb sponge ; a great poet would, doubtless, have made us swallow even it for a moment ; but not Trench. The short lyric, ' I seek Thee in the heart alone,' does survive its subject, because it is swift and sonorous enough to please us without our bothering particularly what it means ; but poems on the Battle of Marne, twenty pages long, all leading up to this King Charles' head at the end, are

insufferable. It is so easy, every time one's own side wins
a victory, to discern the finger of Providence in the pie.
But, as Montaigne wrote, with an unusual touch of
spleen for him, ' Those which on a cocke-horse will
pearche themselves on the Epicicle of Mercury, and see
so farre into heaven, they even pull out my teeth.'

In fact, Trench was one of those extravagant poets who
have beaten out their metal thin to make sieves to hold
moonshine ; yet the true metal was there. His rigmaroles on the war can be forgotten in the lilt of lyrics like
the ' Requiem of Archangels for the World,' his apotheoses
of the family in the pure poetry of ' Deirdre Wedded,'
and some of the best love poems of their decade. Trench
admired Arnold, but he had not Arnold's depth. His
long odes echo Meredith, but they have not Meredith's
wit. It is Wilfrid Blunt, if any one, that these love
lyrics recall—that undertone of fierceness, that slight
but stirring sense of the fanatic's bitterness beneath the
lover's kiss. Such is the ' Bitter Serenade '—

> The very stars grow dread with tense forefeeling
>   Of dawn ; the bell-towers darken in the sky,
> As they would groan before they strike, revealing
>   New day to such as I. . . .
>
> A man can take the buffets of the tourney,
>   But there 's a hurt, lady, beyond belief ;
> A grief the Sun finds not upon his journey
>   Marked on the map of grief. . . .
>
> Was I not bred of the same clay and vapour
>   And lightning of the universe as you ?
> Had I the self-same God to be my shaper,
>   Or cracks the world in two ?

It cannot be, though I have nought to merit,
   That man may hold so dear, and with such
      pain
Enfold with all the tendrils of the spirit,
   Yet not be loved again ;

It cannot be that such intensest yearning,
   Such fierce and incommunicable care
Starred on your face, as through a crystal burning,
   Is wasted on the air.

Alas, we know that indeed it can ; but for a moment it
is easy to forget. The hyperbole of that first verse might
have failed grotesquely, but it succeeds. Bacon observed
in his dry way that it is only in love that perpetual hyperbole is considered comely. He thought it to love's dis-
credit ; but it is the strength of love-poetry, that there
at least men can talk as if they were gods or devils and
yet not seem absurd.

Others of the poems, like ' She comes not when noon
is on the roses ' and ' Come, let us make love deathless,'
have been made by anthologies deservedly familiar to a
wider world ; and it is a few lyrics like these that will
longest keep the name of Trench alive. That is so
often the way. What the man piques himself on, time
disregards ; what he threw off lightly, it keeps and
treasures. So Theophrastus gave his life to philosophy
and botany, but the world cares only for the humorist
whose leisure has left us thirty thumb-nail sketches of
human character. And similarly it was on earth, not
on the ' Epicicle of Mercury,' in the swing of strong
simple rhythms, not in the massed music of his odes, that
Trench found himself. For the intricacies of metre he

had no gift ; there are times when he seems to have no
ear at all—

> Or wave-like, shall Man, enkindled, and mirrored from
>   glass unto glass
> Become at length aware of an audience divine ? Who
>   knows ?

> .   .   .   .

> And drift over the blue turf so nigh dumb
> They startle not from 's gloom e'en the airy fawn.

More often the metre of the longer pieces is not so much
bad as nondescript ; as stanza after stanza passes, one
wonders when the orchestra will cease tuning up and
begin to play. But in this respect, too, the shorter poems
redeem the longer, and fragments, sometimes, the wholes
in which they are contained. If amid the welter of
cuckoo anthologies that are hatched out on us every
season, some one would only give us a collection not of
perfect poems, which are so few and so familiar, but of
the best moments in poetry, which are so many and un-
explored, there would be room there for utterances of
Trench like these—

> O put not on my singing lips
> The proud seal of your hand.

> .   .   .   .   .   .

> Speak not of me nor give my beauty praise,
> Whose beauty is to follow in thy ways,
> So that my days be numbered with thy days.

> .   .   .   .   .   .

> Fame ! When thy thousand graces ask no praise—
>   When all that perfect soul shall disappear,
> And leave no footprint of thy lovely ways,
>   Save in the desperate heart that held thee dear !

What 's Fame to me, when thou wilt smile and pass
    Dew-like ?   For mean lives trumpets shall be blown ;
Thou wilt go wandering through the gate of grass,
    And thy place after thee be all unknown.

Fragmentary ? Yes, like most of the poetry, we remember, that lives with us in silence and comes echoing
back to consciousness at the moments when we ourselves
are most alive.

The third volume of this edition contains Trench's
one finished play, *Napoleon*, which was acted by the
Stage Society in 1919. It is a medley somehow effective
in its own despite—with a plot impossible, yet exciting ;
characters wooden, yet of a certain sculptural impressiveness ; a fundamental idea that is preposterous, yet moving
in its absolute sincerity. The comic relief alone is an
unrelieved nuisance. Trench had little humour—he
would have been a very different being if he had. And,
of course, as the climax of the play, King Charles' head
rises in a wet blanket from the waves of mid-Channel,
whither the typically Trench-like hero has decoyed
Napoleon in order to turn him into a pacifist by applying
the usual apparatus of ' spirals ' and ' chalices ' and ' the
Family.' Here we have the old problem of fanaticism ;
the fanatics, not the intelligent, are the people who do
things ; only, they generally do the wrong things. The
world has always a lurking tenderness for idealists who
persuade it that it is only necessary to dream something
pretty in order to wake up reformed to-morrow morning.
There is a story, which I feel is too good not to be true,
of Mr. Shaw lecturing long ago at Cambridge, on the
economics of the millennium. When he ended, a clerical
person, a little suspicious of his general tone, approached

and said, 'Well, Mr. Shaw, and on what great force do you rely for accomplishing these beneficent results?' 'Oh, human selfishness, human selfishness.' Opposite extreme as this is to idealism like Trench's, it has a refreshing honesty about it. For the world will never be much bettered by talking to its Napoleons about the Family, by sitting on stiles and smiling at its cows. It is neither quite good nor quite stupid enough. Trench was a gifted writer ; too much of his work he spoiled by making it a playground for a sentimental idealism ; still, his own life was probably only the happier for it, and the loss less his than ours.

'*AH, DID YOU ONCE SEE SHELLEY PLAIN?*'*

Not long ago Signor Croce fluttered a portion of the learned world by a violent attack on all biographies of Shakespeare, all studies of Shakespeare's England. The plays are there, he urged, and the plays are all we need, and the rest is but leather and prunella. And others, too, before Croce, have felt and uttered a like annoyance at all our preoccupation with the private lives of poets. What do these accidental details matter—the suburbs they were born in, the dates on which they teethed? Is not this craze for biographies a mere trooping to empty sepulchres, a thinly disguised form of that vulgarity which makes Stratford an everlasting bank holiday and Burns's Cottage a shrine for all Philistia? 'Oh the flummery of a birthplace! Cant! Cant! Cant! It's enough to give a spirit the guts-ache.' The style is unfamiliar; but thus wrote Keats after visiting Ayrshire, with a disgust curiously, though unconsciously, echoed half a century later by Rossetti: 'Fancy carrying about grasses for days and hours from the field where Burns ploughed up a daisy. Good God! If I found the daisy itself, I'd sooner swallow it than be troubled to carry it twenty yards.' And with the same instinctive distaste, no doubt, Matthew Arnold implored that his bones might be left untroubled by any biographer at all.

The reaction is human enough. Even Croce's ex-

---

* *The Life of James Elroy Flecker.* By *Geraldine Hodgson, Litt.D.* Blackwell.
  Collected Prose of J. E. Flecker. Heinemann.
  Hassan. By *J. E. Flecker.* Heinemann.

travagance finds some excuse in all those second-best-bedlamite lives of Shakespeare, built on conjecture resting on conjecture resting on conjecture, which are far more disgusting to the reasonable mind than any mere desecration of his dust. But the reaction, as usual, 'empties out the baby with the bath-water'; it is in biographies, not in biography, that the badness lies. A poet's life does matter—intensely. Indeed, there is only too much at present of that deadly tendency to dissociate literature from life, to talk as if the creation and appreciation of Art consisted in playing a sort of transcendental skittles by oneself in the attic of an Ivory Tower. But reading poetry is not a higher form of solitary soaking; it involves, also, gaining contact with another human being. Perfect appreciation means perfect understanding; and it is therefore unattainable. But we can at least approach it, we can at least penetrate more deeply into a poet's mind by discovering the right things about him; just as what our friends say has shades and tones and subtleties for us, that no stranger's eloquence can ever give. To talk then, like Croce, as if the lives of poets were irrelevant and better ignored, is mere obscurantism. True, the relevance varies vastly bteween poet and poet. Byron's life is the most poetic of all his works. Wordsworth's is a necessary corrective and comment to his text. Arnold's enlightens us far less than theirs. Tennyson, relieved of his clumsy halo, has become human and to some, in consequence, readable for the first time; and Rossetti cannot ever be properly seen except against the gloomy background of his life; but the record of Browning's career has no such significance. The curse of biography is that biographers will tell us what we do not

want to know, and will not tell us what we want to know.
They are, as a class, so strangely incompetent—partly,
perhaps, because biography has a deceptively easy air
about it, partly because it is far too often ' art with a
purpose.'

Actually, indeed, it remains one of the hardest of
literary forms ; for it requires an extremely rare combination of the gifts of the scientific investigator and the
novelist, of the bookworm and the man of the world.   A
historian may nowadays be concerned merely with things
like the price of eggs under Edward I, which does not
make great demands on the imagination.   And he may
be far more literary and humane than that, and yet still
have a less subtle task than the biographer ; just as it is
easier fully to grasp and convey a campaign than an
emotion, the vicissitudes of an empire than of a soul.

But it is with such difficulties that the biographer must
cope, if he aims at more than chronicling small beer.
And the finally desperate thing about most biographers
is the ease with which they seem to think they can accom-
plish this ordeal.   ' You would seem to know my stops ;
you would pluck out the heart of my mystery ; you
would sound me from my lowest note to the top of my
compass ; and there is much music, excellent voice in this
little organ, yet cannot you make it speak. 'Sblood, do
you think I am easier to be played on than a pipe ? '   ' Can
these people ever have introspected ? ' one wonders, amid
their glib, clumsy motive-mongering.   And there are,
too, other almost incompatible qualities which the biographer needs no less—the drudge's gift of not minding
what is boring and what not, combined with a tact that
feels, like ice, the first touch of boredom in the reader ;

that sense of what matters, which is so rare within the walls of libraries ; and not only imagination, but the power to keep fact and conjecture rigidly severed, not only in the writer's, but in the reader's mind. (It is the lack of this which makes the imitators of Mr. Strachey often so maddening, and him the most perilous of models.) Then, again, there must be a fine sense of human fineness, together with an absolute detachment about morality, a Thucydidean power of being shocked by nothing on earth ; and lastly, a good taste which is yet free from that Mary-Annish discretion which is always drawing veils or dabbing whitewash over lives like Swinburne's or Rossetti's. This combination of rare gifts must inevitably be, in its fullness, ten times rarer still ; and we are lucky to have seen the appearance, so close together, of *Queen Victoria* and *Louis Napoleon*. But is it too much to expect that there might by this time be some sort of tradition in English biography as a whole which would deliver us from its worst faults—its banality, its aimless theorising, its absurd reticences ? From these the present life of Flecker suffers typically—nursery anecdotage about his dreaminess in putting on his stockings or his annoyance at being 'progged' at Oxford, premonitions of greatness from his being born 'with masses of long black hair,' letters from school full of his marks in the last grammar paper, testimonials from the mothers of school-friends, asseverations by the author that, whatever 'decadence' means, Flecker was not 'decadent,' only untidy, and not irreligious either, because he was sensitive to the beauties of nature. For all this *fatras* the reader is ill comforted by being told, of a period in 1913, ' it would be futile, and even wrong, to publish passages in his private letters in which from time to time his weariness, temporarily intolerable, escaped.' This is a curious sort of censorship. Are people only to be photographed smiling? No doubt this is all only partly Dr. Hodgson's fault. The book is very markedly written *in piam memoriam*; and it is not easy to write well under such circumstances, with a due insistence on that excellent motto of the *Dictionary of National Biography*, 'No flowers, by request.' We must wait. Meanwhile, little emerges to throw any real light on Flecker the poet.

He was born in a fog in Lewisham in 1884 and reared in Cheltenham; he was jealous in the nursery, according to the best Freudian principles, of his later-born sister ('A nice aunt you will make for my children!'); he went to Uppingham and hated it, to Oxford and liked it moderately, to Cambridge and liked it less. A prig at first, very much in the style of the young Clough ('I should think I am the only person in the 'Varsity, save clergymen, Wycliffe people, and the like, who has got a text hung up in his room. I am taking up missionary work, though I hate it.'), later in his time at Oxford he became 'an agnostic with a firm belief in the immortality of the soul'—failing to realise, in the words of an Oxford friend, 'how Christianity embraces the whole of life with all that is beautiful, artistic, and hilarious.' On Cambridge, where Flecker next went to work for the Consular Service, Dr. Hodgson is a little hard. 'Conventional standards in morals and religion,' she quotes, 'had broken down badly; the "New Hellenism" of Lowes Dickinson and Gilbert Murray was fashionable.' But, though thus abandoned to the iniquities of Mr. Dickinson, Cambridge in 1908 had not on that account anything gay or 'hilarious' about it. 'The Cambridge climate,' Dr. Hodgson pursues, 'is said not to suit everybody. More probably he chafed under the almost Puritan seriousness of the place.' Unfortunate University! The rest is brief—consular appointments in the East, a chill through bathing, when heated, in the Black Sea, consumption, marriage, Switzerland, and in January 1915 the sudden end.

Of the Flecker who seems real enough flesh and blood in his poetry, little survives here; either he had not a great deal of personality outside his writing, or it has escaped this portrait of him. As a human being it may be that he really was something of a bore; as a poet, though I doubt if many read him now,* he remains a pathetic, but a sympathetic figure still—

O friend unseen, unborn, unknown,
  Student of our sweet English tongue,
Read out my work at night, alone;
  I was a poet, I was young.

Since I can never see your face,
  And never shake you by the hand,
I send my soul through time and space,
  To greet you. You will understand.

To the poems, then, for the present at all events, we must still turn to understand the essential Flecker; and it is as yet another approach to the poems that the *Collected Prose* has likewise its main value. Quite attractive journalism, it shows more what Flecker was than what he could do. This collection falls into three parts—

---

* *This fear was proved to be groundless, I am glad to say, by a subsequent letter from Flecker's publishers, on the convincing evidence of steadily increasing sales.*

'Tales and Sketches,' fantastic or Levantine; 'The Grecians,' a treatise on education; and ' Critical Studies.' In the first section, ' The Last Generation,' a vision of the future resembling not so much Wells (the comparison moved Flecker to fury) as the whimsical irony of Butler, is curious for its resemblance to *Hassan* in one thing— the way in which its dreamy fantasy quickens all at once into gruesome reality, as Moses' rod into the sudden horror of its venomous life. Flecker, like his admired John Davidson, combined the extremes of visionary and realist; he soars into futurity not on the ingenious mechanism of a Time Machine, but on the yellow and purple wings of the poet's Wind of Time; and yet, if he starts in the clouds, he comes most solidly to earth on his arrival in the unborn Birmingham. There is, indeed, in this compounding of clay and fire something not unakin to the earthy unearthliness of Mr. Chesterton (who should approve ' The Ballad of Hampstead Heath '), but of a sadder and wiser Mr. Chesterton. Flecker's daylight when he returns to it, is of a greyer hue.

It is this greyness that clouds for him even the Eastern sun. ' Candilli ' utters the fundamental sadness of the gazer on some splendour of mountain or of sea. Here is beauty—yet we can never seize it or possess—it is like a heap of treasure in a wilderness.

But who am I to enjoy this high gift of the gods ? What can I do with it, how make it my own ? Why is it there, part of my foolish daily life; can I treat it as a common thing ? . . . A poet might sing of it, and find peace; or a painter paint it; glorious would it shine to a man returning from a long journey, if among those countless lights one light meant home.

And as here in the presence of Levantine beauty, so in
' The 'Bus in Stamboul ' his heart is heavy with the sense
of absence and the past ; and the exiled Flecker, to whom
that understanding of the East, which Orientalists owned
that he possessed, brought no love for it, is stirred by the
sight of a fellow-exile, a Vanguard motor-'bus, to a
longing, not the less real for the wry laughter that expresses it, for the West and home and fellowship.

> And you, too, O Cricklewood, lovely Cricklewood of the
> idle evenings, not so far from Hampstead Heath, Crickle-
> wood, where clerks, returning from toil, eat their suppers
> and kiss their young wives, and sleep at peace with God
> and all the world, you are worth all the golden East,
> obscure and lovely Cricklewood, whatever those literary men
> say—and forget it not.

These sketches are the least serious part of the book ;
but, for all that, they are the best. In ' The Grecians '
the ex-schoolmaster in Flecker turns to building in a
Platonic dialogue the cloud-image of his ideal school, an
educational ' Republic.' Eloquent in passages, it yet
suffers from that curious donnish pompousness which
seems usually to attack imitators of Plato ; still it over-
flows with good sense. As might be expected, Flecker
believes literature with its criticism of life to be the best
basis of education in the art of living, as distinguished from
making a living—not, indeed, literature after the present
beggarly standard, an arbitrary patch of the Classics, some
English, small French, less German, and no Italian ;
not linguistics—' any half-breed dragoman can gabble
six or seven tongues and sometimes gabble them correctly ' ;
not science—' science brooks no rival in her house ' ;
but a modernisation of the Renaissance humanism of

Vittorino da Feltre. It is at least a far more significant contribution, especially in its ethics, than most of the periodical screaming on the subject of public schools.

The ' Critical Studies ' matter less. Flecker was too good a lover and hater to be the perfect critic. John Davidson's blank verse is not ' the best since Milton ' nor the work of William Watson limited to ' pompous out-cries.' Still, these Johnsonian tantrums are redeemed by some Johnsonian common sense ; and all is said in his neat ruling on that weary controversy about art and purpose, ' It is not the poet's business to save man's soul, but to make it worth saving.'

But Flecker remains before all things the lyric poet. His prose is a by-product ; and even *Hassan*, by his own account, was written to lead up to its epilogue, that long-familiar lyric ' The Golden Journey to Samarkand.' Two readings are really needed before one can even begin to criticise this fine but eccentric play. For its atmo-sphere reels and quivers from scene to scene like a mirage of the desert—now comedy of manners, now opera or masque, now farcical buffoonery, now agonising tragedy. No less Proteus-like are the characters. Comic con-fectioner, amorous greybeard, poet, artist, man of action, voluptuary, philosopher—all these by turns is Hassan ; and yet remains Hassan still. It is as if one mixed *Le Bourgeois Gentilhomme* with *Bajazet*, or Shaw's Cæsar with Shakespeare's, or *Kubla Khan* with *The Mikado*. The combinations are amazing, and yet no mere *tour de force* ; only at moments does Flecker go too far in mingling his incompatibles ; the prolonged persiflage, for instance, of his Gilbert-and-Sullivan chief of police and captain of military is cheap in itself (Flecker's humour is not his strongest point) and still more of a nuisance in its context.

But the distinction of the play lies in its poetry, its philosophy, its style ; for the plot, simple as a whole and with plenty of fine situations, is not always convincing in detail. Hassan, the confectioner, by good fortune and common sense saves Haroun al Raschid from the conspiracy of Rafi, whose beloved, Pervaneh, has been kidnapped for the Caliph's seraglio. He becomes the Caliph's friend ; and there his disillusionment begins. Yasmin, who had scorned his love, fawns now upon his greatness ; his friend the Caliph proves but a pitiless savage. To Rafi and Pervaneh he gives the choice of eternal separation or of one day of love, with a death of torment after. They choose the second, and when Hassan pleads for pity, the Caliph flings him back into his obscurity after forcing him first to watch the victims' tortures. Agonised and broken, he turns from 'this Bagdad of slaves, this city of fornication,' to take with his fellow-poet Ishak, the most charming figure in the play, the Golden Road of pilgrimage to Samarkand.

So it ends. 'This rose has faded and this rose is bitter and this rose is nothing but the world.' What began in laughing fantasy closes in a sadness that is only not despair. In the prison of the King of the Beggars, while the Caliph beat vainly on the walls, Hassan had turned quietly to examine the beauty of the carpet on the floor ; now, in the vaster prison of the world, cast off by the Caliph, there remains for the pilgrim still the wild beauty of the desert, the sands of the Golden Road. The very ghosts of the lovers, dead in their agony, have faded before us into forgetfulness. Only in the beauty of the moment for the moment's sake, in the splendour of the tragedy of life, in the sublimity of human folly, lies its last, its single solace. How brief and precarious are these! And yet the race goes on; and the ghost of Pervaneh in the garden, agony behind her and oblivion before, when the rustling voices of the unborn question her, 'What of Life, O dead?' answers with a great cry, 'Why Life . . . is sweet, my children.'

Some will wince at this touch of Maeterlinck. But Flecker, at least, does not dally with his pessimism, does not burke the bitterness of life with amiable saving clauses, nor smuggle in Dr. Pangloss by a side door to honey the final scene. 'Dost thou hope for a revelation? Why should the dead be wiser than the living? The dead know only this, that it was better to be alive.'

When the play is performed, the British public, who will always flock in far greater numbers to see a live camel on the stage than all the plays of Ibsen, expecting from this Oriental drama a repetition of the cheery crudity of *Chu Chin Chow*, or of the sanctimonious vulgarities of *The Garden of Allah*, and even encouraged in this expectation by the comedy of the early scenes, will perhaps be rudely pulled up by the bitter realism of such a close. Indeed, a preliminary wail has already been raised in a distinguished weekly by a writer who complains of the unbearable pessimism of *Hassan*, on the ground that 'the greatest poets dwell on the permanence of beauty rather than on the passing show,' and suggests that there is 'a certain weakness in the constitution of art which predisposes it to pessimism.' It might be urged that the weakness lay in the constitution of the universe. But it is clearly vain to point out, if people cannot see it for themselves, that vastly more great poetry has been written in the mood of the *Iliad* and the *De Rerum Natura*, of the *Inferno* and *Lear*, than in that of *Pippa Passes*. Let those who find *Hassan* 'unbearable' leave it alone ; in this picture of life, as in life itself, the terror is redeemed by the beauty and by nothing else.

> We are the pilgrims, master ; we shall go
>   Always a little further : it may be
> Beyond that last blue mountain barred with snow,
>   Across that angry or that glimmering sea,
>
> White on a throne or guarded in a cave,
>   There lives a prophet who can understand
> Why men were born : but surely we are brave
>   Who take the Golden Road to Samarkand.

And so if 'the Caravan starts for the dawn of Nothing,' if there is no prophet and, at the last, no Why—what of it ? These things the pilgrim knows already in his heart. The goal is vanity and the gold at the rainbow's foot a dream. But the road and the rainbow are ours for a little while, as we go our ways to the dawn of nothingness.

JOHN MASEFIELD*

In 1902 Mr. Masefield published *Salt Water Ballads*; in 1922 *Berenice*. From the brazen altar of Kipling to the marble shrine of Racine is, even for twenty years, a lengthy pilgrimage. Very opportunely, however, for tracing the pilgrim's progress there appears also Mr. Hamilton's *John Masefield*. It is no doubt more usual to bury our saints before we praise them to the length of 155 pages. But here is no unmixed idolatry; no Pan-belabouring Arcadian ever trounced his divinity more soundly than Mr. Hamilton on occasion. Only at the end does he testify to the faith that Mr. Masefield in his next phase will 'perhaps dazzle and delight us as never man before, or as never this man before.' One may hesitate before subscribing to this creed, even when qualified with so judicious an anti-climax. None the less Mr. Hamilton's is an interesting handling of an intriguing but difficult subject; and, apart from teaspoon tempests of indignation with his author for borrowing plumes in youth and parodying parsons later, he leaves an impression of fairness as well as sincerity.

To say nothing, however, of Mr. Masefield's future, his past is not easy to appraise; nor is it made easier by the frenzies of his critics and his own versatility. Between Charles Sorley's youthful preference of him to Homer and Shakespeare and of *The Tragedy of Nan* to *Œdipus*, on the one hand, and Miss Jameson's hysterics over *Nan* as 'a tale of evil, most evilly told,' on the other, there is no fence for the judicious to sit on, only a great gulf.

* *John Masefield. By W. H. Hamilton. Allen and Unwin.*
Berenice. Translated by John Masefield. Heinemann.

159

Again, a writer who plunges in turn into poetry lyric and narrative, fiction long and short, drama, criticism, and the history of seventeenth-century piracy and twentieth-century war, needs a wide net to contain him.

This infinite variety is perhaps a mixed blessing to an author ; in Mr. Masefield it is not the only feminine characteristic. Indeed, it may be perilous, but also not without interest, to trace some of the most distinctive vices and virtues of his work to a certain femininity, strangely persistent through all the toil and hard experience of his life.

It is this quality that makes one feel of Captain Margaret and Edward Herries, of Pompey and The Dauber, that each has, in Stevenson's phrase, ' a comb at the back of his head ' ; it is this that gives his work a touch of rustic shyness and tenderness, recalling another writer whom his fellows called ' The Maiden ' twenty centuries ago— Virgil, poet likewise of the country, of battles, of the sea. And a misogynist might go on to ascribe to the same cause his false sentiment, his lack of humour, his mixture of brilliant intuition and illogicality, of acuteness and *naïveté*, of the weakness and strength of the highly-strung—all that capriciousness which has so delivered him into the hand of the parodist. The lapses into bathos recall Dr. Johnson's lady whose mind was ' all wiggle-waggle ' ; and the simple sentimentality of such a passage as, in *Gallipoli*,—' The Germans boasted that our troops would never be able to land. But English soldiers and sailors are not Germans ; they are, as Carlyle says, " far other " ' —is equally in the vein of that other unfortunate female who once incurred a douche of the coldest realism by saying to the Great Duke, ' But surely, dear

Duke, *British* soldiers never run away !' Set beside Mr. Masefield those three other great names in English poetry to-day, Hardy, Housman, and Walter de la Mare, and you feel at once how intensely masculine in comparison are the first two, while as for the third, he, we know, is really a fairy and not mortal at all. There is indeed scarcely a book of Mr. Masefield's in which this succubus which haunts him has not collaborated.

Yet there are moments when this evil genius is silent, as in the splendour of ' D'Avalos' Prayer '—

And let me pass in a night at sea, a night of storm and thunder,
In the loud crying of the wind through sail and rope and spar.

There are moments when it turns from womanishness to a womanly tenderness that does not repel, as in one of the loveliest of all English dirges—

She has done with the sea's sorrow and the world's way
    And the wind's grief ;
Strew her with laurel, cover her with bay
    And ivy-leaf.
Let the slow mournful music sound before her,
Strew the white flowers about the bier, and o'er her
    The sleepy poppies red beyond belief.

On the black velvet covering her eyes
    Let the dull earth be thrown :
Hers is the mightier silence of the skies
    And long, quiet rest alone.
Over the pure, dark, wistful eyes of her,
O'er all that's human, all that dies of her,
    Gently let flowers be strown.

And after all what matters most is that, whatever his faults and their gender, he is one of the not numerous living poets who could afford to have them.

L

Mr. Masefield's main achievement is undoubtedly his revival of narrative poetry, and his most fruitful years, so far, the period 1911-13 which produced *The Everlasting Mercy, The Widow in the Bye-Street*, and *Dauber*. Since then only *Reynard* has reached high-water mark. The most popular, no doubt, is the first of these. It is the most startling, the most facile, the most optimistic ; it provides the best of both worlds, at its beginning the ' Hell for company ' of the adage, the ' Heaven for holiness ' at its close. In fact much of its attraction is not literary at all. A hearty vote of confidence in the government of the Universe will always carry the day, though not, perhaps, the day after. The odd thing about it is that it should have been found shocking—(who *does* give the British public the hint when to be shocked ?)—and the great thing about it is that, as often with Mr. Masefield, however bearish and cubbish and unlicked, the thing is not a plaster-cast, but alive. But as an example of the suicide which his Muse is always attempting, it is enough to take any few lines from the irrelevant and fatuous six-page flyting of the woman Jaggard—

> For Minnie whom I loved the worst
> Died mad in childbed with her first.
> And John and Mary died of measles,
> And Rob was drownded at the Teasels.
> And little Nan, dear little sweet,
> A cart run over in the street ;
> Her little shift was all one stain,
> I prayed God put her out of pain.
> And all the rest are gone or going
> The road to Hell. . . .

Here, indeed, may be raised the whole question of Mr.

Masefield's language, not his profanity (for horrific as his
expletives are, by their very exaggeration they prevent the
reader from feeling them as more than ' protests of pepper-
gingerbread ' and, in effect, his ruffians swear like sucking
doves) but his vulgarisms. It is interesting to contras
the view of the greatest critic of antiquity, the so-called
Longinus. After giving other instances of journalese
that writer continues : ' The expression in Herodotus
for beautiful women—" stunners "—is not much better.
Still, he has some excuse, for those in whose mouth he
puts the phrase are barbarians and in their cups ; but
even with such mouthpieces it is a pity for a writer to be
so trivial-minded as to make an exhibition of himself
before posterity.' We have changed all that, of course ;
still, even now in *his* handling of ' barbarians in their
cups ' Mr. Masefield might remember Longinus. This
is the difficulty of every Romantic trying to annex new
territory to poetry ; Wordsworth lamed much of his
work by attempting to flog it on over the rubble of
prosaic and ludicrous associations ; and for Wordsworth's
whips, Mr. Masefield plies scorpions.

A cat sidling on to the stage at the critical moment has
ruined the crucial scene of a tragedy ; it shows, no doubt,
what a foolish flibbertigibbet the human mind is ; still,
this is the instrument on which the poet has to play, and
he neglects its stops at his peril. It is at least a definite
mark of progress that in Mr. Masefield's subsequent
poems the neologisms tend to fade away.

An advance in other ways too is shown, in spite of the
parodists, by *The Widow in the Bye-Street*. Here too a
certain number of the cats of bathos stalk the stage ; but
one has to discriminate between all the *simplesse* and

moments, especially at the end, of a simplicity as poignant as Lear's last ' Pray you undo this button.' One may feel resentfully now and then that just to make our eyes water, Mr. Masefield is stripping an onion with no real heart at all. But one knows that life can be just as tragic. And to Dr. Johnson's view, in his criticism of *King Lear*, that literature at all events should not be, Mr. Masefield's reply in his *Shakespeare* is just : ' Tragedy is a looking at fate for a lesson in deportment on life's scaffold. If we find the lesson painful, how shall we face the event ? ' It is with a touch of the quiet nobility of *Hamlet* that the poem ends. The old woman goes mad and, a withered Ophelia, sings flower-garlanded across the summer fields as the mowers go to work—

> Dully they watch her, then they turn to go
> To that high Shropshire upland of late hay ;
> Her singing lingers with them as they mow,
> And many times they try it, now grave, now gay,
> Till with full throat over the hills away,
> They lift it clear ; oh, very clear it towers
> Mixed with the swish of many falling flowers.

A companion piece, as fine in thought, if not quite equal in expression, is the close of *Dauber*, when his ship, the Horn outfaced, has slipped into the peace of Valparaiso Bay, though he lies on the seafloor far to south, killed by falling from the mast. Above, the Andes tower—

> Silent the finger of the summit stood,
> Icy in pure, thin air, glittering with snows.
> Then the sun's coming turned the peak to blood,
> And in the rest-house the muleteers arose.
> And all day long, where only the eagle goes,

> Stones, loosened by the sun, fall ; the stones falling
> Fill empty gorge on gorge with echoes calling.

The silent thunders of that desolate falling haunt one long after the book is closed.

Dauber is another step forward. In English fields Mr. Masefield has to face comparison, not unfair, but unfavourable, with the intellect, the restraint, the craftsmanship, the terse intensity of *A Shropshire Lad*. But the sea is his and all that is in it —

> It 's not been done, the sea, not yet been done,
> From the inside, by one who really knows ;
> I 'd give up all if I could be the one.

Here is a poem of the central sea, the sea as the mariner, not the landsman, knows it, scarcely surpassed in its way since the *Odyssey*. It is the coming true of the dream of Fitzgerald, when, thrilled by that glimpse, at the fall of Amphipolis, of Thucydides the admiral behind Thucydides the historian, he wrote, ' That was the way to make men write well. Oh, Alfred Tennyson, could you but have the luck to be put to such employment ! ' This is the difference between life and pastiche, between *Dauber* and *Enoch Arden*.

Only once since has Mr. Masefield recaptured his highest level—in *Reynard the Fox*, the most faultless of his poems. This indeed wears best of all. It was almost too good to be true that some fool should dismiss it the other day as of interest only to sportsmen. Precisely the extraordinary thing about it is the way it fascinates people of the most alien temperaments. I suppose, were we perfectly humane and reasonable, foxes would be exterminated once for all ; even if a plebiscite of foxes preferred the continuance of their hunted life to extinction, there can be no question on which side all the geese in the country would make themselves heard. Yet despite these painful views, *Reynard* has once more given me extreme pleasure. It has all the strength of the other narrative poems at their best (though not the magnificent anger of the seas about the Horn in *Dauber*), with none of their lapses into ugliness or mawkery or false psychology. The character-sketches at the Meet can be measured with Chaucer's *Prologue* itself without absurdity, though a little provincial beside that masterpiece of smiling urbanity. The downland setting is perfect, and the Homeric roll of its English place-names a perpetual joy—

> By Tencombe Regis and Slaughter's Court,
> Through the great grass square of Roman Fort,
> By Nun's Wood Yews and the Hungry Hill,
> And the Corpse Way Stones all standing still.
> By Seven Springs Mead to Deerlip Brook,
> And a lolloping leap to Water Hook.
> Then with eyes like sparks and his blood awoken,
> Over the grass to Water's Oaken,
> And over the hedge and into ride
> In Ghost Heath Wood for his roving bride.

And then the dramatic stagger home of the exhausted fox to the refuge of his lair on the Wan Dyke Hill—

> One last short burst upon failing feet—
> There life lay waiting, so sweet, so sweet,
> Rest in a darkness, balm for aches.
>
> .   .   .   .
>
> The earth was stopped. It was barred with stakes.

And though in the end there is perhaps, emotionally, a

little sharp practice—a certain running with the fox and hunting with the hounds—in letting Reynard escape, while consoling the Hunt with a vicarious and unknown victim, yet the reader more than forgives Mr. Masefield for hitting so cleverly the one dramatically right conclusion. It is the sort of solution which would have gladdened the heart of Aristotle, as he pointed out that on the one hand the slaughter of the fox with whom we have come to sympathise, would have been repulsive, while on the other hand seventy huntsmen, described to us in Homeric catalogue, returning empty-handed would have seemed, if not laughable, certainly an anti-climax.

Since then Mr. Masefield has been disappointing. *Right Royal* was inferior to *Reynard the Fox* ; *King Cole* with its attempt to desert the firm English ground of realistic narrative on which Mr. Masefield has followed Chaucer and Crabbe, for the visionary and fantastic, marked a further decline. Nor have the later dramatic experiments succeeded better now than the earlier. Compared indeed with his narrative poems, neither the novels, the short stories, nor the plays possess much importance. The secret of creating character with any subtlety is not among Mr. Masefield's gifts. *The Tragedy of Nan* leaves its readers unhappy in more ways than the author intended. *Pompey* and *Philip* are too soft ; *The Faithful* too hard, disfigured by what Dr. Johnson would have called such ' enormous and disgusting hyperboles ' of heroism, as a child killing itself to leave its father free to set about murdering some one else. Only its lyrics live in the memory—

> Sometimes, in wintry springs
> Frost, on a midnight breath,

> Comes to the cherry flowers
> And blasts their prime.
> So I with all my powers
> Unused on men or things
> Go down the wind to death
> And know no fruiting-time.

It might have seemed not unpromising in past years to recommend Mr. Masefield to go to school with Racine, and try his hand at translation : but none made wise by the event could recommend it since the publication of *Esther* and *Berenice*.

He remains, then, a narrative poet, with an uncertain, plaintive, but sometimes haunting lyric gift. He can be so outrageously second-rate and unintelligent that among the *intelligentsia* it is hardly decent to mention his name. Few of them have troubled to compare their opinion and his pages, or to look far for the flashes of beauty they contain. Yet the words of one of his sonnets are true of their poet himself—

> For this my body with its wandering ghost
> Is nothing solely but an empty grange,
> Dark in a night where owls inhabit most ;
> Yet when the King rides by, there comes a change,
> The windows gleam, the cresset's fiery hair
> Blasts the blown branch, and beauty lodges there.

And these beauties of a moment are real, though the owls may not see them.

When Goldsmith wrote, indeed, like a gentler Lucian, his allegory describing that small vehicle which carries men of letters to the Temple of Fame, there was one point he failed to remark—the heavy excess-payment that is always exacted from those who begin their journey with an over-weight of popularity. For pay they always do, and ruinously ; indeed, some poor wretches, unable to meet that charge, have never arrived at the Temple at all. At the moment it is Mr. Masefield, in the company of greater men such as Tennyson himself, who is having to pay. And those who wonder by what whimsy of criticism his *Collected Poems* should rouse sneering references to Tupper, must seek the cause of it not in the pages of that volume, but in those pre-war days when Mr. Masefield was all the rage and the *Everlasting Mercy* became a temporary torment. The main reason, in short, for his unpopularity with some persons is, simply, his popularity. Of course he has also written a good deal of verse which is not only bad but—what is far worse in these days when even Heine and Housman are considered not above suspicion—sentimental. But just as Wilde defined vulgarity as ' other people's manners,' ' sentimentality ' is too often merely ' other people's feelings ' ; and even if Mr. Masefield has written on occasion almost as badly as Wordsworth, poets are not judged by the size of their rubbish-heaps. Admit that four-fifths of his work is sad stuff. There still remains more than can be written off as happy freaks of composition ; and ours is not such a peculiarly poetic era, in anything beyond quantity, that it can afford to be supercilious about the author of some of these lyrics and of *Reynard the Fox*.

A RECENT writer on Tennyson has suggested, as an
explanation of the hero-worship of the Victorians, that
'the more the scientists shook their faith in God, the
more did they invest their contemporaries with divine
attributes.' One may suspect that the cause lay rather
in the seriousness with which that age took things generally. But at all events that motive has ceased to work
with us, and in a Cambridge teeming with savants who
split, not the traditional hair, but the atom itself, no devout
hand lays wreaths of bay on the steps of Whewell's Court.
And whereas enthusiasts swarmed stealthily up the very
elms of Farringford to watch a short-sighted laureate
disport himself at battledore and shuttlecock, not a head
turns now as down King's Parade passes the author of
the *Shropshire Lad*. Not that, in this particular case, one
would recommend the most undaunted American 'big-
game' hunter to attempt closer approaches ; or that in
general any one need sigh for Victorian *Schwärmerei* here
again. But there are other extremes. We have learnt
to take Professor Housman for granted as a poet ; perhaps
we have learnt the lesson a little too thoroughly. Must
we wait to bury Cæsar before we praise him to the full,
for the earth to swallow it before we realise how much
has meant to us this shadow of a great rock in the weary
land of modern verse, so boundless and so bare ? Professor Housman has given us his 'last' poems ; so that
we can see his work, it is to be feared, already as a whole,
if not so steadily as posterity. For that posterity will
read him, seems to me as (humanly) certain, as it is

dubious if there are more than four other living English
poets of whom the same can be said. When *Last Poems*
appeared, the reviews paid indeed their tributes to his
verse and style and beauty—such tributes as adorn the
wrappers of half a hundred other poets, in the inflated
currency of to-day ; but when it came to certain other
characteristics, there appeared in their criticisms a tone
ludicrously like the reluctant testimony of conjured devils.
The view of life that breathes through these poems, the
essence of their being, was passed gingerly over, with a
mild deprecation, perhaps, of some particularly defiant
utterance, or a pious wish that Professor Housman were
less pessimistic—much as one might sigh what an agree-
able play *Hamlet* might be without that depressing prince.
Indeed it recalls the advertisement I received the other
day of a selected edition of Voltaire : ' Tout en repro-
duisant la physionomie du poète philosophe, l'auteur s'est
appliqué avec le plus grand soin à ne rien laisser passer
qui pût choquer les susceptibilités de qui que ce soit,'—
a recommendation well calculated to make the creator
of *Candide* chuckle in his grave.

But one cannot believe that our posterity, if our states-
men allow us that luxury, will fall into this half-hearted,
impertinent folly. Wondering what the Georgians
really thought and felt about existence, turning wearily
from piles of little poets who busied themselves scribbling
illuminated miniatures in the margin of the book of life,
and with slight disgust from such typical Georgianisms
as Sir Oliver Lodge and Canon Barnes exchanging
bouquets of pious nothings before edified audiences at
the British Association, they will find here one answer
to their question, one personality among so many echoing

masks, one reading of life, hard maybe, but blurred and
corrupted at least with no optimistic emendations, and
rendered into English of a purity that English literature
has not surpassed. Some, rejecting his interpretation,
will yet recognise, if they are human, that in moods, at
least, they too have felt the same ; and will hope, if
they are wise, that though differing they enjoy him none
the less. And some, sharing his view of life, will know
that they enjoy him yet the more. And nobody will
deprecate.

In pre-war Cambridge, which seemed so much more
exciting than it does now (though this is doubtless mere
middle age), one of the greatest of excitements was the
newcomer's discovery everywhere, in its little red bind-
ing, of the *Shropshire Lad*—the expression, so long in-
articulately wanted, here found at last, of the resentment,
the defiance, the luxuriant sadness (sentiment, I suppose,
some will call it) of youth. With what expectation one
waited in the Lecture Theatre of the Arts School amid
an audience that seemed unworthily sparse, for the first
sight of the poet—and in what perplexity one went away !
Could this quiet, immaculate figure, setting straight, with
even-voiced, passionless, unresting minuteness the jots
and tittles of a fifth-rate ancient whose whole epic was not
worth one stanza of his own—could this be the same ?
Only the lines about the mouth with their look of quiet,
unutterable distaste, only the calm, relentless, bitter logic,
as of destiny itself, with which some sprawling German
commentator was broken into little pieces and dropped
into the void, seemed in the least recognisable. One came
away feeling as if one had been watching a disguised
Apollo picking the oakum of Admetus : divinely—but

oakum !   Had I known them then, I should surely have
thought of those lines of Matthew Arnold to (of all things
in this connection !) a Gipsy Child—

> Is the calm thine of stoic souls, who weigh
>   Life well, and find it wanting, nor deplore :
> But in disdainful silence, turn away,
>   Stand mute, self-centred, stern and dream no more ?

And had I been a prophet, I should have thought too of
the verse that follows it—

> Once ere the day decline, thou shalt discern,
>   Oh once, ere night, in thy success thy chain.
> Ere the long evening close, thou shalt return,
>   And wear thy majesty of grief again.

But in those days *Last Poems* were beyond our hopes, and
none dreamed of a second sunrise that should make this
Sphinx of the desert once more a Memnon of the dawn.
It was cause for gratefulness enough that the *Shropshire
Lad* was there—that and the poetry of Morris—to bear
one through the war.

Arnold, indeed, the poet-professor of the sister University, with his classicism and his Virgilian majesty of
sorrow, is Professor Housman's nearest kin in English
literature ; and for a third to join with these, we must
look to the disdainful yet tender brevity of Landor.   In
no other three of our poets have the spirits of Greece,
Rome, and England found that happy mixture of their
elements which lives in them—the grace and lucid sadness of the flutes of Hellas, the proud glitter and the stab
of the short Roman sword, the sweetness and strength of
the English countryside.   Arnold doubted more, and

wailed because he doubted, till harder men lost patience
with his ' nibbling and quibbling ' about belief ; he was
sometimes prim ; and, unsurpassed as his best work is,
and far wider in its range, he had not, technically, the
sureness of the modern poet's touch.   Landor was less
subtle and, likewise, less sure.   It is a curiosity of literature that so late in the development of English poetry it
should have been possible to bring harmonies so new, so
invariably perfect, out of some of its most hackneyed
metres.   Swinburne produced many of his miracles by
brilliant modifications of old metrical forms.   Beddoes
recaptured, as no one since has done, the secret magic
of Elizabethan blank verse.   But Professor Housman
modifies little and recaptures nothing ; though the Carolines used some of his verse-forms to perfection, they
are not like him.   And when one sits down and puzzles
where one has seen anything really akin to this Melchizedek, there comes only the unexpected half-answer :
' In Heine.'   The belief that there is here more than
coincidence is strengthened when one recognises in the
flower of ' Sinner's Rue ' no other than the German's
Armesünderblum—the blue floweret that grows at
cross-roads on the mounds of the slayers of themselves.

But this does not go far towards explaining how his
effects are produced.   It is easy to docket the artifices he
so boldly and openly uses, such as the assonance and
alliteration of—

> Ah, *p*ast the *pl*unge of *pl*ummet,
>   In *s*eas I cannot *s*ound,
> My heart and *s*oul and *s*enses,
>   World without end, are drowned.

His *fol*ly has not *fel*low
　　*B*eneath the *b*lue of day
That gives to man or woman
　　His heart and soul away.

There flowers no balm to sain him
　　From *ea*st of *ea*rth to west
That 's *lost* for ever*las*ting
　　The heart out of his breast ;

or the haunting

　　From *all* the *w*oods that *aut*umn
　　Bereaves in *all* the *w*orld.

And it is simple enough to note the repetition carried even
beyond Roman bounds, till, once, it becomes a little self-
caricaturish in

　　The goal stands up, the keeper
　　Stands up to keep the goal.

But the charm endures where these devices are not ; there
are so many strings to this bow with its sweet swallow-
song—pause and shift of stress, fingering and vowel-play ;
above all, the skill which keeps the diction of these lyrics
so simple and close to the directness of prose, without ever
transgressing that fatal boundary, and the perfect inter-
mingling of the unexpected word with the speech of
everyday, of the unexpected thought with the looked-for
conclusion. These Shropshire lads talk with just that
' wild civility ' for which Herrick praised his love—

　　There flowers no balm to *sain* him . . .

　　From far, from eve and morning
　　And yon *twelve-winded* sky . . .

> But men at whiles are sober
> And think by fits and starts,
> And if they think, *they fasten*
> *Their hands upon their hearts.*

But perhaps the supreme example of the sudden sting the verse leaves in the hearer's heart, as with all the wonder of a serpent's suppleness it glides away, is in the last but one of *Last Poems*—

> Tell me not here, it needs not saying,
>   What tune the enchantress plays
> In aftermaths of soft September
>   Or under blanching mays,
> For she and I were long acquainted
>   And I knew all her ways.
>
> On russet floors, by waters idle,
>   The pine lets fall its cone ;
> The cuckoo shouts all day at nothing
>   In leafy dells alone :
> And traveller's joy beguiles in autumn
>   Hearts that have lost their own.

In the later volume as a whole, indeed, if there is any development, it is an extension of this device of sudden check and unexpected pleasure, from the thought to the rhythm also—

> ' What sound awakened me, I wonder,
>   *For now 'tis dumb.*'
> ' Wheels on the road, most like, or thunder :
>   Lie down ; 'twas not the drum ' ;

or best of all—

> Wenlock Edge was umbered,
>   And bright was Abdon Burf,
> And warm between them slumbered
>   The smooth green miles of turf ;

> Until from grass and clover
> The upshot beam would fade,
> *And England over*
> Advanced the lofty shade.

And with this, there goes a growing boldness in the surprises of the thought itself, a use of metaphors quite 'metaphysical,' such as that ironic 'foolscap' wherewith night's cone-shaped shadow crowns the earth eternally, the last mantle which cured Dick's lifelong hatred of the cold—

> Fall, winter, fall : for he,
> Prompt hand and headpiece clever,
>   Has woven a winter robe,
> And made of earth and sea
> An overcoat for ever,
>   And wears the turning globe.

These things produce their complete effect just because the power to contrive them is controlled with a rigid economy ; so that the general impression these lyrics leave is of a strength that never needs to strive or cry, a beauty whose quality is never strained. 'Schiller,' observed Coleridge, 'sets you a whole town afire. But Shakespeare drops you a handkerchief.' And, as there is no strain, so there are no collapses ; if we could spare anything, it would be some of the poems on soldiers and on gallows. But such exceptions are few, and the most serious challenge to Housman's position will be his want of bulk. I do not think that need trouble us greatly ; the poems of Sappho, said Meleager, are ' few, but roses.' The poems of Catullus are likewise few.

But the spell of this poetry does not live merely in its technical perfections, in its pure beauty, in the happy way

Mr. Masefield's main achievement is undoubtedly his revival of narrative poetry, and his most fruitful years, so far, the period 1911-13 which produced *The Everlasting Mercy, The Widow in the Bye-Street*, and *Dauber*. Since then only *Reynard* has reached high-water mark. The most popular, no doubt, is the first of these. It is the most startling, the most facile, the most optimistic ; it provides the best of both worlds, at its beginning the ' Hell for company ' of the adage, the ' Heaven for holiness,' at its close. In fact much of its attraction is not literary at all. A hearty vote of confidence in the government of the Universe will always carry the day, though not, perhaps, the day after. The odd thing about it is that it should have been found shocking—(who *does* give the British public the hint when to be shocked ?)—and the great thing about it is that, as often with Mr. Masefield, however bearish and cubbish and unlicked, the thing is not a plaster-cast, but alive. But as an example of the suicide which his Muse is always attempting, it is enough to take any few lines from the irrelevant and fatuous six-page flyting of the woman Jaggard—

> For Minnie whom I loved the worst
> Died mad in childbed with her first.
> And John and Mary died of measles,
> And Rob was drownded at the Teasels.
> And little Nan, dear little sweet,
> A cart run over in the street ;
> Her little shift was all one stain,
> I prayed God put her out of pain.
> And all the rest are gone or going
> The road to Hell. . . .

Here, indeed, may be raised the whole question of Mr.

Masefield's language, not his profanity (for horrific as his expletives are, by their very exaggeration they prevent the reader from feeling them as more than ' protests of pepper-gingerbread ' and, in effect, his ruffians swear like sucking doves) but his vulgarisms. It is interesting to contras the view of the greatest critic of antiquity, the so-called Longinus. After giving other instances of journalese that writer continues : ' The expression in Herodotus for beautiful women—" stunners "—is not much better. Still, he has some excuse, for those in whose mouth he puts the phrase are barbarians and in their cups ; but even with such mouthpieces it is a pity for a writer to be so trivial-minded as to make an exhibition of himself before posterity.' We have changed all that, of course ; still, even now in *his* handling of ' barbarians in their cups ' Mr. Masefield might remember Longinus. This is the difficulty of every Romantic trying to annex new territory to poetry ; Wordsworth lamed much of his work by attempting to flog it on over the rubble of prosaic and ludicrous associations ; and for Wordsworth's whips, Mr. Masefield plies scorpions.

A cat sidling on to the stage at the critical moment has ruined the crucial scene of a tragedy ; it shows, no doubt, what a foolish flibbertigibbet the human mind is ; still, this is the instrument on which the poet has to play, and he neglects its stops at his peril. It is at least a definite mark of progress that in Mr. Masefield's subsequent poems the neologisms tend to fade away.

An advance in other ways too is shown, in spite of the parodists, by *The Widow in the Bye-Street*. Here too a certain number of the cats of bathos stalk the stage ; but one has to discriminate between all the *simplesse* and asking for the building without the foundation, the body without the life. If there were not the despair, there could not be the passion ; if there were not the tragedy, there could not be the majesty of grief—

> The troubles of our proud and angry dust,
> Are from eternity and shall not fail.

THE POETRY OF WALTER DE LA MARE

An hour's contemplation, three days ago, of the head of Mr. de la Mare, against the framing background of Watts' 'Tennyson' in the Hall of Trinity has left a memory that the writer will henceforth hug as pleasantly symbolic, laying it up against his anecdotage for the unhappy youth of 1960. Watts' handiwork, indeed, even over-coloured the actual contrast; in himself the author of 'Claribel' or 'Mariana' need find no great strangeness, except of delight, in the haunted gardens and forsaken homes of Mr. de la Mare, nor feel that his own 'Sleeping Beauty' had passed into ruder hands. But that damp, moping mystic enshrined in Watts' portrait seemed only to glower with an exaggerated consciousness of the estrangement between Now and Then, the old song and the new, himself and his posterity.

For some there are three poets, above all, who seem to utter the thoughts that thrill or trouble us to-day. This, indeed, is one advantage, the only one, that the living poet possesses over the dead; only a contemporary, minor though he be, can bring to his contemporaries the solace of hearing uttered just what they dumbly feel, in a way no age has ever quite felt before nor will again. There are moods when the near valley is dearer than the distant summit, and *Satires of Circumstance* mean more than *Paradise Lost*, *Last Poems* than *The Prelude*; there are times when *The Listeners* is more, far more, than *In Memoriam*.

On the pure poetry of Tennyson time lays no hand;

ferred the continuance of their hunted life to extinction, there can be no question on which side all the geese in the country would make themselves heard.   Yet despite these painful views, *Reynard* has once more given me extreme pleasure.   It has all the strength of the other narrative poems at their best (though not the magnificent anger of the seas about the Horn in *Dauber*), with none of their lapses into ugliness or mawkery or false psychology. The character-sketches at the Meet can be measured with Chaucer's *Prologue* itself without absurdity, though a little provincial beside that masterpiece of smiling urbanity.   The downland setting is perfect, and the Homeric roll of its English place-names a perpetual joy—

> By Tencombe Regis and Slaughter's Court,
> Through the great grass square of Roman Fort,
> By Nun's Wood Yews and the Hungry Hill,
> And the Corpse Way Stones all standing still.
> By Seven Springs Mead to Deerlip Brook,
> And a lolloping leap to Water Hook.
> Then with eyes like sparks and his blood awoken,
> Over the grass to Water's Oaken,
> And over the hedge and into ride
> In Ghost Heath Wood for his roving bride.

And then the dramatic stagger home of the exhausted fox to the refuge of his lair on the Wan Dyke Hill—

> One last short burst upon failing feet—
> There life lay waiting, so sweet, so sweet,
> Rest in a darkness, balm for aches.

> The earth was stopped.   It was barred with stakes.

And though in the end there is perhaps, emotionally, a

little sharp practice—a certain running with the fox and hunting with the hounds—in letting Reynard escape, while consoling the Hunt with a vicarious and unknown victim, yet the reader more than forgives Mr. Masefield for hitting so cleverly the one dramatically right conclusion. It is the sort of solution which would have gladdened the heart of Aristotle, as he pointed out that on the one hand the slaughter of the fox with whom we have come to sympathise, would have been repulsive, while on the other hand seventy huntsmen, described to us in Homeric catalogue, returning empty-handed would have seemed, if not laughable, certainly an anti-climax.

Since then Mr. Masefield has been disappointing. *Right Royal* was inferior to *Reynard the Fox* ; *King Cole* with its attempt to desert the firm English ground of realistic narrative on which Mr. Masefield has followed Chaucer and Crabbe, for the visionary and fantastic, marked a further decline. Nor have the later dramatic experiments succeeded better now than the earlier. Compared indeed with his narrative poems, neither the novels, the short stories, nor the plays possess much importance. The secret of creating character with any subtlety is not among Mr. Masefield's gifts. *The Tragedy of Nan* leaves its readers unhappy in more ways than the author intended. *Pompey* and *Philip* are too soft ; *The Faithful* too hard, disfigured by what Dr. Johnson would have called such 'enormous and disgusting hyperboles' of heroism, as a child killing itself to leave its father free to set about murdering some one else. Only its lyrics live in the memory—

> Sometimes, in wintry springs
> Frost, on a midnight breath,

felt always ambushed there, there lives beside the paganism the teeming grotesqueness, the haunting mystery, the laughing exaggeration of the Middle Ages.

Thus the charming lines of Gavin Douglas before his version of *Æneid VI*, with its similar wedding of the Classic and the Gothic spirit—

> All is bot gaistis and elriche fantasies,
> Of brouneis and bogillis full this buke,

might well stand on the title-page of *Down-Adown-Derry* * as of several of Mr. de la Mare's earlier works. And his bright, childish fancifulness brings back to mind the clear, unearthly colours of a mediæval illumination or such playful imaginings of a simpler age as the Giant of William Dunbar—

> He wald apon his tais† stand
> And tak the sternis‡ doune with his hand
> And set them in a gold garland
> Above his wyfis hair.

Not, indeed, since Thomas the Rhymer has there been such a poet of Faerie. Shakespeare's fairies are more human ; Drayton laughs at, rather than with, his ; Herrick's are more like Mr. de la Mare's, but vaguer ; Irish fairies are marred by a sinister touch of Irish ferocity ; while the pantomime variety, though they seem to have succeeded in sitting for their portraits to the illustrator of *Down-Adown-Derry*, are best left to the scientific camera of Sir Arthur Conan Doyle. Even the supernatural of Poe, though his ghost rises in the memory when one comes to the ' Dark Château ' or the stone house ' named only Alas,' or to the Ivory Tower in 'Time Passes,' or

---

* *Down-Adown-Derry. By Walter de la Mare. Constable.*
† *Toes.* ‡ *Stars.*

the mere name of ' Alulvan,' suffers in comparison from a touch of theatrical garishness. The strange thing is that Mr. de la Mare's lightness of touch keeps unstaled his repetition of gaunt houses with something lurking behind their blank, glazed stare ; of the rank, sequestered beauty of gardens in decay ; of doors that never open to the knocker or open only on a void. Always this Lilliputian delicacy, like the gift of Melampus, who could hear the growing of the grass and the whisper of the worm —now watching the shadow that a bubble casts, or hearkening at the fireside to the ' tiny crooning ' of the flames, or seeing in ' Remembrance ' how—

> The sky was like a waterdrop
>   In shadow of a thorn,
> Clear, tranquil, beautiful,
>   Forlorn,—

now dancing in its fairy ring to the music of a metrical inventiveness unequalled since Swinburne. Mr. de la Mare indeed gets his effects not so much, like Swinburne, by devising regular new metrical schemes, as by loosening the limbs of long-familiar forms. It is his artful irregularity and variation of length with monosyllabic and quadrisyllabic feet that restores to verse arrangements almost decrepit, a youth and spring in his hands, as different from their usual jog-trot as a living thing from the mechanical duck of the *encyclopédiste*. It is hard to choose examples, there is such abundance, from the playful

> Someone came knocking
>   At my wee, small door,
> Someone came knocking,
>   I 'm sure—sure—sure,

A RECENT writer on Tennyson has suggested, as an explanation of the hero-worship of the Victorians, that 'the more the scientists shook their faith in God, the more did they invest their contemporaries with divine attributes.' One may suspect that the cause lay rather in the seriousness with which that age took things generally. But at all events that motive has ceased to work with us, and in a Cambridge teeming with savants who split, not the traditional hair, but the atom itself, no devout hand lays wreaths of bay on the steps of Whewell's Court. And whereas enthusiasts swarmed stealthily up the very elms of Farringford to watch a short-sighted laureate disport himself at battledore and shuttlecock, not a head turns now as down King's Parade passes the author of the *Shropshire Lad*. Not that, in this particular case, one would recommend the most undaunted American 'big-game' hunter to attempt closer approaches; or that in general any one need sigh for Victorian *Schwärmerei* here again. But there are other extremes. We have learnt to take Professor Housman for granted as a poet; perhaps we have learnt the lesson a little too thoroughly. Must we wait to bury Cæsar before we praise him to the full, for the earth to swallow it before we realise how much has meant to us this shadow of a great rock in the weary land of modern verse, so boundless and so bare? Professor Housman has given us his 'last' poems; so that we can see his work, it is to be feared, already as a whole, if not so steadily as posterity. For that posterity will read him, seems to me as (humanly) certain, as it is

dubious if there are more than four other living English
poets of whom the same can be said.   When *Last Poems*
appeared, the reviews paid indeed their tributes to his
verse and style and beauty—such tributes as adorn the
wrappers of half a hundred other poets, in the inflated
currency of to-day ; but when it came to certain other
characteristics, there appeared in their criticisms a tone
ludicrously like the reluctant testimony of conjured devils.
The view of life that breathes through these poems, the
essence of their being, was passed gingerly over, with a
mild deprecation, perhaps, of some particularly defiant
utterance, or a pious wish that Professor Housman were
less pessimistic—much as one might sigh what an agree-
able play *Hamlet* might be without that depressing prince.
Indeed it recalls the advertisement I received the other
day of a selected edition of Voltaire : ' Tout en repro-
duisant la physionomie du poète philosophe, l'auteur s'est
appliqué avec le plus grand soin à ne rien laisser passer
qui pût choquer les susceptibilités de qui que ce soit,'—
a recommendation well calculated to make the creator
of *Candide* chuckle in his grave.

But one cannot believe that our posterity, if our states-
men allow us that luxury, will fall into this half-hearted,
impertinent folly.   Wondering what the Georgians
really thought and felt about existence, turning wearily
from piles of little poets who busied themselves scribbling
illuminated miniatures in the margin of the book of life,
and with slight disgust from such typical Georgianisms
as Sir Oliver Lodge and Canon Barnes exchanging
bouquets of pious nothings before edified audiences at
the British Association, they will find here one answer
to their question, one personality among so many echoing

his imagination moves with the swift certainty of a child's. The supernatural legend that to Morris, for instance, would have been a damned good story, to Mr. de la Mare would remain also a fascinating possibility. And when, in the music of his verse, we forget for the moment our inbred disbeliefs, our illusion becomes all the more perfect because of this. Our ears are opened. We too hear the breathing of faint presences that beat unheard at other hours against the gross walls of our worldliness, as the traveller in ' The Listeners ' beats with ghostly hands in vain. Again and again through the poems these *revenants* return—

> Who knocks ?   I who was beautiful
>   Beyond all dreams to restore,
> I from the roots of the dark thorn am hither
>   And knock on the door.

> So when with fickle heart
> I joyed in the passing day,
> A presence my mood estranged
>   Went grieved away.

To some this sense of hauntedness and mystery will seem only the broken plaything of a childish and outworn past : to others less pedantic there is a strange fascination in this door of escape unexpectedly opened in this factory which imprisons us, in such a magic circle inscribed in the flat map of our modern world with the legend— ' Here be dreams.' But have these hauntings, these presences any objective reality ?   Mr. de la Mare might answer ' Perhaps yes ' : others of us, quite unhesitatingly, ' No.' But what does it matter to the poetry ?

Indeed this is where Poetry has the laugh of her old

foe Philosophy.   Whatever the weary facts of existence,
whatever the ultimate reality, at least the feelings of
man's heart are real for him and no cheat, though the
heavens fall and the solid earth dissolve beneath him.
Our dreams, our emotions throw light on nothing beyond ;
they are themselves—the surest thing we know, and
indeed the only one.   The Poet may sigh in vain to
understand it all ; but only the Philosopher is so credulous
as to dream he really can.   It is not that the greatest
poetry has blinked the incurable sadness of the world :
but it is because they realised the hideous tragedy of life
that many of the poets have found in their song their
only anodyne—

> And some win peace who spend
> The skill of words to sweeten despair
> Of finding consolation, where
> Life has but one dark end :
> Who in rapt solitude, tell o'er
> A tale as lovely as forlore
> Into the midnight air.

So Mr. de la Mare has written ; and so he has done.
His is one of the great divisions of poetry, the poetry of
illusion ; just as the other, the poetry of disillusion, has
been Thomas Hardy's.   But with all his elusive mysticism Mr. de la Mare has never been one of those who
load their dream-ships with ponderous cargoes of message
or morality, only to founder in mid-air.   He has not among
all his visions forgotten the ultimate sadness of the earth—

> Walk in beauty.   Vaunt thy rose.
> Flaunt thy transient loveliness.
> Pace for pace with thee there goes
> A shape that hath not come to bless.

wailed because he doubted, till harder men lost patience with his 'nibbling and quibbling' about belief; he was sometimes prim; and, unsurpassed as his best work is, and far wider in its range, he had not, technically, the sureness of the modern poet's touch. Landor was less subtle and, likewise, less sure. It is a curiosity of literature that so late in the development of English poetry it should have been possible to bring harmonies so new, so invariably perfect, out of some of its most hackneyed metres. Swinburne produced many of his miracles by brilliant modifications of old metrical forms. Beddoes recaptured, as no one since has done, the secret magic of Elizabethan blank verse. But Professor Housman modifies little and recaptures nothing; though the Carolines used some of his verse-forms to perfection, they are not like him. And when one sits down and puzzles where one has seen anything really akin to this Melchizedek, there comes only the unexpected half-answer : 'In Heine.' The belief that there is here more than coincidence is strengthened when one recognises in the flower of 'Sinner's Rue' no other than the German's Armesünderblum—the blue floweret that grows at cross-roads on the mounds of the slayers of themselves.

But this does not go far towards explaining how his effects are produced. It is easy to docket the artifices he so boldly and openly uses, such as the assonance and alliteration of—

> Ah, past the plunge of plummet,
>   In seas I cannot sound,
> My heart and soul and senses,
>   World without end, are drowned.

His *fol*ly has not *fel*low
  *B*eneath the *b*lue of day
That gives to man or woman
  His heart and soul away.

There flowers no balm to sain him
  From *ea*st of *ea*rth to west
That 's *lost* for ever*las*ting
  The heart out of his breast ;

or the haunting

From *all* the *w*oods that *au*tumn
Bereaves in *all* the *w*orld.

And it is simple enough to note the repetition carried even
beyond Roman bounds, till, once, it becomes a little self-
caricaturish in

The goal stands up, the keeper
Stands up to keep the goal.

But the charm endures where these devices are not ; there
are so many strings to this bow with its sweet swallow-
song—pause and shift of stress, fingering and vowel-play ;
above all, the skill which keeps the diction of these lyrics
so simple and close to the directness of prose, without ever
transgressing that fatal boundary, and the perfect inter-
mingling of the unexpected word with the speech of
everyday, of the unexpected thought with the looked-for
conclusion. These Shropshire lads talk with just that
' wild civility ' for which Herrick praised his love—

There flowers no balm to *sain* him . . .

From far, from eve and morning
And yon *twelve-winded* sky . . .

those twin paradises of the worm, cemeteries and libraries. Already our minds are getting like that. We are so devastatedly cultured. A writer cannot name us Lethe, but we recall Keats' nightingale ; or Oblivion, without our remembering Sir Thomas Browne. From Oblivion indeed our dreadful diligence has wrested half her poppies ; and they have become in our hands numbing opiates instead, to minds clogged with what they cannot forget. In the end, then, it is clear that either the brains of the living or the works of the dead must be largely reduced to pulp. If the old Egyptian complained that writing had spoiled the art of memory, to-day in revenge memory is spoiling the art of writing. And so, as in the decadence of Greek and Roman literature, it has become again the dilemma of the modern poet—shall he follow Echo, or flee ? She is a dangerous nymph and deceiving and un-fruitful ; yet Narcissus, who scorned her and would dwell on no beauties but his own, died miserably of inani-tion—the eternal symbol of a self-centred fool, and now more immortal than ever since they have made of him in Vienna the name for a new lunacy.

What is to be done ? Hope and compromise and keep poetry alive. So Mr. Bottomley has seen his task ; and so he has fulfilled it. ' Even to continue its living practice in a time of recession is to partake in its next great blossoming, though perhaps only by the work itself becoming part of a soil and compost of dead leaves in which the new seeds shall strike.' Till the next Columbus of poetry finds us a new world or a new egg, the poet of to-day had best own allegiance to the past, trusting to his own personality to keep him an individual, not a slave. And if he has as much personality as Mr. Bottomley, he will not trust in vain. The fanciful reader's pencil may trace in these margins—as parallels, of course, not necessarily sources—the names of Morris or O'Shaughnessy, of Beddoes or Thompson or Frost. Yet Mr. Bottomley still keeps his own place in the tradition of English poetry as the ablest wielder of blank verse in his generation and, in lyric, a last inheritor of the haunting magic of the pre-Raphaelites. He may cry out against the past ; yet his mind dwells there. He may turn to the modernity of a railway viaduct ; but the goods-train trailing across it carries him back at once two thousand years—

> And when I found the narrowing estuary
> I saw a railway bridge through twilit mist ;
> It seemed by veils suspended to exist,
> But a hushed tide washed under clankingly.
>
> A train from London crossed it in the night :
> I woke and saw a tossing, burning mane,
> I felt some tragic woman passed again
> With trailing tresses in dispurposed flight.
>
> Unending luggages dragged past all day,
> Piled trucks, tarpaulin mounds and heavy vans ;
> Considering this monotony, some chance
> Steep contour of its iron, sad array
>
> Made me remember thus it must have been
> That Cæsar's trampling triumphing appeared—
> Elephants heaving, fuming flames upreared,
> Stacked waggons, slow unthinking slaves between.

He may turn, again, from the present to the future ; and even then it is of a return to the past that, like Morris, he dreams—of a time when the hideous industrialism of to-day, with the hemlock festering in its gaunt and blasted yards, shall be but quiet grass again. He may even look beyond to the end of the world itself; yet he beholds that end coming in no more unfamiliar shape than an immemorial fall of snow, just as, it happens, the imagination of pagan Scandinavia had pictured it a thousand years before. And if he writes the best blank verse of to-day, it is in the far antiquity of Troy and Babel and Atlantis, Nimrod and Helen and Cleopatra, that he finds his subjects, despite that cry of a moment since, that such themes are outworn now and 'murdered by much thinking on '—

> These are decayed like Time's teeth in his mouth,
> Black cavities and gaps, yet earth is darkened
> By their deep-sunken and unfounded shadows.

And as he is haunted by the dead past, so he is haunted by Death itself; as his tongue speaks at times with the wild beauty of Beddoes' rhythm, so his mind goes brooding back at moments, in the company of that strange morbid spirit, into the earthy gloom of the grave-house, sifting the thin dust to which even mummies have fallen at last, straining itself in a terrible fascination against the phantom mockery of Death—

> Priests from Bubastis, sellers of love from Tanis,
> With brows like the dusk ivory long-buried
> Nigh mummied queens in lands whose very names
> Are silted in the crevices of time. . . .
>
> .   .   .   .   .   .
>
> When the last bubble of Atlantis broke
> Among the quieting of its heaving floor. . . .
>
> .   .   .   .   .   .

Where is that tomb of Antony's ?
Is Cleopatra there ?
Have the old desert's atomies
Silted among her hair ?
Is even her last throne-room sacked ;
Have delvers hastily unpacked
Some nameless mummy with shut eyes
And sold the vanished fair ?

.   .   .   .

The soul—the little soul, Antinous—
Goes beggared to a realm it cannot rule,
Lost in a terrible equality
And guested in some unimagined way,
And only leaves behind it on my earth
A Greekish tragedy of Ototois,
A Cæsar's pompous head upon a coin.

' *Animula, vagula, blandula* '—the coins of Hadrian—
the cries of Cassandra beneath Athene's hill—the high-
day of Athens and the dusk of Rome—how subtly are
these memories welded and wielded there ! There are,
after all, compensations in being a literary poet ; and
there is strange life to be raised out of the overpowering
past, as well as death. If the literature of our age tends
to be frankly reminiscent, let it be, not with bankrupt
inverted commas, but with a skill like this.

Yet it would be a peculiar one-sidedness that saw Mr.
Bottomley only under this strange green light of the
macabre, running sinister fingers through the dust of kings.
All this is but a mood, not unreal, but less really part of
him than his other simpler side of tenderness and sorrow
for the past with its vain, broken gallantry, and for the
present with its bright, transient beauty hastening into

the shadowiness of what shall never come again. If he mourned before with Solomon that nothing changes, he mourns here with Rossetti and Morris that all things change so ceaselessly. And things like the 'Song of Apple-gathering' bring us to the pre-Raphaelite in him, the lover of the small simplicities and unregarded things, hearing the slight stir of the pillow beneath the bride's smile on her wedding-eve, feeling the hush of evening heightened in the twitching of the rabbits' ears amid the grass, seeing spring and autumn, flower-time and decay in the blossom of the apple, the symbolic tree that the pre-Raphaelites could none of them forget. And the lover of Morris will find here once more, with the sense of a friendly coming-home, Morris's strange dream-mingling of senses clear to sharpness with emotions bemused and misty as the feelings of a dream. By Kelmscott may stand Silverdale, by Sigurd the Volsung Gunnar of Lithend, by the heroines of *The Earthly Paradise* 'The Last of Helen,' with its lingering languor of regret—

> Love, ere the ending I am cold,
> Would I have given all I sold ;
> For my desires are satisfied,
> I know no pleasure to abide,
> My world is mine and used and gray—
> There is nought left but going away.

Yet here, too, there lies a difference. There was in Morris a passion for action, for doing with restless vehemence whatever he set his hand to, whether it was making tapestry or Socialists, killing a man in an epic or teaching him to print one ; but that tireless activity is absent from these quieter, more meditative pages of a writer who has learnt to sit, rather, in a wise passivity, knowing that Beauty slips through the hands that snatch to possess her, or offer a price as to buy. This last mood is as characteristic of Mr. Bottomley as the other two, even more, perhaps. And if it is not merely idle to associate men or books in one's mind above all with some single utterance which seems supremely to express them, linking Nero with ' *Qualis artifex pereo !* ', or Gay with his epitaph, or Lincoln with his definition of democracy, or again, *The Duchess of Malfi* with that one great ' Cover her face,' or Marvell with ' time's winged chariot hurrying near,' or *The Defence of Guenevere* with ' the back-tolled bells of noisy Camelot ' ; then this book of poems, too, may find an epitome in its proud utterance of the creed of all artists and their sure reward—

> Sackt Troy and queens at auction ; if thou wert there,
> Wouldst thou buy Helen ere her husband came ?
> Passing from hand to hand so passively,
> Helen was Helen's secret, Helen's own.
> *Pass thou and gaze, she is more greatly thine.*

MR. W. H. DAVIES *

Iт may seem absurd to say of a poet as firmly established as Mr. Davies that his work shows less performance than promise. In a rather undistinguished age his verse ranks high ; and yet the basis of his reputation is not metrical subtlety, or distinction of style, or profundity of thought—

> This Davies has no depth,
> He writes of birds, of staring cows and sheep,
> And throws no light on deep, eternal things.

His prosody, never ambitious, is not invariably respectable ; the last line, for instance, of—

> Dance, dance, thou blue-eyed wonder, dance !
> I still believe there 's one small chance
> Thou 'lt fall into my arms in a trance,

scans hideously ; and one had ' rather be a kitten and cry " mew," ' than rhyme ' converse ' with ' hoarse,' ' looked ' with ' sucked,' ' sweet ' with ' mute.' Assonance is one thing, rhyme another—they do not live happily together in the same poem. Similarly with his diction ; the comparison of a kiss to a dead fly has indeed ceased to blot ' The Portrait' in its latest form, but the worm-simile of ' The Grief of Others '—

> Once more I see the happy young
> Broken by grief and pain,
> That tears have made like earth's red worms
> Turned white by days of rain,

is almost as intolerable. There is no intrinsic objection

* *Collected Poems (Second Series). By W. H. Davies. Cape.
Secrets. By W. H. Davies. Cape.*

to worms, creatures with a peculiarly distinguished poetic past ; and after the recent plethora of birds, let the worms have a turn by all means ; but not disconnected worms dragged in anyhow. And there is much more evil than genius in the spirit that moves Mr. Davies to write—

> The tyrant Love that after play
> Dribbles on Beauty's cheek.

> The voices and the legs of birds and women
> Have always pleased my ears and eyes the most.

> We 'd rush to strike that monster down
> And drown him in our common spit.

Whence, then, Mr. Davies' reputation ; and his real promise ? It is, partly, that he has an extraordinarily happy, though fickle, fancy, and the mob of his more superficially accomplished contemporaries have not. It is a far cry from Mr. Davies to Aristotle ; but the stress laid by that ancient on the gift for metaphor (and, it follows, simile) above all else in poetic style—'since this alone cannot be taught and is a mark of genius, for it entails a real eye for resemblances '—is itself by now one of the platitudes of genius. That eye lives in Mr. Davies' head and its visions form his greatest charm. The uncut maiden corn that the wind drags by its golden hair towards the darkness of the wood, or, after harvest, the stooks that

> like golden lovers, lean
> Their heads together, in their quiet way ;

the coming of his love's portrait as the swallow before the spring of her own presence ; the poising skylark as the apple of the sun's bright eye; the moths that kiss their shadows on his ceiling; the memory of his youth—

> My youth is gone—my youth that laughed and yawned
> In one sweet breath, and will not come again,

—all these glimpses are slight things, no doubt, but how full of graceful inventiveness ! Such little butterfly moments torn from their context and cold-bloodedly pinned out as specimens may seem a frail claim to poetic eminence. But the point of a butterfly is not its horse-power; and these fulfil their end in the gentle lightness of their touch, while one skims our faces and is gone, or another—

> lying down doth open and close
> His wings as babies work their toes.

Indeed, if Mr. Davies' work is as full of holes as a net, it is a net full of butterflies; and a symbolist might find a subtle fitness in the recurrence through his work of this emblem at once of frivolous lightheartedness and of the soul. His own first poem indeed takes no other emblem of the recurrence of his thoughts from ' higher themes ' to those he loves from of old—

> As butterflies are but winged flowers
>   Half sorry for their change, who fain,
> So still and long they lie on leaves,
>   Would be thought flowers again.

The other thing about Mr. Davies is that genuine spontaneity of his feelings which, though too often he tries (surely not with great success) to make Mrs. Grundy's flesh creep, is the secret of much of his appeal. Here is a modern poet who neither screams nor ogles—

> Come, let us laugh—though there 's no wit to hear ;
> Come, let us sing—though there 's no listener near ;
> Come, let us dance—though none admire our grace,
> And be the happier for a private place.

The pity of it all is that there should be so many good lines, good verses, good ideas ; and yet so few good poems here. In these reviewing days, the fool in Hierocles who carried about a brick as a sample of what his house was like, is become the type of us all ; we are cultivating a pretty taste in bricks rather than in architecture, and it would be particularly easy to write a convincing ' puff ' of Mr. Davies. But it is a commonplace literature that caters only for commonplace books. And that is Mr. Davies' besetting sin. He can begin a poem with a quiet distinction like this—

> When our two souls have left this mortal clay
>   And, seeking mine, you think that mine is lost—
> Look for me first in that Elysian glade
>   Where Lesbia is, for whom the birds sing most,

and then allow it to gutter out in a fourth verse of utter banality. With a repetition of this sort of *felo-de-se* the reader grows embittered. We cannot trust Mr. Davies not to let us down in midstream ; and this feeling that we must be perpetually prepared to wince spoils the enjoyment of the happier moments. Mr. Davies' success is one more testimony to the truth of Ruskin's paradox, ' the utmost a man can do is that which he can do without effort.' But having lustily hammered the iron while hot does not dispense from the after-use of the file when it is cold. ' A great statesman must have two qualities —the first is prudence, the second imprudence. So with

poets.' That is true enough : all the same, Mr. Davies'
imprudence is too imprudent and his artlessness too like
the real thing. It is futile to leave the winnowing of his
work to the casual reader's pencil, and it may be fatal
to leave it to Time. Nothing is quite so dead as promise
never fulfilled.

The trouble is that though other modern poets have
more admirers, none has more adorers than Mr. Davies.
They have erected their conception of him into a sort of
idyllic idol, an inspired natural, a poetic Peter Pan of
bucolic complexion, contemplating, with poesy and a
straw in his mouth, the loves of the butterflies. Infant
prodigy, *enfant terrible*—both aspects are dear to jaded
dowagers of either sex in this our middle-age. Mr.
Davies is *so* original—no one else rhymes ' power ' and
' fire,' ' ever ' and ' together,' or writes—

> Let women long for dainty things,
> Expecting twins ; content am I.

' Fie, Mr. Davies ! Isn't he too delightfully naïve ?
—Oh, Mr. Davies, do be naïve again.' And in a few
months Mr. Davies is naïve again. The thing comes to
seem, if it does not actually become, a trick ; and it brings
him in danger of sharing the fate of that artist so admirably
described by Mr. Graves—

> He found a formula for drawing comic rabbits :
> This formula for drawing comic rabbits paid,
> So in the end he could not change the tragic habits
> This formula for drawing comic rabbits made.

The best thing about *Secrets* is that it contains some
charming poems that are not in this overworked and

overflattered vein, that are not naïve at all, without being
for that, the less characteristic—

> Time bears us off, as lightly as the wind
>   Lifts up the smoke, and carries it away ;
> And all we know is that a longer life
>   Gives but more time to think of our decay.
>
> We live till Beauty fails, and Passion dies,
>   And Sleep 's our one desire in every breath,
> And in that strong desire our old love, Life,
>   Gives place to that new love whose name is Death.
>
> .   .   .   .   .   .
>
> I, who had eyes to wander here and there,
>   No longer have my vision unconfined ;
> Love brings the first grave thoughts of majesty
>   Into the free republic of my mind.
>
> The time is grave with doubting of my power
>   To serve her well, that she may always smile :
> Love-at-first-sight is oft, as hundreds know,
>   Made Love-lies-bleeding in too short a while.

Something has certainly brought here a new majesty
into the democracy of Mr. Davies' style. It is a happy
restoration, that with him will never become a tyranny.
Nor need this dignity prove out of place ; for I do not
believe that the real Mr. Davies is, after all, quite so
simple. When his muse sings, straw in mouth, her most
ingenious praises of infinite beer and skittles, one has
often felt that she had also—ever so little—tongue in
cheek. She had merely discovered that a certain exaggerated *simplesse* in the manner of expressing feelings,
genuine in themselves, ravished a section of the public,
who can discern no new thing in poetry unless it is under-

lined six times.　*Secrets* is better than its recent pre-decessor, because it has less mental morris-dancing and more thought, less thumping on the table with a beer-jug and more of that wide human pity which is one of the deepest and most enduring springs of the world's poetry. In ' Earth Love,' the poet contrasts his own light-hearted joy in living things, in the dancing boughs of green, with the darker thoughts of another at his side—

> My friend, his thought goes deeper down,
> 　Beneath the roots, while mine 's above ;
> He 's thinking of a quiet place
> 　To sleep with his dead Love.

But it is just because Mr. Davies at times ceases to flutter about surfaces, because he himself can go groping deeper among the roots of things and the sweet dignity of their sorrow, that he here wins new successes worth winning, with poems like ' Pity ' and ' The Two Heavens.'　How well his writing will last, it is even harder than usual to prophesy ; if it proves ephemeral, it will be largely because Mr. Davies has been taken too seriously by his public, not seriously enough by himself.

ISAAC ROSENBERG*

Isaac Rosenberg was born in Bristol in 1890. A precocious, eager child, even at his Stepney Board School, writing Byronesque poems and drawing with chalks on the pavement in his spare hours, then a reluctant apprentice to a Fleet Street firm, still struggling to evening Art Classes and writing verse at meal-times, he was fortunate at least in finding, as he grew up, appreciation and assistance which enabled him to attend the Slade School from 1911 to 1914. In 1915 he enlisted, and on 1st April 1918 he was killed in France, after four hated years of Army life which jangled and blunted his gift for poetry, though they never lessened that pathetic devotion to it which lives through his unhappy letters to the end.

If devotion sufficed, he would have done great things ; but the reader, encouraged in his expectations by Mr. Laurence Binyon's introductory memoir, and by a certain quality in Rosenberg's own quoted letters, may find with disappointment in the poems themselves not much fulfilment and only a fading promise. For the earlier pieces are certainly more attractive than the later. It is true that they are full of echoes of other styles ; of Rossetti, for instance—

> What dread, dark seas and perilous
> Lie 'twixt love's silence and love's speech ?

Of Blake—

> I saw the face of God to-day,
>   I heard the music of His smile,
> And yet I was not far away,
>   And yet in Paradise the while.

* Poems. By Isaac Rosenberg. Heinemann.

Of the seventeenth century—

> If you are fire and I am fire,
>   Who blows the flame apart,
> So that desire eludes desire,
>   Around one central heart ?

Of the sixteenth, even—

> Your body is a star
>   Unto my thought ;
> But stars are not too far,
>   And can be caught—
> Small pools their prisons are.

But Echo is a deceiving nymph, and ' there is imitation in the planting of cabbages,' and he was young.   It would be absurd to damn such writing as ' unoriginal ' ; what matters is that it is charming ; less remarkable things have grown and are growing to a reputable age in anthologies.

But the poems of Rosenberg's war period show a change for the worse.   As he grows and comes more under contemporary influence, as he struggles harder and harder to realise his own passionate ambition and the generous hope of those who had backed him, yet feels himself crushed and numbed by army life and the miseries of the front, his ear and his vision seem to grow blunter, his voice shriller and harsher and more strained in its effort to surmount the clangour of his day—until it snaps into sudden silence.   In his own overstrained words—

> The streaming vigours of his blood erupting
> From his halt tongue are like an anger thrust
> Out of a madman's piteous craving for
> A monstrous balked perfection.

The change was, no doubt, partly due to the vampire-sucking of the war, the failing vitality felt in his later letters—'all through this winter I have felt most crotchety,' 'my memory, always weak, has become worse,' 'all I do is without energy and interest.' But there were other causes, in himself, in his time. Mr. Binyon's account of his painting, as now confounding its skill in the covetousness of tangled symbolism, now sacrificing its own qualities in vain efforts after a more modern realism, applies exactly to his later verse. 'The Louse-Hunt' is tiresome and 'The Dying Soldier' ballad-doggerel—

> 'They are gunpits,' he gasped.
> 'Our men are at the guns.
> Water . . . Water . . . Oh, water
> For one of England's dying sons.'

'Moses' and 'The Unicorn,' on the other hand, are fantastic without beauty, wild without strength, obscure without depth—

(Moses speaks) : 'Fire ! Fire !
> See in my brain
> What madmen have rushed through,
> And like a tornado
> Torn up the tight roots
> Of some dead universe ;
>
> The old clay is broken
> For a power to soak in and knit
> It all into tougher tissues
> To hold life.'

Rosenberg's idea of poetry as 'an interesting complexity of thought,' while it serves to describe some kinds of it, is a perilous guide for practice. To emulate Donne,

or Fulke Greville even, by setting out to be complex is
not much better than hoping to become a Beethoven by
eschewing barbers. ' Poets,' said Nietzsche—in this,
as in other ways, often a poet himself—' make their water
muddy, that it may seem deep ' ; if so, the less poets they.
Unfortunately Rosenberg, to take his own favourite
image of the star in the puddle, became too lost in troubling
the puddle, became less complex than perplexed, less
subtle than incoherent.   From his letters one catches the
ring of the Hebrew passion of the young Disraeli shouting
in the teeth of the derisive Commons : ' Ay, and though
I sit down now, the time will come when you *will* hear
me ' ; but in reading his last verse one thinks rather of
the impatient despair of the painter in the story flinging
his sponge at the refractory canvas.   That experiment
may have succeeded once—not more.

Rosenberg's work will hardly win long remembrance,
but that need not mean it was wasted.   How many of
the legion of our modern poets are fools enough to hope
to score a century for their memories ?   Rosenberg was
at least poet enough to write to please himself, for the sake
of self-utterance, without looking to poetry for her loaves
and fishes.   Sometimes in these days, with the petulant
human craving for all or nothing, one is moved to groan
with depressed irritation at the endless procession of half-
poets—from the Press this year into oblivion next—
raising, in the charming words of one of them, ' Shrines
to dream-deities, beautiful and vain.'   But, after all, it
is much that poetry remains so living and so loved.   It
has indeed become the convention that the poet pretends
to immortality—*monumentum aere perennius* ; but literature itself was once Communist, and men used to die

content enough to leave their verses anonymous to the common stock of their posterity, to be plagiarised or to be forgotten. To that attitude perhaps we shall be driven back. It is well that so much verse should be written ; it is less well that all of it should be published ; but if it is ephemeral, that need not convict it of futility. Under the hedgerow last year's thrush lies mute forgotten dust ; but who asks if his singing was in vain ?

I⊤ is a natural desire to wish to attend one's own funeral ; it would be so pleasant (or so we imagine) to read the obituaries, and to shake hands with one's own ghost. After all, it is very tantalising that the most distinguished day in a man's life should come after he is dead, that he should play the chief rôle, for once, on the stage of existence as a mere stage property. This tiresome disability modern poets circumvent by dress rehearsals in which, in the midst of life, they present the world with the apparent finality of *Collected Works*. The other day it was Mr. Masefield ; now Mr. Drinkwater lays himself out for premature interment. Our regrets are sincere ; but these too vivacious dead cannot claim the privilege, *de mortuis nil nisi bonum*. An initial objection to this practice of periodic *Collected Poems* is that it enables the printer's devil to tempt the poet into collecting a great deal too much ; and, in consequence, the present obsequies, for example, seem over costly. No doubt the publishers know perfectly well what they are about, when they set their guinea-stamp on Mr. Drinkwater's work ; but it would be an interesting contribution to that fascinating *Economics of Modern Poetry*, which will never be written, could one but know what kind of purchaser these two handsome volumes will find. Are our ' highbrows ' so well-to-do, or our well-to-do so ' highbrow ' ?

For it is that hideous but expressive epithet that comes, uncalled-for, to the reader's mind. Here are culture, talent, a generous and sympathetic personality, funda-

---

* *Collected Poems. By John Drinkwater. Sidgwick and Jackson.*
The Poetical Works of Austin Dobson. Milford.
Poems. By G. H. Luce. Hogarth Press.

mental hard work—so many qualities, but not what we politely call ' inspiration,' to make decent our ignorance of what poetry really is. Doubtless among the prophets of Baal on Mount Carmel was many a thoughtful good Samaritan ; doubtless Elijah was violent, narrow-minded, a little mad ; but it was on his offering that the fire from heaven descended. And I cannot conceive Mr. Drinkwater girding up his loins and running before the chariot of Ahab to the entrance of Jezreel. How unfair ! No, it is not this that is unfair, but the Muses, who regard not reason nor virtue, whom no man wins by deserving. And the comparison is not so inapposite ; for that strange, fanatical Tishbite, who shoots like flame through the dust and ashes of the *Book of Kings*, had above all what the modern poet has not—has too much good sense to have—intensity. ' *Il pensait*,' says Anatole France of such another portent, Napoleon, ' *ce que pensait tout grenadier de son armée ; mais il le pensait avec une force inouïe.*' That is the difference. The great poetic ages, when men like Mr. Drinkwater, not great geniuses, have been swept into writing great poetry, were times when it was possible to feel an enthusiastic passion about the state of the world, without being a complete fool. At the end of the sixteenth century, in parts of the nineteenth, it was so ; but it was not so in the eighteenth, nor is it now, unless, with the paradox of Hardy and Housman, a man burn with a passion of despair. That, we may console ourselves, is in our world always possible.

So what is fatal here is not that Mr. Drinkwater can be banal enough to write—

> By Athenian rivers while the reeds
> Made love melodious for the Ganymedes ;

or—

> Once Athens worked and went to see the play,
> And Thomas Atkins kissed the girls of Rome.

Nor need it be disastrous in itself, that he is derivative and over-read, and the past world too much with him. Theft does not matter if a poet is clever enough to make his readers enthusiastic accessories after the fact. It is certainly awful to write—

> And silver arrows of the moon
> Were splintered in her hair,

after Arnold's—

> While the deep-burnish'd foliage overhead
> Splintered the silver arrows of the moon.

But it is not the imitation that is bad, but the bad imitation. And these things would be as nothing, if Mr. Drinkwater had but a touch of that *force inouïe* of Anatole France, if he were dæmonic where he is merely earnest, passionate where he seems only sensible. If Mr. Lawrence had some of Mr. Drinkwater's sense and knowledge of his craft, or if Mr. Drinkwater had some of Mr. Lawrence's insensate energy, like Victor Hugo's cannon hurling itself up and down a ship at sea, then we might look for some new poetry ; but, divorced, their qualities are sterile. The bull lacks the china-shop, the china-shop the bull. And so it is not surprising that Mr. Drinkwater's best work should be found in those love-sonnets where his feeling does succeed in making itself felt, and in those lighter pieces where feeling is not needed, like the deservedly familiar ' Mamble.' For in the rest there is neither intellect enough to be interesting in the absence of metre, nor feeling enough to justify its presence, nor the sheer metrical skill that justifies itself; and if the author wins, unconsciously almost, our sympathy and respect, it is for himself, not his work; as a person, not a poet.

Austin Dobson, having the same lack of intensity, was on the contrary clever enough to realise it at once and choose that lighter vein, that primrose path which could alone save his work from a bonfire the reverse of ever-lasting. *Il faut savoir se borner*; and Dobson knew—

> Not mine the march, the counter-march,
> The trumpets, the triumphal arch.
> For detail, detail, most I care
> (Ce superflu, si nécessaire !).

That enthusiasm which the nineteenth century could hardly inspire in any sensitive person, he deliberately sought and found elsewhere—in its predecessor, just as the pre-Raphaelite poets had found it, more seriously, in the thirteenth and fourteenth. What Lamb threatened —' Damn the age, I will write for antiquity '—Dobson did; and did so well, that his filigreed cherry-stones keep more than a fancy-value still—

> As much, in short, as one may hope
> To cover with a microscope.

One comes to love this little man, so sensible, so urbane, gentle in disillusion, ceremonious yet pitiful, though expecting little yet giving much; just as one flees from the depressing ' uplift ' of optimists and reformers to the quiet wisdom of his two great masters, Horace and Montaigne. All their strength and self-possession he has not; there are moments when his eighteenth-century reserve slips into the sentimental, when specks of alloy

show in his 'golden mediocrity.' But in the present
classical revival he ought not to lack readers among those—

> That like along the finished Line to feel
> The Ruffle's flutter and the Flash of Steel.

And if there are no great discoveries to be made in this
definitive edition, if, as so often, the general taste proves
to have been sound, and the less-known pieces to have
been deservedly so, yet completeness has a value of its
own, and this is certainly the edition to possess, and itself
the best answer to the doubt of its familiar closing lines—

> In after days when grasses high
> O'ertop the stone where I shall lie,
>   Though ill or well the world adjust
>   My slender claim to honoured dust,
> I shall not question or reply.
>
> I shall not see the morning sky ;
> I shall not hear the night-wind sigh ;
>   I shall be mute, as all men must,
>   In after days !

But mute that still, small voice is not as yet.

To pass from Dobson to the third of these poets is to
circle half the globe. Here is no neat little garden of a
Queen Anne cottage. Larger than human, with the
jungle creepers fastening on his moveless hands, the jungle
mists curling like incense before his heedless eyes, the
Buddha seems to sit and hear, unlistening, the strange
praises of a Western tongue that has half forgot the spirit
of the West. Be it said once for all that this is no easy
book ; it expresses a mystical casting adrift of the reason
on the shoreless ocean of the Imagination in a style ex-

tremely obscure. Yet it is possible to abominate mysticism and obscurity alike, and none the less to own after half a dozen readings the power, the cloudy fascination of this small book. The originality, if also eccentric, is real ; and in the rare experience of finding, not one more Georgian poet, but a person who feels, thinks, and writes with a natural individuality that does not echo nor ogle nor prettify, one forgives much, even the incongruity of being summoned to glide into Nirvana by way of a verbal obstacle-race of the severest sort. Here at least is a ' hard acorn of thought,' and no chestnuts. And murmuring ' Luce *a non lucendo*,' persevering readers will set sail into the mist, in the faith that at intervals sudden vistas of splendour will reward them, that at moments they too may—

> Lean on the night, and hail,
> All guilty though they are,
> On the dark seas a sail,
>   And through the horror of the heavens, a star.

After all there is little mistaking what poetry is going to matter to one—heroic efforts to sympathise, stern suppression of intellectual hatreds may acquire one a few new tastes, but not many. For tastes in poetry are rather born than made ; and either there comes at once that curious cold shiver down the spine, *le frisson du beau*, or all is blank ; either snatches begin to haunt one or the book lies dead where it dropped. So it is : one can do little to change it. By those tests these *Poems* deserve their name. Those among them that are philosophical should please despite their difficulty (if not because of it) all who care for the Metaphysical Poets. The descriptive pieces that form the other half are much easier ; and one, ' In Na-lin Village,' is perhaps the most graceful thing of all. The book, with its charming cover, remains a wild and wilful beauty ; to make it, West and East, vision and dream, personality and denial of personality, have met and mingled in a strange, passionate confusion.   Thence its faults, but thence also its qualities—

> For as he may, not as he ought,
> Man takes the honey of his thought,
> And o'er his heart his vision closes
> As bees upon the heart of roses
>   And butterflies on stones.

Talk not to me about the Book of Sin,
    For, friend, to tell the truth,
That is the book I would be written in—
    It is so full of youth.

So runs a quatrain of Hafiz, as rendered by Mr. Le
Gallienne ; and it contains the essence of all there is to
say of *The Flaming Terrapin.* For this, too, is a book of
sins against the laws of poetry : and yet—' it is so full
of youth.' To open a volume of modern verse and
stumble straight on lines like—

Her shadow smeared the white moon black : her spars
Round wild horizons buffeted the stars,

or

And down upon the crackling hull beneath
Toppled the white sierras of the sea,

or

Round the stark Horn, the lupanar of Death,
Where she and that fierce Lesbian, the Typhoon,
Roll smoking in the blizzard's frosty breath,
While, like a skinny cockroach, the faint moon
Crawls on their tattered blanket, whose dark woof
Of knitted cloud shrouds their dread dalliance, proof
To the white archery of the sun and those
Thin javelins that cold Orion throws—

this sort of thing stifles in its infancy the reader's premonitory yawn. We wanted air ; and here is a south-
wester straight from the sea. So, it appears, many have
felt in the last few weeks ; it is excellent that such work
should win its recognition ; but it throws also a strong

* *The Flaming Terrapin. By Roy Campbell. Cape.
Heliodora. By H. D. Cape.*

light on the shabby gentility of modern poetry as a whole, that this book should have been immediately so feverishly praised and overpraised. Yet it is natural that this should happen; we are so tired of the confessions of second-rate sensitive minds with nothing to confess and no gift for confessing it, of lyrically bleeding hearts on every sleeve, which the poor daws can scarcely summon the appetite to go on pecking. There are times when niggling subjectivity becomes an infliction and whoever breaks a window in that stuffy salon earns gratitude beyond his due. So it was that Whitman came to the young Chesterton choking in the air of the 'nineties.

And, the Green Carnation withered, as in forest fires that
    pass,
Roared in the wind of all the world ten million Leaves of
    Grass.

And so men acclaimed *General Booth enters into Heaven*, clear though it was that Mr. Lindsay had, unfortunately, the mentality, as well as the vigour, of a dancing dervish.

The Flaming Terrapin has no form worth the name; its philosophy is neither deep nor new; why then does it stand apart from the usual abortions of modern poetry? Partly because Mr. Campbell has lungs, imagination, and an ear; but much more because he has a personality —the charming, laughing, laughable earnestness of youth, that vigour which is still unwearied, that intensity unblunted by too much experience, that spontaneity which has not learnt to suspect. You can feel most of our versifiers feeling their audience, perspiring under their evening dress with self-consciousness and solicitude to please. Hence the blessed relief of a writer who has clearly written to please himself, and enjoyed it, because he loved shouting his thoughts in galloping rhythms that he liked none the less for being—like all the things that move us most deeply—old as the changeless hills to which men lift their hearts.

The poem is in six parts. The first is a kind of prologue, identifying the Terrapin with that energy of life which was before living things, whose thoughts are the blowings of the winds, the sweep of the sea—' this sudden strength that catches up men's souls,' the inspiration of Bellerophon and Samson and Noah. In II the Ark is built and launched and meets the Terrapin, which is harpooned by Noah with his stone anchor and drags him headlong round the world through shrieking hurricanes. In III the storm is renewed and the crew's agonies of despair are only dispelled by the inspiration of the Terrapin. In the meantime, while they are tossing about the Southern Pole, the Devil, as the spirit of neurotic decadence, with a fine disregard of chronology establishes the reign of Mediocrity and Corruption upon an industrialised earth —all, in fact, that the poet most loathes in this present age. IV opens with a second prelude, bidding avaunt the bookish Muses ; then, as the Ark sails at last northward from the Pole, the Terrapin snaps the cable and, cannoning across the world, butts the Devil once for all into the Bottomless Pit. The last two parts are occupied with a lyrical unlading of the Ark and an epilogue—Noah standing on the peak of Ararat with the Universe wheeling about him, defiant and alone—

> There as amid the growing shades he stood
> Facing alone the sky's vast solitude,
> That space, which gods and demons fear to scan,
> Smiled on the proud irreverence of Man.

This comparatively sober summary can give little idea of the gallimaufry of the original, with its wild digressions, its mixture of the atmospheres of *The Apocalypse*, Lucan, and *The Ancient Mariner*, *Moby Dick*, Dryden, and the Sitwells.   This amorphousness is a fault that will escape no reader ; no reader, indeed, will be able to escape it. It is the redeeming qualities that matter—the mere sound of the verse, as in the old play Miramont says of Greek—

> Though I know no Greek, I love the sound on 't,
> It goes so thundering as it conjured devils ;

the imagination which can drag by main strength likenesses from the uttermost ends of thought to flash and combine in some thunderous metaphor ; the vividness of vision that can prod the sleepiest mind awake and make it feel and see.   Often enough Mr. Campbell's taste fails him, his ambition overleaps itself, and the reader relaxes to a smile, as

> Enormous lice, like tiger, hog and bear,
> Go crashing in the jungles of his hair.

or

> Gigantic copulations shake the sky.

Quite a number of our contemporaries could have written that, with one smirking eye upon their audience ; whereas Mr. Campbell, I suspect, wrote it just because his eye was not on his audience, because it gave him a childish amusement to say it.   And that makes all the difference in the world.   And in any case these *bêtises* are forgotten in the hollow thunder of the trees that fall to build the Ark—

When star by star, above the vaulted hill,
The sky poured out its hoarded bins of gold,
Night stooped upon the mountain-tops, and still
Those low concussions from the forest rolled ;

or in the whistling of the Antarctic gales, where

Its four sad candles dripping from their wicks,
The Southern Cross disconsolately swung,
And canted low its splintered crucifix,
While all around the wolfish winds gave tongue ;

or in the silence of Corruption's descent upon the smoky
cities of the earth—

With movements as of one
Who, diving after pearls, down from the sun
Along the shaft of his own shadow slides
With knife in grinning jaws ; and as he glides,
Nearing the twilight of the nether sands,
Under him swings his body deft and slow,
Gathers his knees up, reaches down his hands,
And settles on his shadow like a crow.

That was worth writing. Things such as this do not
make *The Flaming Terrapin* a great poem ; but they
make it a very interesting and hopeful one. Time will
calm that vehemence which at present makes even his
nightingales 'ferocious' ; experience may teach him to
send into the world poems with backbones, not unlicked
bears' whelps. If he can learn without losing his spontaneity, we shall hear more of Mr. Campbell.

There could be no more complete contrast in every
way than *Heliodora*. 'H. D.' has reputation ; she is,
Mr. Untermeyer assures us, 'the only true Imagist' ;
what is more important, she is clearly devoted to the spirit

of Greece as she imagines it, and to the idea of making
it live again.   But the result seems to me hopeless, desic-
cated, dead—a wire-jerked mummy—and the mummy
a forgery and a travesty at that.   Here are parts of a
rendering of the opening of the *Odyssey*—

> And all the gods pitied him ;
> But Poseidon
> Steadfast to the last
> Hated
> God-like Odysseus.
> The sea-god visited
> A distant folk,
> Ethiopians,
> Who at the edge of earth
> Are divided into two parts. . . .
>
> Let us swiftly send
> Hermes, slayer of Argus,
> Your attendant,
> That he state
> To the fair-haired nymph,
> Our irrevocable wish,
> That Odysseus,
> Valiant of heart,
> Be sent back.

It does not matter that the translation is not even particularly accurate ; but it is grotesque that half-educated
people who know no Greek should be led to suppose that
this funeral march of flies in glue, this parody of a hen
drinking, bears any relation to Homer.   This again is
from an original poem on Peleus and Thetis—

> He asked for his youth,
> And I, Thetis, granted him

Freedom under the sea,
Drip and welter of weeds,
The drift of the fringing grass,
The gift of the never-withering moss,
And the flowering reed,
And most,

Beauty of fifty nereids,
Sisters of nine,
I one of their least,
Yet great and a goddess,
Granted Pelius [*sic*]

Love under the sea,
Beauty, grace infinite. . . .

It dies very hard, this notion of Greeks as Pale Young
People in eurhythmic attitudes ; yet it is fantastically
false. A Greek might have made something of the
Terrapin—'Certainly this young man is a barbarian,
and often frigid in his straining after effect (our Æschylus
was sometimes that) ; certainly he sows not with the
hand, but with the whole sack ; but there is something
attractively Dionysiac about him.' But, confronted with
this gutless, asthmatic ghost of himself, he would probably have felt the angry contempt of William Morris
for a rich person with similar ideas of the essential anæmia
of high art, who once came to buy dyed stuffs of him.
When, after being shown all the hues of the rainbow,
the rich person said in pained tones, ' But I thought you
went in for faint colours,' he heard himself being bidden,
in a bellow of Morris fury, if he wanted dirt, to go and
look for it in the street. *Heliodora*, I fear, is a sham
reproduction of an original that never existed.

THERE is still to be found among the public and publishers a belief in that almost extinct monster—the
reviewer, who, as a sort of disinterested understudy of the
Devil, goes about like a roaring lion seeking whom he
may devour. If they only knew the thrill there was in
making what seemed but the slightest of discoveries, in
sighting, after weeks of tossing on an extremely ' un-
harvested ' deep, even the tiniest of *terra firmas*, of islands
perhaps enchanted, uncharted at the least !

Yet even this pleasure is brief. For the happy critic
is sure to have some critical friend who, being led to a
private view of the new Eden, responds with a lift of the
brows that obviously tumbles the miserable enthusiast
down several degrees at once towards the cold zero of
his estimation ; so that the victim once more ruefully
remembers Meredith's—' slave is the open mouth beneath
the closed.' Was the island after all but a fog, a Fata
Morgana, a twilit haze in the dwindling dusk ? The
reviewer may elude the public ; who shall save him from
his friends ?

This familiar process repeated itself over the poems of
Miss Millay. Here, it seemed, for the first time since
let us not say how long, was a new versifier, who was
actually a real poet. True, much of the work was thin
or rather obvious or a little sentimental, while some of it
seemed imitative ; but—— To say this was enough ;

* *Poems. By Edna St. Vincent Millay. Secker.*
The Harp-Weaver. By Edna St. Vincent Millay. Secker.
Sonnets and Verse. By Hilaire Belloc. Duckworth.
Poems (Selected). By Wilfrid Scawen Blunt. Macmillan.

up went the eyebrows and down the wet blanket came. And yet from beneath its chilly, smothering folds, I still protest that those hopeful souls who have not long since abjured modern poets and all their works, should turn to these small volumes.

Their faults are obvious and on the surface. 'For all that he was worth,' 'like the mischief,' 'yanked both ways' are not phrases that will pass muster in serious poetry, even transatlantic poetry. But more and more, after allowing for the first cloudy enthusiasms to evaporate, since first coming on Miss Millay's verse two years ago I feel that here is more promise than any other of our younger poets has shown. As poetry and its readers and its world grow older and more sophisticated, brains and brevity matter more and more ; and these she possesses as conspicuously as most of her rivals lack them. Consequently she does not lie under their necessity of being eccentric for lack of originality, of using the muddy to conceal the shallow. On the other hand, intellect has left her sensitiveness and her emotions unspoiled, unatrophied, and sane. If her moods are shot through with a red thread of bitterness, that is but natural in the time and the universe we inhabit. The twentieth century has not been peculiarly rich in good poets, even good minors ; but at least they have not paraded that complacent and obtuse satisfaction with human life, which Browning once flaunted as fashionably as a white tie. Better any wormwood than that saccharine.

German critics have maintained that one can tell the work of one Elizabethan dramatist from another, even in composite plays, by reading them aloud and noting the change that spontaneously affects the voice in passing from one writer's work to another's. That is very German. But it is true that a certain clear defiant ring of suppressed resentment does make itself heard in the voice that reads the most typical verse of Miss Millay—

> Beat me a crown of bluer metal,
>   Fret it with stones of a foreign style.
> The heart grows weary after a little,
>   Of what it loved for a little while.
>
>   .   .   .   .   .
>
> He laughed at all I dared to praise
> And broke my heart in little ways. . . .
>
>   .   .   .   .   .
>
> That April should be shattered by a gust,
> That August should be levelled by a rain,
> I can endure, and that the lifted dust
> Of man should settle to the earth again ;
> But that a dream can die, will be a thrust
> Between my ribs for ever of hot pain.

As we grow older, we become more resigned than this to life, it may be ; but I do not see why we should think the better of ourselves for that. There is no very exalted cause of self-congratulation in this only too facile loss of the fire and the generous anger of youth. But the ring of steel in the tone of Miss Millay does not therefore mean a monotony of mood. She combines with her other gifts a saving sense of humour which ranges from lighter laughter to the grim neatness of 'Humoresque'—

> 'Heaven bless the babe !' they said ;
> 'What queer books she must have read !'
> (Love, by whom I was beguiled,
> Grant I may not bear a child.)

' Little does she guess to-day
What the world may be,' they say.
(Snow, drift deep and cover
Till the spring my murdered lover.)

The pregnant brevity of these asides is no ill epitome of
an age when youth has, for better or worse, so emphatically
determined to be ' something better than innocent.'
Miss Millay has found and made her own style—
rapid, ruthless, direct—being well aware that five words
can say more than fifteen, quiet understatement than
hyperbole—

Spring will not fail nor autumn falter ;
    Nothing will know that you are gone,
Saving alone some sullen ploughland
    None but yourself sets foot upon.

Oh there will pass with your great passing
    Little of beauty not your own,—
Only the light from common water,
    Only the grace from simple stone.

From her own verse, that light, that grace, that beauty
will not pass so easily away.

In the sonnet some poets have excelled because its
rigidness tightened their own tendency to looseness and
prolixity ; here too Miss Millay succeeds for the opposite reason that restraint is hers by second nature from
within.

Oh, my beloved, have you thought of this :
How in the years to come unscrupulous Time,
More cruel than Death, will tear you from my kiss,
And make you old, and leave me in my prime :

How you and I, who scale together yet
A little while the sweet, immortal height
No pilgrim may remember or forget,
As sure as the world turns, some granite night
Shall lie awake and know the gracious flame
Gone out forever on the mutual stone;
And call to mind how on the day you came
I was a child, and you a hero grown?—
And the night pass, and the strange morning break
Upon our anguish for each other's sake!

How much further this writer may go it is even harder
than usual to predict.   For the carefully perfect is seldom
prolific, and the branches that even in youth need little
pruning fail often to spread widely in the end.   And if
disillusion makes a writer's work all the more intense and
poignant, it tends often to induce, too, the feeling that
there are few things it really is worth while to write.
This indeed is part of the price to be paid for becoming
too intelligent in this world which has bred so unthink-
ingly—amid its beasts and, like them, to perish—that
marvellous aberration, the brain of man.

Mr. Belloc and Wilfrid Blunt both share Miss Millay's
passion for the sonnet—that disdainful and often faithless
mistress, to master whose fourteen lines so many poets
have laboured their seven years only to gain a Leah in the
end. And both have likewise done their best work in other
forms. Mr. Belloc's sonnets, indeed, without being ever
quite perfect, do contain perfect lines, perfect quatrains—

The tiny, stuffless voices of the dark.

.   .   .   .   .   .

Where large oblivion in her house is laid
For us tired children, now our games are played.

. . . . . .

Your life is like a little flute complaining
A long way off, beyond the willow trees :
A long way off, and nothing left remaining
But memory of a music on the breeze.

. . . . . .

Now shall the certain purpose of my soul
By blind and empty things controlléd be
And mine audacious course to that far goal
Fall short, conferring mere mortality.
Limbs shall have movement and ignore their living,
Brain wit, that he his quickness may deny.
My promised hope forswears in act of giving,
Time eats me up and makes my words a lie.

Yet the sonnet-writer is like a mediæval knight in panoply
of proof ; one stumble, and his proud plumes are soiled
in the dust from which the warrior cannot lift himself
again. So close-knit is its unity that one blemish stains
the whole. But of Mr. Belloc's lyrics three are supreme
—that ' Tarantella ' which is like nothing else in English
poetry, the ' Stanzas written on Battersea Bridge,' and
' Ha'nacker Mill.' Indeed, the whole volume is worth
stealing for the sole sake of the last of these. ' Battersea
Bridge ' would be spoilt, if it could be, by its last stanza ;
it is the least perfect of his three Graces, but for that very
reason lends itself best to the dismembering hand of
quotation ; and the curious, reading its first shouting
verse—

The woods and downs have caught the mid December,
    The noisy woods and high sea-downs of home ;
The wind has found me and I do remember
    The strong scent of the foam—

may feel again the wonder of the enduring freshness of English poetry, and marvel how custom cannot stale, not the infinite variety, but the eternal sameness of English rhyme. How many hundreds and hundreds of times have both the rhyme-pairs of this stanza recurred in the history of our poetry, how hackneyed already in Keats' day must have been this use of -ember months ! Yet here once more, 'remember' and 'December' take hands, as fresh, though as familiar, as the spring ; and only those who in criticism have lost their innocence, are even conscious of the presence of these repetitions which in the right hands seem never vain. And the same life, too vital to reck of novelty, runs through the rest of this utterance of homesickness for the sea, which must surely move even the unseaworthiest of men—

> There is no Pilotry my soul relies on
>   Whereby to catch beneath my bended hand,
> Faint and beloved along the extreme horizon
>   That unforgotten land.
>
> We shall not round the granite piers and paven
>   To lie to wharves we know with canvas furled.
> My little Boat, we shall not make the haven—
>   It is not of the world.
>
> Somewhere of English fore-lands grandly guarded
>   It stands, but not for exiles, marked and clean ;
> Oh ! not for us.   A mist has risen and marred it :
>   My youth lies in between.

It has become impossible to think of Mr. Belloc without his 'Great Twin Brother' ; and with that thought comes the feeling that Mr. Belloc's poetry lacks Mr. Chesterton's furious splendour.   Mr. Belloc writes the better prose, he never gives that impression of a devilishly clever, but maddeningly monotonous machine.   But in verse ' The Ballad of Val-ès-Dunes ' fades beside ' The Ballad of the White Horse ' ;   and similarly, for all its fascinating description of the plutocrat's outfit for the next life—

> The working model of a Burning Farm
> (To give the little Belials) ; all the three
> Biscuits for Cerberus ; the guarantee
> From Lambeth that the Rich can never burn—

' To Dives,' and the ' Verses to a Lord,' make one long even more for the shrivelling scorn, the superb gasconading of Chesterton on the theme of Mr. Walter Long.   For if Mr. Belloc has elements of Athos with his melancholy and of the ecclesiastical Aramis, it is to G. K. C. one must look for the weight of Porthos and the fire of D'Artagnan.

To this Poetry of Anger, ' the scorn of scorn,' belongs, like much of Chesterton, the best of Blunt.   The love-sonnets to Esther and Juliet and the rest have largely lost their savour.   To begin with, sonnets that like many of these call themselves 'The Same Continued,' thereby deny their own nature ; for a sonnet, even in a sequence, must be complete also in itself, or stultify the completeness of its form.   And to read Blunt's sequences at length is too like climbing endless flights of barrack-stairs, all with the regulation fourteen steps.   Once more we have, in short, not sonnets but fine fragments.   Such is the last line in the book, which recalls the epitaph of Landor, in his Roman imperiousness so like Blunt himself—

> Now I ask silence—my ambition ends.

Throughout life that same ambition had set the word below the deed, with all the scorn of Johnson or the late Sir Walter Raleigh for the mere man of letters —

> I would not, if I could, be called a poet ;
> I have no natural love of the ' chaste muse.'
> If aught be worth the doing, I would do it ;
> And others, if they will, may tell the news.

And still less was Blunt a philosopher—

> I long have had a quarrel set with Time
> Because he robbed me.   Every day of life
> Was wrested from me after bitter strife,
> I never yet could see the sun go down,
> But I was angry in my heart.

Here was no lover of the happy mean ; no lover either that would content himself with the funeral-bakemeats of passion, living on as his own ghost and his mistress's ' friend '—

> What is this prate of friendship ?   Kings discrowned
> Go forth not citizens, but outlawed men.

But of one mistress at least he never wearied ; and in these days when, according to Signor Mussolini, ' the truth is, men are tired of Liberty,' it is like a trumpet-blast in a funeral vault to hear again his praises of that dishonoured name, his denunciation of

> Man the oppressor who with pale lips curled
> Sheds blood in the high places of the world.

' Wind and Whirlwind ' cannot indeed approach the magnificence of the poem it most recalls—Swinburne's ' Mater Triumphalis.'   For Blunt's personality is always

more striking than his poetry—so that he lived in deed,
what Swinburne wrote—

> I have no spirit of skill with equal fingers
>   At sign to sharpen or to slacken strings ;
> I keep no time with golden-perched singers
>   And chirp of linnets on the wrists of kings.
>
> I have ear at least, and have not fear, and part not
>   From thine unnavigable and wingless way ;
> Thou tarriest and I have not said thou art not,
>   Nor all thy night long have denied thy day.

Yet his sympathies were wider, as well as more steadfast,
than Swinburne's. For they were not limited to the
human victims of human oppression ; and though ' Satan
Absolved ' is a dreary poem, it quickens into fiery life
for a moment when the Accuser pleads before God against
Man the Exterminator—

> And Thou hast clean forgot the fair great beasts of yore,
> The mammoth, aurochs, elk, sea-lion, cave-bear, boar,
> Which fell before his hand, each one of them than he
> Nobler and mightier far, undone by treachery.

The same anger burns more coldly in the distich, with its
sneering feminine rhymes—

> Assassins find accomplices. Man's merit
> Has found him three, the hawk, the hound, the ferret.

Such a poet was not made to be an amorist. His love-
sonnets are the measured turnings and returnings of an
untamed leopard in an incongruous cage ; and the really
characteristic love-poem of this best of haters is to be
found in what is the finest of the lyrics in the book, the

utterance of a woman's feeling for the first who ever
won her—

> If I forget thee ! How should I forget thee ?
> Sword of the mighty ! Prince and Lord of War !
>   Captive I bind me
>   To the spears that blind me,
> Rage in my heart and love for evermore.
>
> If I forget thee ! How shall I forget thee ?
> One man there is no woman dares despise.
>   Hate him it may be,
>   Wound him if the way be,
> Nay, but forget him ? Not before she dies.

The leopard is loose ; the rhythm is the rhythm of his
uncaged stride.

TWO POETESSES *

'THERE is but one thing certain,' says Pliny, with his
curious mixture of matter-of-fact and melancholy, ' that
nothing is certain ; and there is nothing more wretched
or more proud than man.' Human unhappiness and
the pride that half causes it and half redeems—of the
union of these two eternal contrasts *Flame and Shadow* is
made. It is the utterance of a mood which all feel sometimes, some always ; which all the generations have
repeated, yet each of them yearns to hear expressed anew
in the special accents of its own day—that particular kind
of pessimism which feels the vanity, and yet the value, of
life. And it needs to be restated still. For the present cannot
live on the past, on dead men's words, alone ; its own
literature may be inferior, much of it must be, inevitably,
minor ; yet, as Homer had already learnt, men love the
song which is new, and a living voice has in some ways
an appeal that no dead eloquence can bring. This is the
value of *Flame and Shadow* ; not that it contains new
ideas, but that a view of life which our age in part accepts,
in part struggles to avoid, is here once more expressed
with sincerity and skill—the feeling that for all the agony
of transience, all the disillusion of hopes in vain fulfilled,
there are no consolations, but the bitter beauty of the
Universe, and the frail human pride that confronts it,
for a moment, undismayed. 'There is nothing more
wretched or more proud than man.' It is always strange
that sorrow should possess this higher beauty than laughter,

* *Flame and Shadow.* By Sara Teasdale. Cape.
  The Forsaken Princess. By Alberta Vickridge. *Preface by W. Gibson.*
Swan Press.

235

even children's or lovers' laughter, can possess ; that
Tragedy is so fundamentally a greater thing than Comedy.
But for this, the sadness of the world would be unbearable ;
thanks to this, from sorrow itself there is wrung a kind
of joy—

> Let it be forgotten, as a flower is forgotten,
>> Forgotten as a fire that once was singing gold,
> Let it be forgotten for ever and ever,
>> Time is a kind friend, he will make us old.
>
> If any one asks, say it was forgotten
>> Long and long ago,
> As a flower, as a fire, as a hushed footfall
>> In a long forgotten snow.
>
> . . . . . .
>
> Even love that I built my spirit's house for
>> Comes as a brooding and a baffled guest,
> And music and men's praise and even laughter
>> Are not so good as rest.
>
> . . . . . .
>
> It is strange how often a heart must be broken
>> Before the years will make it wise.

With a suspicion of insincerity the effect would be what
Arnold called 'a horrid falsetto ' ; some, perhaps, will
suspect ; but that is not the impression left by the book
as a whole. For the quietness with which the passion is
controlled throughout is perfect, like the quiet of a small
unruffled pool clasping its dark reflection of a lowering
heaven in stillness to its heart. And with this gentleness
goes hand in hand another quality which makes the
writer's attitude, though so familiar, new and individual
—her deliberate restraint from bitterness. Bitterness
has been the very salt of some of the intensest poetry from

Archilochus and Juvenal to Hugo, from Wyatt and Webster to Hardy and Housman. It may be exaggerated or hideous or morbid—it is at least never insipid. And yet superb as scorn can be in its vibrant intensity, there is something a shade finer still in the ideal, though not, of course, therefore in the work, of a writer who rises above cursing the world for its cruelty to recognise its indifference, its lack of evil intent as well as good, and therefore to take alike its buffets and its beauty, in her own fine phrase—

> with gay unembittered lips.

This indeed is one difference between Mrs. Teasdale and Edna St. Vincent Millay, whose general attitude and tone are so similar, though Miss Millay's is an intenser and more brilliant gift. It is easy, for instance, to seize the contrast between the resilience and resonance of—

> White with daisies, and red with sorrel,
>   And empty, empty under the sky !
> Life is a quest and love a quarrel.
>   Here is the place for me to lie,

and the quieter resolution of *Flame and Shadow*—

> With earth hidden and heaven hidden,
>   And only my own spirit's pride
> To keep me from the peace of those
>   Who are not lonely, having died.

One other piece in this new volume stands out as being not only charming, but true and new as well—

> There never was a mood of mine,
>   Gay or heart-broken, luminous or dull,
> But you could ease me of its fever,
>   And give it back to me more beautiful.

In many another spirit I broke the bread,
  And pledged the wine and played the happy guest,
But I was lonely, I remembered you ;
  The heart belongs to him who knew it best.

It is good that this kind of poetry should go on being
written.   It is not only good as poetry ; it keeps alive
an attitude to which the human mind is perhaps destined
to be more and more driven back—the poetic philosophy
of life.   So, at least, Arnold thought, when he wrote :
' In poetry the spirit of our race will find, as time goes
on and other helps fail, its consolation and its stay.'
Theologian and philosopher have always tended to look
at everything as means to some end ; and it has been
the poet and the artist who valued things, not for the
uses they can be put to or the promises they hold, but
for the interest and significance of what they are.   In
that mood we know we cannot possess ; we do not
desire to possess ; the verb ' to have ' ceases to torture,
and our pleasure is for once at least not a satisfaction
that must be preceded and followed by the pain of
craving.   And if all is transient, transience too must
be endured—

  Denn aller schöner Dinge Schönheit ist
  Dasz sie vergehen.

This is disinterestedness—loving life for its own sake.
It is not a road for all, but for many ; not an abiding
place, but a refuge.   It too is a blind alley in the end,
but no mean or sordid one, nor one that is trodden with
blinded eyes.

  If *Flame and Shadow* flings this answer in the face of
life, *The Forsaken Princess* turns a dainty back on reality.

The book consists of three fairy tales in delightfully smooth and graceful verse. It has been pointed out that the authoress has clearly read Keats (one may also suspect, Morris). But, after all, it would be odd if she had not ; and the obligation is not clearer than it ought to be. Of the tales the first is the most charming, but the one that goes deepest is the last, which tells how three women were once changed into flowers. One of them, however, used nightly to return in her own shape to her husband's arms ; and when at last, weary of the separation each dawn brought, he besought her to tell him how to keep her always, she told him of the meadow where the three flowers grew ; he had but to pluck her flower and she was his for ever. But how to know her from her two companions ? There would be no dew upon her petals. So it was ; but when he had found the place and there the three flowers grew at his feet, an unlooked-for temptation came. Should he not pick another new love in his old love's stead ?

> ' Familiar grown,
> Joy turns to staleness. . . . I have known
> All she can teach me, yea, too well.
> Romance, like silvery dew, is shed,
> And never more may crown her head,
> Though pitying love should break the spell.
> Now let me choose a fresher bloom
> Whereto the spangling dew still clings—
> Renew my dream and reillume
> The rapture, the imaginings,
> The magic of forgotten springs. . . .
> O Bride unnamed, O Dream, O Dew,
> O veiled Ideal, I turn to you ! '

And then with hand half-stretched, at pause,
He chid himself. ' What fool is here,
Dream-dallying in a fateful hour ?
Is not my dearest doubly dear
Because familiar ?—yea, because
There is no veil upon her flower ? '

There, from amid the flowers of her fairyland, *The For-saken Princess* casts over her shoulder a glance that goes to the heart of the real world after all.

PROBABLY every reader who has not entrails of brass, knows sated moods in which he half loses faith in literature : and every critic who has not a forehead of that substance, goes through times when he doubts of all criticism, *even* his own. There are moments when I remember with half-regretful amusement a former self who used to progress gaily enough through the villages of the Somme, carrying nothing but an unread Homer in his valise, and reading nothing—*O tempora, O mores !*— but *The Bystander*. That recurrent blue devil has this time been exorcised in a quite unlooked-for way. *Plays and Controversies* seemed at first sight attractive, but not thrilling. Mr. Yeats' plays are charming. But how many times has not *The Countess Cathleen* already made her bow before us ? And the ' Controversies ' which fill half the book—(newspaper articles twenty years old, taken from a periodical, *Samhain*, that few have ever heard of, and reprinted now in the hope that the Free State Government may soon be considering a National Theatre)—hardly promised ecstasies.

That was where the deception came in. For these quite occasional pieces of dramatic criticism contain not only admirable sense, but, what is far rarer still, admirable prose. When Mr. Yeats, explaining how failing sight made dictation necessary, adds that here fell his hope of mastering a real style, the modesty is clearly genuine, but the fear was clearly false. In these papers, written for

* *Plays and Controversies.* By *W. B. Yeats.* Macmillan.
Love Poems and Others. By *D. H. Lawrence.* Duckworth.
Birds, Beasts, and Flowers. By *D. H. Lawrence.* Secker.

an ordinary, intelligent public, there are no striking novelties of dramatic theory—how should there be ?— only an unfailing patience and good sense in defending his theatre against those eternal enemies, the politician, the priest and, more dangerous still, the commercial vulgarian. Patriots cried for stage-propaganda and howled at the suggestion of *In the Shadow of the Glen* that an Irishwoman could be immoral as well as a Saxon ; bishops, draping themselves with pompous ignorance in the rags of English puritanism, pontificated against the treatment of ' the degrading passion of love.' ' Nothing,' as Mr. Yeats says, ' has ever suffered so many persecutions as the intellect, though it is never persecuted under its own name.' The liberty of literature has been pleaded for through the ages by our best ; but that cause always needs repleading ; and few writers have done it with a simpler dignity, a nobler intensity of suppressed passion than find utterance here. Take, for example, his handling of that almost decrepit question, the relation of art and morality. Of course, we cannot impose morality on the writer : and yet is the divorce so complete as some would have it ? If literature be not itself divorced from life, we must perforce pass some judgments on its figures as they pass before us. Yet the code we judge by is not the maid-of-all-work morality that serves our unsatisfactory society in the common light of day—

The character whose fortune we have been called in to see, or the personality of the writer, must keep our sympathy, and whether it be farce or tragedy, we must laugh and weep with him and call down blessings on his head. This character who delights us may commit murder like Macbeth, or fly the battle for his sweetheart as did Antony, or betray his country like

Coriolanus, and yet we will rejoice in every happiness that comes to him and sorrow at his death as if it were our own. It is no use telling us that the murderer and the betrayer do not deserve our sympathy. . . . Complain of us if you will, but it will be useless, for before the curtain falls, a thousand ages, grown conscious in our sympathies, will have cried, *Absolvo te*. . . . We understand the verdict and not the law; and yet there is some law, some code, some judgment. If the poet's hand had slipped, if Antony had railed at Cleopatra in the tower, if Coriolanus had abated that high pride of his in the presence of death, we might have gone away muttering the Ten Commandments.

There is a brave ring about this that is not often heard in the writing of to-day. Many of his views we have now learnt to accept—in theory : and twenty years have given a less original air to Mr. Yeats' hatred of realism, to that dislike of conventional acting with its excess of gesture (which once goaded him to ask to rehearse a company in barrels on castors that he could push about the stage with a pole), to his protests against the huge, commercial theatre with its sacrifice of the acting to the scenery, and of the poetry to the acting. But here, on the other hand, is a newer idea, though I doubt if it be altogether true—

There are two kinds of poetry and they are commingled in all the greatest works. When the tide of life sinks low there are pictures, as in the ' Ode to a Grecian Urn ' and in Virgil at the plucking of the Golden Bough. The pictures make us sorrowful. We share the poet's separation from what he describes. It is life in the mirror, and our desire for it is as the desire of the lost souls for God : but when Lucifer stands among his friends, when Villon sings his dead ladies in so gallant a rhythm, when Timon makes his epitaph, we feel no sorrow, for life herself has made one of her eternal gestures, has called up into our hearts her energy that is eternal delight. In Ireland, when the tide of life is rising, we turn, not to picture-making, but to the imagination of personality—to drama, gesture.

And if Mr. Yeats writes bitterly of the general want of youth and personality in our bleached and middle-aged civilisation, he writes in no despair of the future. ' For has not Virgil, a knowledgeable man and a wizard, foretold that other Argonauts shall row between cliff and cliff, and other fair-haired Achæans sack another Troy ? '

I have dwelt long on these ' Controversies ' : but I am unrepentant about the length of these quotations from a collection of criticism that seems to me unsurpassed in English since Pater and Stevenson for its combination of truth and beauty. For it is seldom indeed that one finds criticism which cries out, in the tense beauty of its rhythm, to be read aloud. As for the plays, *The Countess Cathleen* and *The Land of Heart's Desire* have charmed audiences and readers long ere this. The four *Plays for Dancers* at the end are, on the other hand, so odd and shadowy and ghostlike, that one wants them acted according to the author's elaborate directions, rather than to read. For on the reader they leave a certain disquieting doubt lest Mr. Yeats' palely beautiful muse be not growing a little too bloodless and in peril of falling into a decline.

There is no bloodlessness about the ' barbaric yawp ' of Mr. Lawrence. In *Love Poems*, first published eleven years ago, a certain mania for blood already shows itself in the poet who delights to scent a lover's hands in a passionate embrace with the fur of the rabbit he has come from killing. The women themselves wilt and wince in the arms of their Orlando Furioso. They are expected to ; if they did not, it would mean they were tainted with enfranchisement and such devices of the devil. And this mental twist of mere brutality infects work that is finely vivid in itself—

> Under the long, dark boughs, like jewels red
>> In the hair of an Eastern girl,
> Shine strings of crimson cherries, as if had bled
>> Blood-drops beneath each curl.
>
> .   .   .   .   .   .
>
> Under the haystack a girl stands laughing at me,
>> With cherries hung round her ears—
> Offering me her scarlet fruit : I will see
>> If she has any tears.

The poems as a whole show, as this one does not, that Mr. Lawrence has a too careless ear ; but they show also that peculiar imaginative vigour he has, which stamps his pictures as with a graven die.

In the new *Birds, Beasts, and Flowers* the verse has become Whitmanese ; the vigour remains ; and the general bloodiness has waxed. A few of the better pieces would have been better still in Mr. Lawrence's prose. The rest is sound and fury. Mr. Lawrence is angry, he prides himself on being angry, and he wants to make as many other people as possible angry. He wants, much more than Whitman, to turn and live with the animals, to smash this universe of sickly intellectuals—

> I shall be so glad when it comes down.
> I am so tired of the limitations of their Infinite,
> I am so sick of the pretensions of the Spirit.
> I am so weary of pale-face impotence.
>
> .   .   .   .   .

See if your skies aren't falling !
And my head, at least, is thick enough to stand it, the smash.

But Mr. Lawrence is a far too warm-blooded animal for his bite to be really venomous. After all, his emotion is common enough. Little Hartley Coleridge, a guest once, in the prim silence of a Nonconformist minister's household, and unable to bear it any longer, leapt from the sofa, kissed the daughter, and fled from the house. But he spared the world a volume on the subject. This passion for blood and ' red, angry men,' this absorption in the sexual relations of goats and tortoises, may win a cursory reading for curiosity's sake ; but such nine-days' wonders are merely nine-days' wonders. The Philosopher's Stone is not to be discovered by stamping like an enraged alchemist round a den full of stale simples and stuffed crocodiles. Mr. Lawrence ' believes in life ' like any anti-Malthusian ; and he is as little able to explain what he means. Revolutions of this sort are mighty fine and giddiness the main result. It all brings back a story of Edward Lear's sojourn in a south Italian town during some mushroom political upheaval. When he went back to his hotel and asked the waiter ' Where is the *chiave* of my *camera* to get at my *roba* ? ' he was met with the ecstatic answer : ' *O che chiave ! O che camera ! O che roba ! Non c'è più chiave ! Non c'è più camera ! Non c'è più roba ! Tutto è amore e libertà ! O che bella rivoluzione !* ' But the world seems to continue much the same.

NEW POETRY*

Poets should eschew prefaces. If their verses please, there is no more to be said : if they do not please, prose will not help them. Mr. Wolfe introduces his poems by asserting that there is no such thing as 'modern verse.' This is not true, and not very judicious ; for no reader is conciliated by being told that he daily uses a phrase which signifies nothing, and is by implication an idiot. Next, Mr. Wolfe explains that he is thus violent because he has been accused in the past by somebody of new-fangledness in his use of commas. 'I was almost assured that I could not change a comma without troubling a star.' It was very tiresome, no doubt; but, after all, should criticism of his commas so trouble a poet ? He then proceeds to defend his half-rhymes from the charge of being new (as though it mattered if they were), and to tell his readers that he will not tell them how his verses ought to be read. Fortunately, however, the preface is speedily forgotten in the poetry ; and it would be negligible if it did not betray a certain excess of self-consciousness and lack of self-criticism which are the only weaknesses in one of the most remarkable volumes of verse published for some time.

What exactly, one asks on laying the book down, made these poems so enjoyable ? To begin with, their unusual pleasantness as pure sound—

> I shall no longer wander
> your goose-boy—for I shall be
> with the Greek, with the young Alexander
> when he rides to Galilee.

---

* *The Unknown Goddess. By Humbert Wolfe. Methuen.*
The Espalier. By Sylvia Townsend Warner. Chatto and Windus.

And you will change as the way is
from the girl I knew to a Queen—
Flora the Roman, or Thais
or Mary the Magdalene.

The debt to Rossetti's Villon is clear ; the meaning, even with the context, is not clear at all ; and yet this fragment serves to illustrate the writer's gift for melodies that cling in the memory, like the burs carried unconsciously from a meadow all a June day long—

When all that wonder
this loveliness
of heart lies under
the sleepy grass,

And slow are the swift
and dark the fair,
and sweet voices lift
not on the air,

When the long spell
of dust lies on
all that was well
bethought upon

And all that lovely,
and all those brief
hopes that went bravely
beyond belief . . .

These deft, short lines are characteristically dear to Mr. Wolfe, as they are also, by a curious coincidence, to Miss Warner, and as they used to be, before he began to starve us with his silence, to Mr. de la Mare. Or is it, after all, no mere coincidence ? And have we here a typically ' modern ' (with Mr. Wolfe's pardon) sensitiveness to the brevity both of time and of modern patience, a fear of dwelling long or pressing heavily on thoughts that can no longer hope to be very new? For these four- and five-syllabled lines do give this impression of figures stealing by us with quick, short, tiptoed steps, a little deprecating, a little anxious lest we should turn impatiently away, or lest some old worm-eaten board should creak beneath them in the House of Thought and groan out 'Commonplace!' One of Mr. Wolfe's critics has objected that a form so slight cannot carry the weight of philosophy he puts upon it. But it is not easy to establish this sort of mathematical relation between length of lines and depth of thought; and in fact, Æschylus has packed some of his profoundest meditation into verses no longer. The metre, like any other, can be made ridiculous by abuse; but there is no reason to feel that it has been. In short lines or long, this is a poet with an ear. And with it goes a definite gift for phrase and imagery—

> And she can sing—the blackbirds hear her—
>   those little coals with throats of flame—
> and they can find, alighting near her,
>   no sweeter practice than her name.

There are austerer minds by whom such things will be dismissed as merely pretty. And yet why 'merely'? Is it so easy? Is a Herrick so much more? And this, at least, has a deeper charm—

> On a dream-hill we'll build our city
> and we'll build gates that have two keys—
> love to let in the vanquished, and pity
> to close the locks that shelter these.

.   .   .   .

There 'll be a London Square in Maytime
with London lilacs, whose brave light
startles with coloured lamps the daytime,
with sudden scented wings the night.

A silent Square, could but a lonely
thrush in the lilacs bear to cease
his song, and no sound else—save only
the traffic of the heart at peace.

There is something extremely pleasing and skilful in the
way the verse leads up, with growing excitement of rhythm
and break, to the climax and sudden quiet of the perfect
crowning line and phrase.

The third attractive thing about *The Unknown Goddess*
is its sense of personality. This is an elusive quality ; it
has to be felt rather than demonstrated ; and its absence
in a writer is sometimes more obvious than its presence.
But it is to life what style is to language ; and a poet must
have this secret too if he is to do more than spend his time
beating on a beautiful tom-tom—

I have had great gifts—the cool clear brow of a queen
  that for a moment was mine to crown from afar,
hands for a moment outstretched for mine to rest between,
  as in the hands of his love the hands of the lover are.

Well ! she has tired of the crown. Do you think I shall
  blame her ?
  She has folded her hands together. Shall I protest ?
She has only done those things that well became her
  at the time and in the way that they became her best.

Here seems to me to reveal itself, above all in the last
line, that indefinable quality which the poetaster always

lacks. After all, one of the essential things about poetry is that it provides one of the most perfect means of self-revelation ; in the half-light of its convention the shyest souls have been emboldened to stand naked and unashamed. The poet can show himself without fear of being caught ; for the secret remains always his own, where exactly fact ceases and imagination begins. It was typical of that detestable vein of vulgarity in Browning to pretend that it was degrading for a poet to unlock his heart ; for that matter, his own career consisted of little else. But for this very reason it is essential that poets should have some personality to reveal, some sense of value to convey, some attitude to the universe, some form, not muddle, in their minds. You cannot communicate a chaos ; you cannot get contact with a mind ' all wiggle-waggle.' The danger to the more intellectual part of modern literature is, it is true, rather different ; the tendency there is not to muddle values, but to deny their validity, not to live in a chaotic world, but in one reduced to such a devastated state of order that everything in it is worth as much as everything else, that is to say, precisely twopence. But here, too, Mr. Wolfe is happy. He does not live in a mental jungle like Mr. Lawrence ; nor yet in the desert disillusion of the too intelligent. He holds, it seems, a sort of Platonism, struggling to believe in a more perfect reality of ideal things, to hope against hope that the Universe will satisfy

> The heart's desire for what will lend
> To love that ends love without end.

One may neither believe, nor much want to believe, in the absoluteness of love and beauty ; that is a matter of personal opinion ; the point is, that this philosophical attitude of life, the having thought about these things, does add a unity to his work, a form to his reactions, that is not common in modern verse.

There are indeed dangers too, which have shown themselves already in the preface. The danger of personality is over-self-consciousness. And 'Oxford,' for instance, which describes the emotions of travelling back to the University years after, leaves a feeling of slight discomfort, as if the writer felt he was being sentimental, and laughed with you at his own sentimentality, and yet meant by this frankness to convey the impression that he was not really sentimental at all, and would resent it if you continued to think him so. The danger, again, of the idealistic philosophies of sensitive minds is that they tend to become easily a little factitious. In struggles to get 'beyond the mind,' as the thrush's song is beyond it, to feel that love and beauty are absolute and eternal, to believe that love lost or unconsummated is somehow better than perfect possession, there lies always this risk of muddle and of cheating. Loudly 'Moonlight Sonata' protests that the mistress held for a moment is won for ever in the best of ways. And yet . . . If the lady changed her mind, would the lover not change his ? If the wind had blown down a bunch of 'sour' grapes into the fox's mouth . . . Such a poem may indeed be the utterance of a mood of genuine conviction ; suspicion of it may be quite unfair ; and yet the feeling recurs, as one turns again these pages, so gifted, but somehow not quite self-critical enough. 'The Sheeted Living,' for instance, is just such a poem, where for the dried-up emotions of later life the consolation is offered that, at least, he who has no longer a heart cannot break another's. This would be very well ; only it does not happen to be true.

But, just or unjust, these cavils are of minor importance compared with the effect of the book as a whole. The reader desires nothing better than to shut critical eyes for the moment in the pure enjoyment of such music as the opening lines of ' Iliad '—

> False dreams, all false,
> mad heart, were yours.
> The word, and nought else,
> in time endures.
> Not you long after,
> perished and mute,
> will last, but the defter
> viol and lute.
>
> Sweetly they 'll trouble
> the listeners
> with the cold dropped pebble
> of painless verse.
> Not you will be offered,
> but the poet's false pain.
> Mad heart, you have suffered
> and loved in vain.

Miss Warner's volume has less pure poetry in it ; for one thing, the writer is probably some years younger. And yet her view of life seems older in some ways than Mr. Wolfe's. She has no Platonic consolations for her green Dorsetshire world, brooded over by the sardonic melancholy of Hardy and Powys, except a wry, good-tempered humour. The fact that she imitates Hardy at times with a closeness within the forbidden degrees, cannot disguise her originality. Less skilful technically than *The Un-known Goddess*, her work lends itself less to quotation. Yet there is the firm impress of a personality one likes and respects in the allegory of 'The Virgin and the Scales,' or the brief, bold strokes of the narrative in 'Nelly Trim,' with its swift, Homeric opening—

> ' Like men riding,
> The mist from the sea
> Drives down the valley
> And baffles me.'
> ' Enter, traveller,
> Whoever you be.'

Some will complain that Miss Warner, like most happy possessors of both youth and cleverness, overdoes the second ; but time will cure. Some, again, will find her view of life too ironic ; but so is life. Miss Warner should be heard of again.

CRITICAL UNREASON*
OR, DR. COTTARD'S SATURDAY NIGHT

IN this book Mr. Graves beats a number of bushes and starts a number of interesting hares—so interesting, indeed, that the reviewer is tempted to go running after one or other of these light-footed creatures on his own account, instead of following the hunter as he continues to beat about his bushes ; for Mr. Graves does not seem to me to make a very successful field-day of it, and to follow him through his brakes of analysis is by no means always easy going. But though there was always much to be said for Macaulay's method of reviewing books simply by snatching the subject out of the author's mouth and chewing it himself, still it is never quite fair to the reader, who wants to know what the book itself is like, nor to the author, unless his opinions are quite negligible. Now, Mr. Graves's opinions are not negligible. One may wish, in the present case, that they were. But many people believe, with reason, in Mr. Graves, and many people believe in the application to literature of psychoanalysis. Together, the two must be reckoned with ; and so it seems best to try to give an intelligible summary of his not always very intelligible line of argument.

His first chapter, then, discusses what constitutes poetry, and bad poetry. He answers that poetry is a means by which a poet gets rid of some *conflict* in his ' subpersonalities '—just as, I take it, an oyster gets rid of the irritation of a foreign body by turning it into the smooth roundness of a pearl. The poet, according to Mr. Graves,

---

* *Poetic Unreason and Other Studies. By Robert Graves. Palmer.*

knows no more than the oyster what he is doing. And he may find relief merely by a clearer expression of a conflict muddled and inarticulate before, as well as by the discovery of some means of actually harmonising the discord. Good poetry is poetry which relieves some conflict in us. Consequently all poetry is good in the poet's eyes as he writes it ; for the reader it is good when it ministers to a similar dis-ease in his own mind, bad when the conflict is one outside the range of his experience. Shakespeare, for instance, on this theory, wrote *Hamlet*, because he was miserable and at war with himself about Mr. W. H. and the Dark Lady. Now Hamlet, Miss Winstanley has argued, is so self-contradictory a character just because he is really two people, James I and the Earl of Essex ; and though Shakespeare did not, of course, know what he was doing, *we* know that he was symbolising one side of his own personality by the generous Essex, the other side by ' the scholarly, retired, mean, timorous nature of James.' In fine, poetry, one gathers, is just mental medicine ; the poet is a physician who heals first himself, then others ; and for those who do not share his mental conflicts, he is ' bad.'

In his next chapter Mr. Graves makes more precise his idea of the kind of conflict which produces poetry. It is a battle between the good Dr. Jekyll and the disreputable Mr. Hyde in every human being. Yet they never meet hand to hand, because if the angel in us is speaking consciously ' on the intellectual plane,' our familiar devil will be down below, ' on the emotional plane,' subconsciously twisting meanings or inserting symbols in his own favour ; or *vice versa*, if the devil is dominant, then the angel will be secretly countermining. As instances, Mr. Graves takes religious poems of Herbert and Francis Thompson, and finds in them the symbolism of repressed sexual desire. One may grant that this sort of transference frequently occurs, without being particularly convinced by his examples.

After a defence (which the reader is beginning to need badly) of the application of psycho-analysis to poetry, the author proceeds to analyse some poems of his own. This part is curious and entertaining. Then he at last reaches his title-subject—the illogical in poetry. It is possible, he argues, to utter a series of ideas connected logically or connected by mere association, such as, I suppose, in Proust, Dr. Cottard's imbecile ' blanche '— ' Blanche de Castille.' That is to say, one may talk (I trust Mr. Graves would allow the examples) on the one hand, with the self-conscious self-criticism of an Aristotle or, on the other, like Lamb drunk and making puns, or Falstaff delirious and babbling of green fields. The first sort of utterance Mr. Graves calls ' Classical,' the second ' Romantic.' ' All romantic poetry is automatic writing.' He instances Edward Lear's nonsense-verses, or Miss Sitwell's : and quotes with enthusiasm from an American exponent of this style, Mr. Edmund Wilson—

> Quinctilian enjoyed the quince-buds
> (Which he couldn't distinguish from peach),
> He was brooding on asyndeton, astyanax,
> And other figures of speech.
> Nero and his sycophants
> Were violating their uncles and aunts.

Having expounded this lyric to his own satisfaction, Mr. Graves turns to a similar analysis of *The Tempest*, which proves in his hands another masterpiece of 'associative thinking.' The play, we are told, was inspired by Shakespeare's own unhappy love-affair, and by that strange chapter of *Isaiah* where we find Jerusalem spoken of as 'Ariel,' and the prophet's vision as 'a sealed book.' For *The Tempest* is likewise 'a sealed book.' Sycorax (really almost the most important person in the play) reveals herself as the Dark Lady, who kept Prospero (Shakespeare) twelve years imprisoned in the cloven tree of misery. But it was Ariel, you exclaim, that was thus imprisoned, not Prospero. Little that matters to the associatively thinking Mr. Graves: 'I believe that really it was Prospero whom Sycorax oppressed for twelve winters.' Caliban, one learns with resignation, is Mr. W. H., Trinculo and Stephano are Chapman and Ben Jonson. In the light of all this, Caliban's attempt on Miranda becomes crystal-clear as the emblem of Mr. W. H.'s seduction of the Dark Lady: true, the Dark Lady a moment since was not Miranda, but Sycorax. It is merely a matter of a little more 'associative thinking.' Again, in 'Full fathom five thy father lies,' 'thy father' is Shakespeare's older embittered self who had contemplated suicide by drowning. Even better things are in store. For at this point Mr. Graves discovered that his ally, Miss Winstanley, had produced a quite different interpretation of the play, which she had proved to be purely political propaganda; Sycorax symbolising Catharine de' Medici, Caliban the Jesuits, Prospero both James I and Henri IV (who is also Ariel), and Miranda the Reformed Faith. All this, however, so far from disputing it, Mr. Graves greedily adopts; the more 'keys' to jangle, the merrier. Shakespeare, he points out, certainly lodged with a Huguenot family. Probably he was engaged in counter-espionage against Spain. That would account for Philip II's anger with the English stage, Shakespeare's acquisition of wealth, and the legend that he died by poison. Yet other interpretations of *The Tempest* are welcomed by Mr. Graves with a hasty benediction as the chapter closes. For this unhappy play is also, we are told, an allegory of religious mysticism, and 'full fathom five' an emblem of the rite of baptism.

After this supreme effort, the writer draws to his conclusion on a quieter note, explaining the vicissitudes of poetic fame, and why Shakespeare may be dead indeed in a hundred years from now ; and adding in a final chapter, the best in the book, some notes on the particular senses to which different poets appeal.

Thus baldly summarised, this work may seem to some readers, in part at least, a practical joke ; it is not that, I am afraid. But the Shakespearean criticism is really impossible to discuss. One could as soon think of arguing in detail with the interpretations which kindred minds used, more frequently once than now, to produce out of the books of *Daniel* or *Revelation*, proving with the same devastating ingenuity that their particular *bête noire* was the little horn of the Beast or the mystic 666.

Nor is it possible to take very seriously the suggestion that 'Romantic' poetry is really trance-poetry, written in an ecstasy that does not know what it is doing ; or to agree that to 'think' associatively, like a mind in delirium, is not, as Rivers thought, 'infantile,' but just as advanced and grown-up and 'responsible' a way of thinking as any logical process, because analysis reveals orderly cause and effect in both. In life, throwing the reins to one's mind, as it were, and letting it wander at will, is, I have sometimes found, good for insomnia, but for little else ; in literature likewise. Little of the poetry commonly called ' Romantic ' can have been written in this trance-fashion—some of Blake, *Kubla Khan*, a certain amount of ' mad ' or nonsense verse ? Mr. Graves's resource is to swell the amount by making nonsense of perfectly self-conscious and sane writing in the flickering light of psycho-analytic symbolism. But it is at least worth remembering that it was the author of *Kubla Khan*, by which Mr. Graves sets such store, who said : ' Poetry is certainly something more than good sense, but it must be good sense at all events ; just as a palace is more than a house, but it must be a house at least.' And ' good sense,' I take it, does not mean a heap of illogical associations to be expounded to the common man by a priesthood of analysts. It is rather fashionable at the moment to be tired of logical thinking, and to want to be ' whimsical ' and ' wayward ' instead. Indeed Mr. Graves writes at times as if he thought common sense a nuisance invented by Aristotle. But if most of the great writers of the world have chosen to make their sentences follow logically upon each other, it was partly perhaps because they had a prejudice that it was a better thing to reason than to ramble. But there were certain other grounds for it also. They wished to be understood : and they wished to please. Much of the pleasure of literary appreciation consists in seeing that the artist has solved his problem—whether of finding an epithet or framing an epic—with a fitness that no alternative solution could have given. Granted that the 'automatic' writer may sometimes achieve this, the difficulty remains that, like Mr. Edmund Wilson above for instance, he remains extremely obscure. Where half a dozen meanings are equally possible, they are not likely to be all first-rate or to seem 'inevitable'; and authors who cultivate the obscurity of oracles, generally share the oracles' motive of wishing not to be found out. Style, the most lasting of all literary qualities, is the antithesis of 'automatic writing'; and had Mr. Graves realised that a little more clearly, he would not have presented us with such sentences as 'Of course there are the *Sonnets*, but being the man we have just assumed him, we can only conclude that they are purely impersonal and abstract conceits in the fashion of the day.'

The other suggestion that all poetry is due to the conflict of 'sub-personalities' in the poet's mind is much more interesting, and, I think, partly true. But it is surely far too sweeping; and that Mr. Graves should discover in——

> Stumbling on melons as I pass,
> Ensnared with flowers, I fall on grass——

a conflict in Marvell's mind between hedonist and ascetic, merely reveals what sham-fights some of his 'conflicts' are. After this one is hardly surprised to be told that Wordsworth's 'Nutting' symbolises his seduction of Annette Vallon. Surely the essential thing about the production of poetry is emotion; and emotion often, but not always, involves mental conflict. But to attribute all poetry to mental conflict in this hard and fast way is like arguing, because one finds bottles on the seashore, that the sea came entirely out of bottles.

Lastly, as to 'bad' poetry, Mr. Graves, regarding poetry as a drug, calls it 'bad' when it has no relevance to his own complaints ; and says we all do likewise. But one may accept his denial of any absolute good or bad, without falling back on so narrow a criterion as this. What, after all, have Mr. Graves's mental conflicts to do with his enjoyment of the lines he so admires from *St. Agnes' Eve* ?

> The arras rich with horseman, hawk, and hound
> Fluttered in the besieging wind's uproar,
> And the long carpets rose along the gusty floor.

And may not a poem be disgustingly bad, though it deals precisely with our own heartache of the moment, because its style is ugly or its rhythm jolts ? Mr. Graves reads Shakespeare to little purpose if he supposes that because the dramatist's 'observations on the history of human relationships are likely to be severely questioned in the coming century,' he may come to lie unread in another hundred years. Who on earth reads Shakespeare for his 'observations on the history of human relationships' ? Who cares if Caliban represents the Man in the Moon or the Binomial Theorem ? Mr. Shaw observed long since that he could not find an idea worth twopence in all the plays of Shakespeare, yet the spell of the most amazing of all masters of language held him still. The trouble with Mr. Graves is that he will look at *Hamlet* with the eyes not of Shakespeare's audience, but of Rosencrantz and Guildenstern. He will pluck at secrets that do not exist, or that omniscience alone could discover. One feels indeed that any one who claims to know so much of the complexities of other people's souls (to say nothing of poets dead three centuries) can have little realised the complexities of his own. The conclusion is Swinburne's : ' A child with any ear or eye for the attractions of verse or art can dispense with analysis ; it were to be wished that adults equally incapable would rest equally content.' Will not Mr. Graves give us some more poetry, instead of losing the world for this psycho-analytical Cleopatra of his ?

GREATNESS IN POETRY*

THE object of this book is to answer the simple question —'What constitutes greatness in poetry?' Professor Abercrombie begins by laying it down that a real difference does exist between 'good' and 'great' poetry. The essential quality of either is 'incantation'—the power, by a sufficiently close succession of magical phrases, of holding the reader enthralled. But 'great' poetry possesses more than this—that is why it survives even translation —and to illustrate the difference, he contrasts six lines of Sedley's 'Knotting Song,' with six lines of Swinburne on Sappho, or again, with Sappho herself. Hence his first main conclusion—that poetry is great when it combines and fuses into one an unusual variety of emotions and impressions. Similarly, he argues, a whole poem is great when by virtue of its form it packs an unusually various and complex range of experience into one harmonious whole. Thus Shelley is a less great poet than Shakespeare, simply because his range of ideas is narrower. Poetry may further be divided, however, into the poetry of refuge which tries to escape from life, like Boccaccio or Theocritus, and the poetry of interpretation, which faces and transfigures it, like Chaucer or *Paradise Lost*. This is the greater kind. Then follows a discussion of the interpretations of life to be found in Wordsworth, in *The Wisdom of Solomon*, and in Milton's two epics. But *Paradise Lost* is greater than *Paradise Regained*. Why? Because it embodies its central idea in the poetic personality of Satan. From this Professor Abercrombie draws his

* *The Idea of Great Poetry.* By Lascelles Abercrombie. Secker.

264

second main conclusion, that the very greatest poetry not only harmonises a wide range of experience, but incarnates this synthesis in a personal figure. That is why *The Dynasts* is inferior to the *Iliad*. After a digression on tragedy, he ends by discussing two poems which satisfy both his conditions of greatness, the *De Rerum Natura* and the *Divina Commedia*.

Poetic greatness, it seems then, consists primarily in complexity—a 'complexity of rich experience,' a 'confluence of all kinds of life,' a 'concentrated wealth of simultaneous impression.' Leopardi had a similar faith in the virtue of multiplicity, of idea crowded on idea, as in the *Odes* of Horace. And yet can we really believe that the greatness of poetry consists in anything so simple as complexity ? A treatise of two thousand years ago, the so-called *On the Sublime* of ' Longinus,' discussed this identical question. And as one of his most famous examples of poetic greatness—famous for its momentary contact between Hellene and Hebrew—Longinus quotes the sentence of *Genesis* : ' God said " Let there be light," and there was light.' Could anything be less complex ? Or take the epitaph on the Spartan dead at Thermopylæ—

> Bear word to Lacedæmon, passer-by,
> That here, obedient to her laws, we lie.

I cannot see much ' confluence of all kinds of life ' in this bare laconic record of men who did as they were told and died. How simple it is, indeed, compared even with that modern ' Epitaph on an Army of Mercenaries ' which history may hereafter set beside the couplet of Simonides ! And when the shade of Ajax, angry even in death, stalks with great strides in silence from Odysseus

across the fields of asphodel ; when Elijah girds his loins
and runs before Ahab to the entrance of Jezreel, or the
dying king of Israel is stayed up in his chariot by Ramoth-
Gilead to the going down of the sun, or his queen dies
with a taunt upon her lips ; when Francesca, describing
the supreme moment when over the book of Lancelot
two souls were made one and lost eternally, says simply,
' quel giorno più non vi leggemmo avante '—' that day
we read no further there '—can complexity be the secret
of these things ?   Or consider Sappho's great ode, ode
of Professor Abercrombie's fundamental instances, where
she describes with burning directness how her body is
seized with fever and shivering, and her ears drum, and
her eyes are darkened in the presence of Anactoria.
' Here,' says Professor Abercrombie, translating Longinus,
' we have " a concourse of passions." '   But this is an
unfair rendering : the Greek word is far wider than our
' passion,' and means ' anything felt or suffered ' ; and
indeed to describe feeling hot as one ' passion,' feeling
giddy as another, and so on, would be absurd.   The only
passion is sheer physical desire.   In fact, this too is
really an amazingly simple poem—a string of symptoms,
that might come straight out of a medical work, transformed by some miracle of style and rhythm and passion
into one of the great poems of the world.   Think into
what genuine complexity Donne or any of the metaphysicals would have twisted it all.   Would it have
become the greater for that ?   The immortal misery
of Catullus is one degree more complex than Sappho's
poem—

> I loathe, yet love. You ask how this can be.
> I cannot tell. I feel. And it is agony.

Here are two passions in place of one : and yet its greatness seems still the greatness of simplicity. This same
mental state Meredith was to expand into the fifty sonnets
of love-knots tangled with scourges, that are *Modern Love*.
Yet we cannot be sure that all his subtleties will be read
as long as the Roman's terrible simplicity. In short, it
is difficult to accept Professor Abercrombie's insistence on
complexity as the essence, or even a necessity, of great
poetry. It is as easy and at least as true to write in exact
contradiction—

> All the loveliest things there be,
> Come simply, so it seems to me.

In the words of Longinus, ' sublimity is often comprised
in a single thought.'

What, then, do we mean when we say of a poem that
we think it ' great ' ? Simply that it gives us the same
feeling as those other poems to which the consensus of
intelligent opinion for generations has given that title.
And what sort of feeling is this ? It consists, I think, in
being not only pleased and delighted, as we are by ' good '
poetry, but impressed also with wonder, even awe—the
sense that this is the doing of genius and it is marvellous
in our eyes. This may be vague : but what more can
we say ? Greatness is no more definable than goodness :
and attempts to define it inevitably end in tautology.
What qualities, then, go to produce it in a writer ?
Longinus believes in three above all—great conceptions
(where the tautology reappears), passion (which he rightly
admits not to be essential), and style. Sublimity, he
adds, is ' the echo of a great soul.' Again the tautology ;
yet the saying is not altogether meaningless. For when

we speak of poetry as great, we do seem to feel some ethical shadow at the back of our minds, some sense that here is nobility. ' Art and morality ! ' some will exclaim in horror. Yet it is so. The divorce between ethics and æsthetics, pronounced so often, cannot be permanently maintained. The mistake in the past has been that too much has been thought about moralising beauty, too little about beautifying morality. The preachers have forgotten the demands of the imagination, to their own cost ; the meek will never inherit the earth, if only because, in spite of a thousand sermons, men have always felt their hearts kindle, not at the thought of turning the other cheek, but of the Paladins of Charlemaine going proudly to their death at Roncesvaux, or Aucassin as proudly into the eternal flame of Hell. And sometimes the poets on their part have forgotten, that it is after all the paradox of a madman to seek beauty everywhere through land and sea except in the lives and deeds of men themselves. It was not merely because he lived among Puritans that Milton wrote that the great poet's life should be itself a true poem : not merely because he lived under the shadow of Victoria that Arnold felt after the same truth with unhappy phrases about ' high seriousness ' ; not merely because he was baiting a professor that Anatole France, after denying the merit of great literature to be either style or imagination or sense of form, concluded—

> Les grands écrivains n'ont pas l'âme basse. Voilà, M. Brown, tout leur secret. . . . La pitié, voyez-vous, Monsieur le Professeur, c'est le fond même du génie.

This is a brilliant *tour de force* and tells us little new : but it is at least better than equating greatness with intense complexities and simultaneous impressions. Is there then nothing in Professor Abercrombie's recipe? To say that would be going too far. Certainly, as humanity grows more and more complex, so must its geniuses and their work. And since one of our tests of 'greatness' is universality and lastingness of appeal—'quod semper, quod ubique, quod ab omnibus'—this test is clearly more likely to be satisfied by a poet so many-sided as to mean something vital to men of a dozen different fashions of thought and feeling; as, for example, Shakespeare, 'the myriad-minded,' has signified something different, but always something, to every century since his death. In the darkest times the diamond, with its hundred facets, will always catch a beam of light from somewhere. But this does not exclude that other type of great poetry, which has hit so truly and simply some of our fundamental, unchanging emotions, that time is powerless against it. Professor Abercrombie praises multiplicity as might one brought up among Gothic cathedrals, who had never seen the great simplicity of Parthenon or Pyramid. As for his second insistence on personality, the importance of that is too obvious to need discussion. We need no demonstrations that human beings are most interested in human beings, that even 'The Nature of the Universe' cannot compete as a subject with 'The Wrath of Achilles.'

The best part of this book is the digressions, including a very interesting one on *The Wisdom of Solomon*. There is no space here to enter into details; but it is impossible to let pass one most extraordinary interpretation of the weakness of Hamlet as an 'inferiority complex,' leading him to reproach himself, but quite unjustly, with pro-

crastination. For, we are told, it was really impossible
for Hamlet to have killed the king, except in that moment
when Claudius was at prayer. This is grotesque. To
kill the king without endangering his own safety, perhaps :
but was this, then, Hamlet's ruling consideration ? Was
he merely being careful of the life of which he was so
weary ? If the obstacles were really physical, it is hard
to see how they were less present in Act V, than in Act I.
Or had Hotspur stood in Hamlet's place, can we believe
that Claudius' first entrance would not have been his
final exit ? Of a crowning comparison here made between
Hamlet and Telemachus, the less said the better.

Further, Professor Abercrombie has a fatal fondness
for superlatives, which shows itself in asserting that 'the
loveliest world poetry has ever attained is the idyllic world
of Theocritus,' or asking if there is 'outside Milton and
Dante, anything really comparable with *The Ode on
the Intimations of Immortality*.' Such comparisons are
meaningless : one cannot establish orders of merit among
incommensurables. And what is one to make of the
statement : 'I know of only one genuinely psychological
poem . . . "Peter Bell"'? Such criticism is on a
level with the grammar of a sentence like this : 'Twice
it (the Faust-legend) has become great poetry ; perhaps,
remembering Lessing and Lenau, more than twice.'
Indeed, the author's strange suggestion that 'perhaps the
accurate man is the only kind of man whose existence is
excusable,' may well seem after this neither very sensible
nor, from his own point of view, very safe.

In the tom-tom lying, silent now, in some museum-gallery the dreaming imagination may discern the cradle of Shakespeare. When some hairy object in a wilderness first found that making a regular series of noises somehow gave vent to something he felt, and, further, that it mysteriously infected with a similar excitement all his fellows who heard it, one of the greatest of all human discoveries had begun. Rhythm had become conscious. The mother of music came now into the voice of man as she had come, even then, thousands of centuries before, into the cry of the cuckoo amid the woods of a yet unhuman world. We can still dimly imagine the strange noises from apelike throats that the quiet stars somewhere heard, while the ice froze thick above the London clay and slow glaciers crept where now whirls the traffic by the Place de l'Opéra. To this day poetry remembers sometimes in our nurseries her own ; as when in that sad, delightful book *Mary Olivier*, ' Dumpling hid her face and sang—

> Aw, dinny, dinny dy-Doomplin',
> Dy-Doomplin', dy-Doomplin',
> Dinny, dinny dy-Doomplin',
> Dy-Doomplin' daay.'

Thus it must have happened in the beginning, that among meaningless noises meaning began to appear, so that chant and thought were wedded and poetry was born. It must have become at once a thing of sorcery. There was no metaphor at first about the ' magic ' of verse ; and the mediæval Dominican whose fanaticism wished to

271

impeach all poets as professors of the Black Art, was only a few thousand years behind his time. These rough voices that chanted their exultation over the harvested fruits of the earth or heads of enemies, chanted likewise, in incantation, when they hungered to harvest more ; just as the artist painted the buffalo he desired magically to multiply, on his sunless cavern-walls. Art, born of play, seems always to have fallen thus at once under the purposeful tutelage of Magic and Religion, till it was of an age to stand alone. But now came the day when Poetry sold herself to Time for immortality. She had expressed the feeling of the moment at the moment for the moment; but soon men found that words set in recurrent rhythm were not only intoxicating, but as easy to remember as drunkenness is to forget. And since what was in metre they could remember, what they wished to remember they began to put in metre. So that now Poetry turned to embrace not the present only, but past and future as well : an artistic tradition became possible—the very life of literature in its early growth, though hereafter to be sometimes its death. Verse had at first been im- provised—like those hoarse raven-croaks of sudden song uttered by the men of the Icelandic sagas when their steel has bitten to their foeman's brain, or their foeman's steel to their own. But now, as metre grew associated with remembrance and the Muses revealed themselves the daughters of Mnemosyne, poetry not only itself gained permanence and the strength and sanctity of age, but it flowered into new forms that could record more lastingly than stone or bronze the long-done deeds of the warrior and the ancient wisdom of the wise. And so beside chants like that worn monument from the well-

head of our civilisation, the *Carmen Saliare* with its
Latin too obscure for even a Roman of Horace's day to
understand, a mingled prayer and dance for the blessing
of the fields of Rome, there grew up also such lays telling
of men's deeds as Homer makes Achilles sing before Troy
fell, such versifications of peasant wisdom as lie embedded
in Hesiod's *Works and Days* ; or, in our own literature, narratives like the ballads, adages like the vividly
terse

> Wikked tunge breketh bone
> Though the tunges self hath none.

And all this while the style of poetry has been becoming
ever more thoughtful, more full of association and analogy,
of ideas first supposed true, then found false, and yet, for
their beauty's sake, dreamed truthful still. It dons
conscious ornament and becomes an art, learning to tell
not only what is actual or actually felt, but beautiful lies
of what might be. There was once a man who, watching how the sun mounted up from the earth to the height
of heaven and then sank westward to earth again, thought
to himself : 'The sun is like a chariot driving up and
down a hill—the sun *is* a chariot driven up and down the
hill of heaven.' He died and his name perished and,
long after, his belief died also ; already to Homer his
vision had more than half become a dream, but a dream
more beautiful than the drier beliefs that replaced it and
therefore by the poets still feigned true. So man's
wisdom, like the wise serpent, casts off dead skin after
skin ; and the artist's imagination adorns itself with the
empty speckled case. It was never so precious until it
became useless—

> The gods are forgotten in Morven of the glens,
>   The sun shines clearly and gentle is the day.
> Like snow from summer corries, like mist upon the bens,
>   The lovely gods of darkness are vanished away—

but not from poetry.   For swift the answer comes—

> Paganisme immortel, es-tu mort ?   On le dit.
> Mais Pan tout bas s'en moque, et la Sirène en rit.

And the same transition from the need of the intellect to the indulgence of the imagination for its own sake has meanwhile been at work also with simile and metaphor, those arts of saying or implying ' this is like that,' which a moment's analysis will reveal to be, still and always, the strangely simple basis of much of the most complicated poetry.   At first the struggling circumlocutions of a language that in its simplicity has not enough single words for all it wants to say, as the vocabulary widens, these devices become unnecessary and so the poet's prize ; and to-day, poor as Midas among the abstract riches of our dictionaries, our writers are driven back to the English of the past or the English that still lingers among the peasantry of Wessex or Connaught, to find a language which has not lost itself in the clouds, but still nests close to the earth amid the rough reality of concrete things.

Up to a point, then, this growth of poetry from its first beginnings has been almost pure gain.   With ever new forms, new devices, new ideas it becomes able to give utterance (there is no prose as yet) to all that men think and feel and do.   It has acquired the gift of immortality and of giving immortality,

> Where breath most breathes, even in the mouths of men.

But already there has been some slight price to pay.
With the conscious art that composes to be remembered,
there cannot be quite the old spontaneity ; and with the
art that succeeds in being remembered, comes artistic
tradition.   The dead singers of the past begin to rise
from their graves to sit by the living poet's side, dimming
his glory, daunting his courage, tempting him to imitate
or to be different instead of being himself.   And from
now on poetry has much more serious losses than these
to set against her still continued gains.   Prose appears
in literature, and gradually annexes all that part of human
experience which has unceasingly widened with the
growth of the critical intellect.   And with prose appears
the prosaic.   Homer could make into poetry the pole-
axing of an ox and his cutting up and cooking ; but
who after him ?   And in our own tongue never again
since Chaucer could the Wife of Bath have ambled in
metre so naturally as she does in his company along the
Pilgrims' Way.   As the human intelligence partly
transforms, partly weakens, the naked human emotions,
as ' the passionate heart ' yields to ' the quiet eye,' poetry
does still share some of the new conquests, becoming
more complex and metaphysical and following the gropings
of philosophy into the outer darkness of human destiny,
or sitting down to grow carefully descriptive, so that as
her infancy was cradled with music, her latter age draws
closer to painting.   Poetry has never been greater indeed
than when, as in Æschylus and Lucretius and Shakespeare,
the vitality of a ruder age has survived to give its energy
to the mind's new subtlety, while the subtlety sobers, but
does not sicken as yet, the old vitality.   But as time goes
on and men think more and act and feel less violently,

some of the old giant vigour dies away, some of the main branches of the tree begin to wither. The verse drama becomes a sapless thing ; epic gives place to prose romance ; and as the exuberance which produced and enjoyed poems that numbered their lines by thousands, begins to disappear, the voice of a Callimachus or a Poe makes itself heard, proclaiming the very idea of the long poem a mistake. The logical evolution of poetry here traced has not, needless to say, gone on as obviously or as uniformly as this century after century. Continually new shoots break out where all seemed dead ; yet slowly the year sets on towards autumn. There may come a real St. Martin's summer, like the Alexandrian Age of Greece and our own nineteenth century, when the older forms of the springtime of poetry revive and the world's great age seems to begin anew, as beautiful as ever—Argo sails once more for Colchis through the pages of Morris and Apollonius, nature reveals her utmost loveliness before the eyes of Theocritus and Keats—and yet on their woodland beauty the touch of September lies. Twice all this has happened in the memory of man, in the Græco-Roman world and in the modern ; with the winter-rest of the Dark Ages in between. Of course our world has now reached a vastness and complexity where analogy cannot be pressed into prediction ; yet there is surely a vivid interest in the resemblance that has already come to be. We have seen poetry begin in momentary lyrics by nameless men ; it becomes remembered ; the growth of a tradition aids it, the growth of thought makes it deeper ; it branches bravely out into forms that embrace all life. Prose appears as its rival, less beautiful, but strong in its swift utility, more versatile to keep pace with the progress of the intellect. Poetry triumphs indeed over growing difficulties and rivalries more splendidly than ever before ; but the difficulties grow. It remains to trace further the working of the forces that have made those difficulties acute to-day—tradition, that once helped, turning more and more to hinder ; thought, without which poetry could never have gained its highest, changing both our life and our poetry more and more to prose.

There is nothing obscure about the influence of the first of these. Thrice in all, Poetry has come to terms with Time—when verse began to be remembered instead of extemporised ; when it began to be written ; when books grew common and it began to be widely read. And the more it has thus secured the future, the more it has become subject to the past. At first, as has been said, the resulting growth of a tradition was essential to the growth of poetry itself ; without the singers before Homer, no Homer. But at the stage in literature when a Theocritus or a Dryden appears, the past is growing a burden. 'Homer suffices all men,' sighs the one ; and the other—

> Then fame was cheap and the first-comers sped,
> And they have kept it since by being dead.

So the fatal attempt begins to make literature out of literature instead of life. A few of the greatest have succeeded. There is no magic more potent than the necromancy with which Virgil and Milton raise to the reader's mind by their allusions ghost after ghost of poets dead before them. Yet the ivy that adds so venerable a beauty ends by strangling the tree ; and poetry in its youth escaped that cancer of literatures in their later age, like Greek in the time of ' Longinus,' like our own to-day, the obsession with the need for novelty.

If this is one of our maladies, the other is likewise middle-aged—disillusion.   It is no mere literary phenomenon, but the reflection of changes in human nature itself.   For even human nature does change.   Heracles gives place to Plato, Hardrada to Hamlet.   More and more, as civilisations mature, men feel about their feelings, think about their thoughts.   It is no new process—it began with the eating of the apple in Eden ; but it is modern to feel it acutely.   The Berserk saw nothing beyond the moment of his own red rage ; it was his limitation yet his strength.   ' C'est une grande force de ne pas comprendre.'   But when the ballad passes from the wild, unrecking swiftness of the cry—

> Is there ony room at your head, Saunders ?
>   Is there ony room at your feet ?
> Is there ony room at your side, Saunders,
>   Where fain, fain, I wad sleep ?—

to the wistful reflectiveness of the not less lovely

> O waly, waly but love be bonnie
>   A little time while it is new,
> But when it 's auld, it waxeth cauld
>   And fadeth awa' like the morning dew,

then the day of the ballad itself is almost done.   It is lost, for it has stopped to think.   And yet that process is only beginning and it is a far cry still to the complexity of Hamlet, the first of modern men who feel that they have grown, somehow, too intelligent—

> Which is a proud and yet a wretched thing.

' I am always insincere, as always knowing that there are other moods '—in that avowal of Emerson's lies the essence of our time. More and more the past and the future force themselves before us, crushing the unhappy present like upper and nether millstones between them. It is this vivid sense of other moods beside those at the moment felt, that makes so true to its title Meredith's *Modern Love*. It is his anguished memory of all that Time has taken, his anguished foreseeing of all it yet will take, that give to the poetry of Hardy that almost morbid intensity which makes it so dominating, so final, so desolate, as though the eye looked on a great precipice where the ends of all the earth sank suddenly sheer to the sea. And meanwhile the critical, scientific part of the human mind, all that was anathema to Blake, has grown like the genie of an Arabian tale. Amid the veering perplexities of our age Science alone sweeps on with its strange, purposeful blindness, it knows not whither, except that it is assuredly to fresh conquests ; and childish scientists perfect for our childish society with childish indiscrimination toys to amuse it, or to murder. We are enabled to hear voices saying across the Atlantic things not worth hearing across a room ; to buzz round the globe like flies round a chandelier, without knowing any better what on earth to do when we arrive, than the jaded Roman noble who had flogged his horses in a whirl of dust across the Campagna from Rome to Tibur, and from Tibur back to Rome. Indeed our society may be likened to that quaint American who spent years constructing a machine which first chloroformed, then decapitated him. And yet Science is at least alive, while Philosophy mopes and Religion mutters. This in itself need not so much matter to Poetry ; but it does matter to Poetry, to all our creative literature, that the thinking section of society has largely lost its scale of values and is thence in danger of ceasing to have any values at all.   It has come to see through so many things.   It is astray in a Sahara of wind-blown, whirling dust into which the rocks of ages have disintegrated at last.   The war was in the intellectual world only one of a series of explosions—an unusually spectacular, but no isolated, one.   When the advanced minds of the last century threw off Christianity and ' Hebrew old clothes,' they were almost ludicrously insistent in repeating that their moral beliefs, so far from being shaken, were merely intensified thereby.   Naturally the orthodox disputed this ; but in fact never prophets preached more devotedly than Carlyle and Ruskin and Arnold ; and the lives of Mill and George Eliot might have done credit in their altruism to the austerest creed. Yet slowly the leaven worked.   There came the sure reaction from Victorian morality, the questioning of Victorian values.   From behind the broken chancel with a broken cross whence Arthur had passed, never to return, came ever more insistently as the century wore to its end, the older, more enduring chant of the Lotus-eaters—

> Death is the end of life ; ah, why
> Should life all labour be ?

Even the present writer can remember a disgusted birthday in childhood, celebrated by the gift of Smiles' *Self-Help*, with its complacent immortalising of men who by lives of unremitting toil rose from five shillings to fifty thousand pounds, and died and went to heaven ; and now to look round at the intelligent undergraduate of to-day is to realise how dead that ideal (if it deserve the name) has become in the eyes of youth, that wants to find Life rather than a living. Is it strange? The new generation is disillusioned about professional success and about politics and about philosophy and indeed about most things. And in some ways it is none the worse for that. For who can read without a cold disgust some of those Victorian lives of people who never lied to any one except, always, to themselves; who lived in a sort of moral Crystal Palace, and stood in queues to fling the first stone at the woman taken in adultery? There is indeed much truth in the remark of some defender of our time—'We are a great deal less moral than you were, but a great deal decenter.'

And yet what a mass of real literature that century produced! Partly because its great men shared its illusions and believed in progress, and felt that many things were worth while; but still more because they did not share its superstitions, and so felt their lives well and nobly filled in fighting against these dragons of their time. And now we sit, a little bleakly, on that battlefield whence the Arnolds and Huxleys and Swinburnes have vanished. Those forts of folly have fallen, those once massive objects of belief been shaken and overthrown—God's Englishmen, and the original virtue of the middle classes, and the value of work for work's sake, and freedom for freedom's sake, and chastity for chastity's sake. And the war and the peace were merely a culmination of this process of cynicising a race which still believed that its governments were honest, and its clergy Christian. Here too there were redeeming things.

While bishops defended the leaving of Zeppelin crews to drown in the North Sea, the kindly cynicism of the British soldier was pressing cigarettes on his captured enemies ; and whatever came of the oaths of politicians, Wilfred Owen could still write in words that might well have bewildered a Victorian—

> I have perceived much beauty
> In the hoarse oaths that kept our courage straight.

And then the Peace. . . . And now the critical reason having devoured so much, has been turning more and more to rend itself ; it becomes ' intelligent ' to disbelieve in the intellect, and to imagine that literature can become young again by learning to have no sense.

> Doch jetzt ist alles wie verschoben,
>   Das ist ein Drängen, eine Not !
> Gestorben ist der Herrgott oben,
>   Und unten ist der Teufel tot.

> Und alles schaut so grämlich trübe,
>   So krausverwirrt und morsch und kalt,
> Und wäre nicht das biszchen *Liebe*,
>   So gäb es nirgends einen Halt.

And so in fact our creative literature has reduced itself to novels, to lyrics, and to plays, which deal almost exclusively with this one surviving passion. The two things that still inspire us are love and disillusion—the disillusion of the poetry of Hardy and Housman, Miss Millay and Mr. Eliot, of novels like *Antic Hay*, of plays like *The Vortex*. No one has better uttered than Miss Iris Tree this blank greyness of our world—

Grey house and grey house and after that grey house,
Another house as grey and steep and still :
An old cat tired of playing with a mouse,
A sick child tired of chasing down the hill.

Shuffle and hurry, idle feet and slow,
Grim face, and merry face, so ugly all !
Why do you hurry ?   Where is there to go ?
Why are you shouting ?   Who is there to call ?

We have jettisoned the old iron that was the Victorian
ballast ; we have torn up the old charts by which they
sailed so hopefully towards the port of El Dorado ; and
in consequence we roll sickly, without steerage-way, in
the trough of an empty sea.   And because everything
in life matters as much as anything else, provided it is
novel enough to distract our *ennui*, there has arisen among
us an ingenious type of fiction which, with many individual differences, has this in common—that it sees
existence through a microscope.   Some of these works
have great qualities ;   they have revealed us things no
eye had seen before ;   their microscopes are marvels of
ingenuity and their observation a miracle of skill and
patience.   With others of these writers one would think
that 'trivial' was a word they were incapable of understanding, and sense a thing of which they had never
heard.   And, when all is said, this art of magnifying the
minutiæ of life and feeling finds scant room for greater
matters ;   and it makes the observer short-sighted.   'Tout
montrer c'est ne rien faire voir.'   Often amused, often
fascinated, I grow weary of this day of small things, of
these acute and highly polished writers lost in their myriad
details like sharp little needles in haystacks, of these in-

coherent characters who derive emotions of equal interest and intensity from the look of a woman and a tea-leaf, or feel that they have found Reality and all 's right with the world, because they caught the eye of a narcissus that morning, walking through the park. Life may be futile ; but such a fiddling as this ? We do not ask, or want, 'one increasing purpose.' Life is worth while, if it is, for its own sake alone. But this sort of life ? This class of fiction is obsessed, to adapt the current jargon, with an *inter*iority complex. Its figures have so much psychology that they have no room for character. It has worked up the weakness of Hamlet and forgotten the fineness ; it has travestied the nobility of the *Odyssey* into that dreary *reductio ad absurdum* of itself, *Ulysses*.

Like such fiction, much of our would-be advanced poetry suffers from the same lust for novelty, the same loss of values, the same lack of sanity. If it is less microscopic, it is equally indiscriminating, and even more anti-rational. The reaction which raves in the novels of Mr. D. H. Lawrence not merely against the abuse, but the use, of the intellect, has found easier expression in whole volumes of metrical incoherence. A single example will more than suffice, from a type of verse much discussed, and sometimes read, in 'intellectual' society—

> When
> > Don
> Pasquito arrived at the seaside
> Where the donkey's hide tide brayed, he
> Saw the banditto Jo in a black cape
> Whose slack shape waved like the sea—

Thetis wrote a treatise noting wheat is silver like the sea ; the
lovely cheat is sweet as foam ; Erotis notices that she

Will

Steal

The

Wheat-king's luggage, like Babel
Before the League of Nations grew—
So Jo put the luggage and the label
In the pocket of Flo the Kangaroo.

It will surely seem very revealing to the future social
historian that in the England of our time it should have
been worth a publisher's while, even with all the resources
of advertisement, to put this sort of verse in print. It
may serve, if for nothing else, as a post-war memorial of
a period when a section of society was so obsessed by the
weight of established tradition, that it was prepared to go
on four legs for the sole reason that its fathers had walked
on two ; yet intellectually so exhausted that it could
only snatch at vulgarity as the best substitute for vitality,
whimsicality as the nearest thing to wit. This is an
extreme case ; but even the work of writers not to be
named in the same breath suffers from a not dissimilar
lack of simple good taste and simple good sense. These
things do not need exemplifying ; it is extraordinary
that they should need saying. A poet may well feel the
need to utter his repulsion at certain sides of our life ;
only, inventorying dustbins does not happen to be the
way to do it. It is the true poet's secret to be able to
touch even pitch without becoming foul ; but to touch,
not to wallow. Dante's *Inferno* bubbles with slime that
might easily have grown disgusting ; but no fleck stains
that haughty, bitter face as it passes through the smother

and the stench of Hell. And were Dante writing of the modern counterpart, do we suppose that he could not or would not make us feel the squalid horror that lives in our cities, without versified exhibitions of typists' combinations drying out of tenement windows? Are such distinctions arbitrary? Of course they are. These things are, in either sense, a matter of taste. They cannot be argued. It is even possible to do in one language what is impossible in another, to say with dignity in Latin or with grace in French what cannot be said without meanness in English. There is no test but the result; and the critic speaks only for himself. But it seems to me a pity that a good deal of modern talent should waste itself because, in the passion for something new, it forgets that in certain directions it cannot go further without faring worse. For there are things that do not readily follow fashions nor admit of innovation. In those words of the Delphic Apollo that became a proverb of Greek wisdom—

> Seek not to move Camarina; for unmoved it had best remain.

Again, even granting that civilised conceptions of what is vulgar may vary over long periods, to cultivate incoherence by way of a change from connected thinking is really an experiment not worth the making. We have developed a veritable somnambulance corps of poets who reel and wander through page on page of dream and trance, with a contempt for the human reason that in some instances they would do better to reserve for their own. In one case out of ten it may be that unintelligible writers are honestly trying to say clearly what is fundamentally obscure ; in the other nine they are trying to put obscurely what, put clearly, would as clearly be nonsense or platitude. We have too many authors who, like cuttlefish, use ink as camouflage.

But it is not merely that the reaction against tradition makes such modern fiction and poetry sometimes squalid, or that the reaction against reason makes it often muddle-headed and occasionally bedlamite ; it is more serious that, helped by both these tendencies, it seems so frequently to have lost the sense that after all some things do matter more than others in human life, some things are finer than others in human nature. The essential thrill that comes in common from the literature of a hundred differing ages, I cannot get from work which seems too indifferent to lucidity and good sense to be good art, too blind to human greatness to be great. Great poetry may be written though a man drab and cheat and rob hen-roosts all his days, if he has yet Villon's sense of the desolate magnificence of the pageant of man's life, of the queenliness of its beauty that fades so swiftly away. It may be written though its writer cry to the deaf heavens that 'all is filth,' if he has yet Leopardi's sense, in that very utterance, of pride in his own clearness of vision and fortitude of soul. Poetry may leave us saddened, yet not unsatisfied, though it search with unflinching fingers the miserable cesspools of our society, provided it gives, like Crabbe's, the impression of a personality behind, that holds with a Roman strength to its sense of form and order, of unexpected beauty and sudden pity, of certain values and certain standards, mistaken it may be, but genuine, amid the chaos of the world. Whatever else such men have disbelieved in, they have believed in the value of the intellect, of courage, of pity, even if they half denied it to themselves. These things are fine, not fashions; and without some touch of them great literature is not written. Whatever else reason may have undermined, it is not reason that has blunted or can blunt our instinctive sense of what is magnificent and what is mean, any more than botany can touch our sense of the beauty of the rose. These things reach on across space and time, while moralities change from frontier to frontier and from generation to generation. Whatever the gulf between West and East, something in us rises at once in answer to the proud spirit of the Japanese saying, 'It is better to be a crystal and be broken than to be perfect like a tile upon the housetop.' And the things that Homer felt splendid move us still. There is a story (a favourite with Sainte-Beuve) how, when after the sack of Corinth the consul was reviewing the captives destined to be slaves in Rome, he was struck by the look of a boy among them and calling him forward, to test his education, bade him write something in the dust at their feet. In silence the boy traced the lines of Homer where Odysseus, in the bitterness of death at sea, cries aloud his longing to have fallen fighting instead on the plains of Ilios—

Τρισμάκαρες Δαναοὶ καὶ τετράκις, οἳ τότ' ὄλοντο
Τροίῃ ἐν εὐρείῃ, χάριν Ἀτρείδῃσι φέροντες.

Ah, thrice and four times blest those Greeks that fell
In Troy's wide land for the sons of Atreus' sake!

Mummius was a Roman, and a plebeian Roman, and is a byword still for his greedy inappreciation of Greek works of art. Yet he realised the boy's mingled pride in his fallen country's poetry and bitterness at not having found, himself, a better end before the disgrace of Greece ; and in pity and admiration gave him his liberty. And we to-day in our distant land and time and civilisation can still feel a sudden sympathy with that touch of greatness in both the Roman conqueror and the Corinthian boy, called forth in its turn by the eternal greatness of Homer. These things that wake the deepest and finest echoes in men's hearts are not the things that change ; they are stronger than custom and creed ; and they are still the only foundation on which men can build themselves a living poetry, and not too prosaic lives.

For these two cannot be wholly separated ; and if much modern writing seems not to respond, not to have eyes for this beauty where life and poetry join hands, that is partly, I suspect, because it is written by men of letters who are nothing more. The division of labour has torn our lives in two. While our workers drudge, our intellectuals become mere intellectuals ; the hand forgets the brain and the brain the hand. George Scudéry is a ridiculous figure enough in literature ; yet literature might have gained much and escaped a great deal, if only more of those who have practised it had been able to echo or even to appreciate his boast : ' I have passed more days in the camp than in the library. I have used more matches to light my musket than my candles.' It was not mere eccentricity that made Æschylus proudly record in his epitaph that he had fought at Marathon, without adding one word of the hundred dramas he had left posterity. And if this is but con-jecture, I cannot but remember how much more it has meant even to my own experience, to have seen the

T

horrible sublimity of that real Inferno stretched under the darkness of the flame-shot sky from Mametz to Ovillers La Boisselle, than even to have read Dante. And anyway, who would not rather never have opened Shakespeare than never have been in love ? It is no service to literature to talk, like Flaubert, as if a perfect sentence was the supreme crown of all the effort of mankind. It is not in libraries that the great books are written. It is better to be Launcelot than the Lady of Shalott ; there is a curse upon her, magic though her mirror be. But of course we need both ; if it is fatal to sever literature from life, life would be a miserably poor thing without literature. None will ever forget it, who has once seen the jagged peaks of Pindus bitten as on steel against the western sky, while the dusk sweeps up from Pheræ across the Thessalian Plain and the low lands that Achilles ruled ; or watched the rising moonlight strike across the Vale of Lacedæmon on the long rampart of the snows of Taygetus ; and yet how much less even that untold loveliness would have been without the memories of the poetry of Greece ! The vividest poetry is that which sets itself like music, generation after generation, to the acts of life, as even Nero died with Homer on his lips, or Taillefer rode chanting the song of Roland up Senlac Hill, or Wolfe passed up the darkness of the St. Lawrence to his last battle, repeating the *Elegy* of Gray. It is true that most of our existence has to be spent on far other and more prosaic levels than this. That active, many-sided beauty of daily life which men have dreamed as existing in Periclean Athens or the Florence of the first Medici, or which makes the life of William Morris as fine and finished as a work of art

among the depressing biographies of most of his contemporaries, has been the lucky gift of only a few in only
a few ages of the world. Not many can hope for the
opportunities of a Morris, still less for the genius which
enabled him both to make his own life what it was, and
to imagine the only Utopia in which poetry could live.
But far better fail to attain that than cease to desire it.
And I cannot believe that much lasting good is to be
looked for from the sort of writer who sees nothing in
the world to chronicle but small beer, or no way of facing
it except an intoxication which refuses to reason.

If these are the besetting faults of the present, it is at
least very understandable in the light of the past that it
should be so. The state of modern poetry is certainly
not satisfactory ; it is limited to a rather dangerously
small circle, so that it is common to find wide and cultivated readers who never look at a line of it. Yet its
technical handling of the established forms is often extremely competent, and we have in fairness to remember
how hard it is becoming to say anything both good and
new. If our time cannot compare in poetry with the
best periods of the last two centuries, it is certainly much
better than the worst. What augurs least well for the
future is the scarcity of younger writers of promise, and
the difficulty of seeing in what new directions poetry
can develop. If the nineteenth century with its succession of revivals of the mediæval and Elizabethan was
our Alexandrian Age, what is to follow now ? Only a
series of slight and exquisitely finished short poems like
the epigrams which the Greek decadence went on producing almost up to the fall of Constantinople ? Clearly
it is fatal for poetry to be perpetually reviving the past ;

and our writers can hardly go on and on, turning, like Hardy and Synge, to the older world of the peasant. It sounds plausible enough to say that poetry must keep pace with the growing complication of modern life. In practice it is not so simple. A hundred years ago Wordsworth looked forward to a new poetry of science ; we are still waiting for it. The truth is, I think, partly, that though poetry can follow science and invention, it cannot keep up —it lags behind. Give time, and flowers will spring even on factory-wall and slag-heap ; but only when a deep enough soil of human associations has formed itself there. These things will not be hurried. Railway and steamship can find a natural place in poetry to-day that would have been impossible a century ago. But it is not merely a question of time. Some things seem to remain prosaic to eternity, resisting the genius and audacity even of a Meredith or a Hardy ; and it is depressing to think of how many of the ugly objects with ugly names that fill our mechanicalised world this seems to be true. It is somehow possible poetically to liken a mountain-peak to a horn, or call it ' *la Dent du Midi* ' ; but not to compare it to a screw-driver or a toothpick, even though it be more like those than anything else. Associations refuse to be ignored, as the more imbecile poems of Wordsworth exist to remind us ; and daring as some of our modernists may think themselves, they are unlikely to go further or fare better than Fracastoro with his poem entitled *Syphilis*. The new constructions which the modern mind so self-consciously puts together do not easily acquire the beauty which we find in immemorial things that seem insensibly to have grown as natural as human nature itself. A factory chimney may on occasion seem beautiful, but it generally does not ; a tree or a team ploughing or a smithy may sometimes not seem beautiful, but they generally do. The reasons of such differences are a tangle of æsthetics and associations ; but it is at least intelligible that, as our view of the world has become ever less anthropomorphic and more inhuman, it should have become correspondingly less poetic. Proteus rising from the sea and a common seal, Iris the messenger of Heaven and the refractive power of drops of water, are conceptions that appeal to the imagination with extremely different intensity. Otherwise, how is it that European poetry after three thousand years still finds repeated inspiration, not in Newton or Einstein, but in the fancied forms with which a few prehistoric Greeks humanised the unknown universe ? The whole march of science has been occupied with hunting down and exterminating everything anthropomorphic in our ideas of the world about us. The process has, indeed, been slow and desperately resisted by the human imagination ; long after men had realised that there was no earthly reason for attributing to God a human beard, they continued, and continue, to think that there must be some reason for crediting Him with a human mind and human feelings. It is not simply because the glamour of the past lies over the world of Athene and Aphrodite, of Odin and Thor, of elf and fay, that it seems more poetical ; it actually was more poetical, because more human and alive ; and let us face that. Poetry has long been living on its capital ; the raw material of which it is made is no longer added to as fast as it once was. And the poetry of science and modern life is more easily talked about than written.

Of putting into verse the complexity of modern emotions

there seems to be much more hope. In that way the sonnet-sequence of Meredith and the poems of Hardy point out a road which still leads somewhere, and may, I think, be considered the most truly modern poetry of high rank that we possess. But there are two ways of treating such complex states of mind—as a welter of incomprehensible ideas and impulses ; or as a battle of desires, incompatible indeed and inconsistent, but in themselves both rational and familiar. The first method leaves the reader in mystery, the second gives the pleasure of new and deepened understanding. There are readers, of course, who ask nothing better than mystification ; that is a matter of temperament ; one cannot argue with owls. But we are, I feel, more complex than Elizabethans, because we are conscious of more moods and more conflicting impulses at once, rather than because the fundamental impulses themselves are much altered. That is the real difference between the hero of *Modern Love* and Othello ; and Meredith's sequence is great as a triumph of passionate intellectual analysis, where the heart never blurs the brain.

It is in fact towards more brain that poetry must probably continue to travel, as it has travelled since it began. There is no going back. If the reason has taken much, it has given other things ; if it destroyed the ballad, it brought us Donne ; we need more of it, not less. Arnold was being extreme, but not unsound, when after criticising Tennyson's lack of intellect, he added : ' No modern poet can make much of his business unless he is pre-eminently strong in this.' There has always been and, one hopes, always will be the poetry of pure beauty beside the poetry of ideas ; if less has been said of it in this discussion, it is because the poets who write it either have or have not the needful gifts of eye and ear and tongue—and in either case there is no more to say. Very few poets, however, have in practice lived by the beauty of the senses alone ; they have felt the need to express ideas, as even Keats came to feel it. And it is in pieces not more than a few pages in length, sometimes lyric, sometimes narrative, which express, glimpse-wise, the emotions of men sensitive, clear-headed, but not cold at heart, in answer to the bitter wit of nature, as Peer Gynt saw her, to the subtle ironies, the sudden flashes of passion and pity that make life so tragic and yet enthralling—it is in such work that I seem to see the most hopeful poetry of the present and future.

As for its form, I have not much faith in experiments which loosen metre into *vers libre*. Often it would be better to turn frankly to downright prose, through which indeed, with its greater freedom and adaptability, more and more of our poetic impulses may come to find expression. This too is only a continuance of a trend we have already traced. A prose novel or play can always soar into poetry at its supreme moments, whereas a verse narrative or drama is spoilt the moment it sinks to the prosaic ; and the more critical we become of verse, and of bathos in it, the more this disadvantage tells. Accordingly the novel has long since replaced the epic, the prose history the verse-chronicle, while the simple cadences of Maeterlinck and Synge and D'Annunzio have produced a far more poetic type of play than would now be possible in metre. There is, in short, more poetry in Gibbon's work than if he had written an epic on the *Decline* in heroic couplets ; there is more poetry in the close of Mr. Strachey's *Queen Victoria* than all the verse elegies on that sovereign put together can have contained. Apart from this, the infinite variety of the English stanza, with the new individuality it will always take in the hands of masters like Housman or Walter de la Mare, should for long yet provide music enough for all we are likely to find to say. There is no question of legislating for genius ; genius can generally look after itself in any epoch ; it is the good writer, not of genius, who is often made or marred by the fashions and tendencies of his age. And thence the importance of clearer writing and thinking, of a clearer sense of some standards or other alike in life and literature, if our progressive poetry is to progress into anything but speedy oblivion.

But though we may grow impatient at times with the flood of little poetry-books written in the old fashion or the new that pours upon us, it is only justice to remember that these writers are at all events contributing to keep the practice of their art, if hardly their own memories, alive. After all, the first singers were content to be forgotten when they had left their great verse to a little clan ; and perhaps some of our present irritable individualism about literary property and literary immortality may drop away, and leave us none the poorer. That the race of poets, however, is in such danger of dying, as some have suggested, I cannot easily believe. We cannot indeed foresee what effect changes in the external world may have on poetry. It is possible, to take a single instance, that when broadcasting has ceased to be a toy, it might be the means of bringing the poet's living voice once more, as in the childhood of poetry, direct to the ears of men. It is possible that another social upheaval might liberate a new flood of hopes and energies like the French Revolution, or another war bring a new Dark Age and eventually the beginning of the whole long cycle over again. Or a new basis of society might transform men's literature together with their lives. Most Utopias indeed might well be the end of poetry, if they ever came to be established ; only, if they ever came to be established, one trusts that human nature would even more speedily be the end of the Utopias. Anatole France has pictured a future world where with the human passions poetry itself has passed away and only music remains. It is not altogether a new idea ; the old-fashioned Heaven was much the same. But in fact, though the founders of cloud-cities almost always forget it, they can never really barricade their shadowy streets against the eternal forces of human unhappiness, love and jealousy and grief and separation, all the sorrows to which man delivered himself and his posterity, when he ceased to live like the beasts that are glad or grieve for the moment only, and laid bare his soul to the past that torments him and the future that dismays. Humanity could only be made perfectly happy by being so changed as to be no longer human, a new race of beings. And towards man's destiny of pain there remain two attitudes which can give at least some consolation, the best that there is to be had—the religious and the poetic. Some take one, some the other, some both. But while men have eyes for transient beauty, while they suffer and pity suffering, while they fear, and cherish courage, while they love and lose and remember, we may believe that the last poet will not find his grave.

οὔπω μῆνας ἄγων ἔκαμ' οὐρανὸς οὐδ' ἐνιαυτούς·
πολλοὶ κινήσουσιν ἔτι τροχὸν ἅρματος ἵπποι.

Printed in Great Britain
by T. and A. CONSTABLE LTD
at the University Press
Edinburgh

A select List
of RECENT BOOKS in BELLES LETTRES
& of GENERAL INTEREST published
by CHATTO & WINDUS
LONDON

ALL the volumes in this List are, unless otherwise described, of Cr. 8vo size, & all prices are strictly NET

By LYTTON STRACHEY

QUEEN VICTORIA. "A masterpiece which will influence the art of biography."—*New Statesman.* Illustrated. Demy 8vo, v1*th Impr.*, 15s. Cr. 8vo, *New Edition*, 7s. 6d.

EMINENT VICTORIANS. "Four short biographies"—Cardinal Manning, Florence Nightingale, Dr. Arnold of Rugby, and General Gordon —"which are certainly equal to anything of the kind which has been produced for a hundred years."— *J.C. Squire.* Illustr. Demy 8vo, x*th Impr.*, 12s. 6d. Cr. 8vo, 111*rd Impr.*, 7s. 6d.

BOOKS & CHARACTERS. Essays, chiefly literary :— "Racine," "Mme. du Deffand," "Sir Thomas Browne," "Lady Hester Stanhope," etc. "Mr. Strachey's is perhaps the finest critical intelligence at work in English literature to-day."—*The Times.* Illustrated. Demy 8vo, 11*nd Impr.*, 12s. 6d.

By H. G. WELLS

THE STORY OF A GREAT SCHOOL-MASTER: "*A Plain Account of the Life and Ideas of SANDERSON of OUNDLE.*" "No book, even of Mr. Wells, is written with more conviction and more fascinating appeal to either educationists or the general public."—*Birmingham Post.* Illustrated. 4s. 6d.

By ARNOLD BENNETT

FROM THE LOG OF THE "VELSA." "One of the happiest and most delightful and amusing travel-books ever penned."—*Evening Standard.* Illustrated by E. A. RICKARDS. Lge. F'scap. 4to. 18s.

THINGS THAT HAVE INTERESTED ME. SERIES I. "The rich variety of this book is astonishing. It is crammed with the intellectual adventures of a life time."—*Sunday Express.* IInd Impr. 9s.
SERIES II. "A perfect book for the many mauvais quarts d'heure that occur in the best regulated existences."—*Time & Tide.* 7s. 6d.

BOOKS & PERSONS. A collection of Mr. Bennett's brilliant "Jacob Tonson" papers. "A book in a thousand."—*Outlook. New Edition.* St. Martin's Library : Pott 8vo : Cloth, 3s. 6d. ; Leather, 5s.

By G. K. CHESTERTON

A SHORT HISTORY OF ENGLAND. "Something like a History of England at last. He is at once the most concise and fullest historian this country has yet found." — *Observer.* VIIth Impr. 7s. 6d.

THE SUPERSTITION OF DIVORCE. "Contains much fine writing and more good sense." —*Sunday Times.* 5s.

By C. E. MONTAGUE

DISENCHANTMENT. "In describing the
progress of a human soul through the purgatory of
the war to the disillusion of the peace, Mr. Montague
has written a very fine book. . . . I have seen no
book about the war so temperate and so human."—
John Masefield. Cr. 8vo, ɪᴠ*th Impr.*, 7s. St. Martin's
Library : Pott 8vo : Cloth, 3s. 6d. ; Leather, 5s.

THE RIGHT PLACE: "*A Book of Pleasures.*"
7s.

By W. N. P. BARBELLION

THE JOURNAL OF A DISAPPOINTED
MAN. With an introduction by H. G. WELLS.
"One of the most remarkable human documents of
the generation."—*Daily Telegraph.* Cr. 8vo, with
portrait, ᴠɪ*th Impr.*, 6s. St. Martin's Library : Pott
8vo : Cloth, 3s. 6d. ; Leather, 5s.

ENJOYING LIFE: "*And Other Literary Remains.*"
With a preface by ʜ. ʀ. ᴄ. "A man of genius."—
Daily Express. ɪɪɪ*rd Impr.* 6s.

A LAST DIARY. With a memoir by ᴀ. ᴊ.
ᴄᴜᴍᴍɪɴɢs. "A truthful, poignant and noble book."
—*Robert Lynd.* ɪɪ*nd Impr.* 6s.

By HARLEY GRANVILLE-BARKER

THE EXEMPLARY THEATRE. "The
most thoughtful book on the theatre that has been
published in England for a long time."—*St. John
Ervine.* Demy 8vo, 9s.

By ROGER FRY

VISION & DESIGN. Essays on Art. "Mr.
Fry is an authority to be respected. It is ours to
learn where he has much to teach." — *Liverpool
Courier.* Illustrated. *Revised and Cheaper Edition.*
7s. 6d.